The Uses of Autobiography

Feminist Perspectives on the Past and Present Advisory Editorial Board

The Uses of Autobiography

Edited by
Julia Swindells

Taylor & Francis
Publishers since 1798

UK   Taylor & Francis Ltd, 4 John St., London WC1N 2ET
USA   Taylor & Francis Inc., 1900 Frost Road, Suite 101, Bristol, PA 19007

First published 1995

A Catalogue Record for this book is available from the British Library

ISBN 0 7484 0365 5
ISBN 0 7484 0366 3 (pbk)

Library of Congress Cataloging-in-Publication Data are available on request

Series cover design by Amanda Barragry

Typeset in 10/12 pt Times
by Solidus (Bristol) Limited

Printed by SRP Ltd, Exeter

'Our whole conception of ourselves as a people, individually and collectively, is based on those pictures and images which may or may not correctly correspond to the actual reality of the struggles with nature and nurture which produced them in the first place. But our capacity to confront the world creatively is dependent on how those images correspond or not to that reality, how they distort or clarify the reality of our struggles. Language as culture is thus mediating between me and my own self; between my own self and other selves; between me and nature. Language is mediating in my very being.'
(Ngũgĩ Wa Thiong'o, *Decolonising the Mind*)

This collection is dedicated to those who use language to comprehend rather than to compete – and for fun rather than funding.

Contents

Acknowledgments

This book emerged from the meeting of minds which occurred at the conference, *The Uses of Autobiography*, held at Homerton College, Cambridge, in the summer of 1994. That, in its turn, was the result of discussions over the months and years between friends and colleagues in Cambridge and elsewhere, many of whom contributed to the conference. They have subsequently done much, in keeping with the collective spirit of the project, to develop thinking and writing for the book, accommodating responses from conference workshops and from editorial readings. Even now, they would probably prefer, like me, to think of the book as still in progress; not an authoritative end to discussion, but a set of beginnings. My thanks go, first and foremost, to them – the contributors.

I would also like to express gratitude to the guest authors who spoke at the conference: Barbara Castle in conversation with Lisa Jardine, Edward and Kate Fullbrook, and Stella Dadzie sharing a platform with Joan Scanlon. Readers will see references to the intellectual and political energy that they brought to the book's discussions. For contribution to conference planning and administration, I would particularly like to thank Louisa Chapman, for her time, her industry and perfectionism. Special thanks are also due to Helen Nicholson, Peter Raby and Brian Ridgers for helping to initiate and sustain the idea. Jean Rudduck and John Gray were also there at the right time, alleviating organizational anxieties. All this contributed to the book's conceptual biography, but the object itself materialized largely because of June Purvis, together with Comfort Jegede, Alison Chapman and Anthony Levings at Taylor & Francis.

Finally, at the risk of sounding an individual note, I offer a shy thankyou to Hazel Clark for a key conversation about personal testimony and the law, and a too rarely expressed thankyou to Ben and Cass Bradnack for paying homage to the editorial computer and making the tea.

Chapter 1

Introduction

Julia Swindells

The tradition of autobiography, or egoists and interlopers

The orthodox version of the Western European autobiographical tradition displays Roland Barthes as the twentieth-century apotheosis, and variously St Augustine or Jean Jacques Rousseau as the revered head of the tradition. It is also held to contain Ludwig Wittgenstein declaring that 'solipsism . . . coincides with pure realism', W.B. Yeats claiming that 'all knowledge is biography', William Blake, 'crying I', the Delphic Oracle, exhorting the listener to 'Know thyself', and Wordsworth (William), Mill, Fox, Newman, Darwin, to name a few.[1] 'I myself am my own symbol', writes Roland Barthes, and this confident comment raises a set of issues to which I shall return, about the entire tradition and the process of its construction.[2]

The comparatively recent but now rapidly growing endeavour, to collect and comment on examples of what for the most part has been a neglected mode in terms of critical attention, has often rendered usefully problematic the idea that autobiography is a naked and transparent presentation of existence. Rather, the stress has been on the idea that all autobiographical statements show some process of mediation between the subject and author of the autobiography, and the ideological environment they inhabit. This demystifies the notion that the autobiographical act stands alone as a testimony to individuals, removed from their relationship to the social world.

> Social man is surrounded by ideological phenomena, by object-signs of various types and categories; by words in the multifarious forms of their realization (sounds, writing, and the others), by scientific statements, religious symbols and beliefs, works of art, and so on. All of these things in their totality comprise the ideological environment, which forms a solid ring around man. And man's consciousness lives and develops in this environment. Human consciousness does not come into contact

with existence directly, but through the medium of the surrounding ideological world.[3]

The problem, though, with this version of the Western European tradition, apart from its obvious maleness (except the Delphic Oracle?), is that both many of the figures recently enshrined in it, and the commentators who pick over their bones, claim that these men articulate, in their autobiographical testimonies, the model relationship between the individual and the social world. These autobiographers, the claim goes, speak authoritatively, either by being so fully integrated into the ideological domain that they inhabit that they can represent it to perfection, or by showing themselves superior to it via a transcendent selfhood. 'I myself am my own symbol' – the autobiographer, in speaking of his own consciousness, which also comes to stand for man's consciousness in general, articulates the 'scientific statements, religious symbols and beliefs, even works of art, and so on' of the social world. He can even, as one commentator would have it, speak for 'an entire ethics and cosmography'.[4] In the very act of writing personal testimony, these autobiographers thus, supposedly, speak authoritatively for 'the surrounding ideological world', either by transcending it with the power of selfhood, or by exemplifying the perfect relationship between consciousness and environment.

In the very process of making room for the necessary connection between autobiography and the social world, for an interpretation of autobiography as something more than a simple presentation of individual existence, this way of analysing autobiography fails to accommodate any sense of tension, struggle, contestation, or outright conflict between consciousness and environment, between people and their surrounding ideological world. Rather, whatever the distinctive characteristics of the different authors included in the tradition, there is a drive towards the inscription of an autobiographical norm. The critical treatment of Roland Barthes gives an example.

In his autobiography, Roland Barthes 'freewheels in language', arguably seeing and making play with the issue of the authority of selfhood. As evidenced in the title of the autobiography itself, *roland BARTHES par roland barthes* plays a game with the autobiographical subject, with the author's name, with the BIG name. He is playing with the authority of the subject too, playing with the 'egoist', playing with himself. Time and again, though, commentators on his work rewrite the title of his autobiography as *Roland Barthes by Roland Barthes*, standardizing in translation the initial letter of forename and surname, cutting BARTHES down to size. They deny, ignore or fail to see the game, turning the fun back into pomposity, inscribing the Western European male name as the autobiographical norm, and as the word-sign of the perfect marriage of subjecthood and authoritative knowledge or expertise.

*

Those who have moved in on the neglected mode of autobiography to construct a Western European tradition also pronounce about history and historiography. For instance, James Olney does not believe that a historical development can be traced through autobiography. Rather, autobiography is synchronic, born of 'the vital impulse to order that has always caused man to create'. Olney also argues that a study of autobiography for its characteristics as a genre would have limitations, as autobiography can appear in many forms and has a tendency to disguise itself or to be cast in another form – as poetry, psychology, theology, political economy, natural science and even history itself.

At first glance, these arguments could appear sympathetic. The challenge to the exclusions which pass in the name of great traditions, and to the circumscriptions which can operate in the name of genre, is welcome. Celeste Schenck has written of '*homo taxonomicus*' policing the borders of genres.[5] The problem which threatens to emerge, though, is that, in the very process of retrieving a neglected mode and freeing it from genre constraints, the proponents and proselytizers of the Western European tradition claw back history for Great Men. There would be a particular problem if this were to happen at the very moment when feminist historians had succeeded in exploding the myth of 'man' as universal subject.[6]

Olney is also one of those who is insistent that autobiography transcends history in marking man's attempt to produce order, constructing homology between 'the formal organization of the human mind and the formal organization of nature.' This is a dangerous proposition not only in its asocial aspect, whereby the individual appears to bypass society in his relationship to nature, but also because the issue of transcendence (here it is again, that strangely mystical term) inevitably raises the question of displacement, or usurpation. If history is being transcended, what is standing in its place – what but the Western European autobiographical tradition? But we have already been told that no historical development can be traced through autobiography, so what do we end up with – what but a collection of male selves, speaking synchronically for history, out of the authority of themselves as subjects?

In that model, the reason why autobiography can appear in the guise of any subject discipline – poetry, psychology, theology, political economy, natural science, and so on – is that any of these disciplines can show the mark of man's need and ability to impose order on his universe. Heraclitus, Socrates, Montaigne and Yeats saw 'ethics and cosmography' as deeply related to each other, both 'raised up from foundations sunk deep in subjective experience'. This need of the individual autobiographer to impose order via subjective experience, then seems to lead directly to uncritical tribute from commentators.

> If autobiography is in one sense history, then one can turn that around and say that history is also autobiography, and in a double sense: the maker of history, or those through whom history is made, could find in

their autobiographies the destiny of their time achieved in action and speech; and the writers of history organize the events of which they write according to, and out of, their own private necessities and the state of their own selves. Historians impose, and quite properly, their own metaphors on the human past.[7]

The challenge to historical empiricism has been systematic in recent years, but equally problematic as a history of facticity which does not recognize its own biases is a version of history which hands us a collection of male selves, 'imposing' themselves as metaphors of the past, as history. This is, powerfully, a political question.

A British and a German historian would disagree deeply on many things, even fundamentals, but there would still be that body of, as it were, neutral fact on which neither would seriously challenge the other. It is just this common basis of agreement, with its implication that human beings are all one species of animal, that totalitarianism destroys. Nazi theory indeed specifically denies that such a thing as 'the truth' exists. There is, for instance, no such a thing as 'Science'. There is only 'German Science', 'Jewish Science', etc. The implied objective of this line of thought is a nightmare world is which the Leader, or some ruling clique, controls not only the future but *the past*.[8]

This may be somewhat graphic as an example, but the passage shows something of the problem of male selves passing as history, men imposing themselves as history. Again, 'ruling clique' may be a little alarmist for this account of imposing historians, but the mention of 'the Leader' who 'controls ... the past' and claims to stand for objectivity, the representative and only truth, provides an analogy (if, admittedly, a somewhat sinister one) with the man imposing himself as a metaphor of the past. By contrast, there are those women, black people and working-class people who speak from what Sidonie Smith refers to as 'a negative position in culture'. When the life-stories of members of these constituencies (if that name will do for the major part of the human race), where these have received critical attention, if they have been published, solicited or encouraged at all, there are not the same claims for their representative or universal status (although there may be claims to represent a certain interest group). It is particularly unusual to hear them acclaimed in terms of an entire ethics and cosmography! Whereas Western European educated man can both speak for his ideological environment and be seen to represent it, women, black people and working-class people, because of their political position, are not placed to conceal the tensions between consciousness and the social world. Speaking from any kind of subordinate position in the culture reveals a contested and often highly embattled relationship between the two.

In short, members of the major part of the human race are positioned to lack authority, to start from a position of incoherent subjecthood, in which subjectivity cannot be subsumed in or stand in for the surrounding ideological world. But the work to retrieve members of oppressed groups from 'a negative position in culture' has more than begun, as Sidonie Smith comments:

> One by one, individual autobiographers are being retrieved from the gaps in literary history and reread from a perspective that insists on the significance of gender in the autobiographical process and product and that challenges the naive conflation of male subjectivity and human identity.... While women have been relegated to 'a negative position in culture', they have nonetheless resisted this *'assignment'* ... by becoming 'subject[s] *in* discourse' rather than remaining 'subject[s] *of* discourse'. From their position of marginality, women have spoken. They have written public autobiography. Nonetheless, when they engage in the autobiographical project, they do so as interlopers.[9]

Estelle Jelinek describes her own discovery, after a decade of reading, teaching and studying women's autobiographies, that most of the theory of autobiography written by men could not be applied to the women's texts. This took her in the direction, after a period of comparative work on women's and men's texts, of constructing a separate tradition of women's autobiographies.

> The reader should understand at the outset that this is not a comparative study. While I sometimes refer to men's autobiographies or the male autobiographical tradition, that tradition is already adequately documented and analyzed in dozens of critical works on autobiography.... My intention is to trace the history of women's autobiographies.[10]

She is right about the male autobiographical tradition, and her desire to abandon the superabundant men is more than understandable, but does this then raise questions about whether the men can be dropped, and into what? 'I myself am my own symbol', however playfully ROLAND barthes intends it, does not suggest a shrinking violet, or a problem that will simply disappear. Whilst the men have undoubtedly been over-exposed, has it been to the type of critical argument which would show and challenge the intricate workings of male claims to authority? I, for one, would welcome more of that, at the risk of further coverage. More importantly, though, there is that range of testimonies by women, black people and working-class people, which it would not have been possible to have access to without going via the educated, male-authored account. It may not be possible to retrieve significant numbers of the individual testimonies of the dispossessed peoples of the past, without looking at the writings of those male commentators and interpreters who have solicited and made use of such testimonies, for whatever purpose. This may mean that certain 'texts' can only be read in a context heavily circumscribed by and contained within the mediations of Western European educated men. It would be nice to think that this was only a problem with history, and that the contemporary context sees members of oppressed groups acquiring access to texts and to literary production processes on their own terms – operating as autonomous individuals and able to take control of the means by which autobiography represents communities beyond the individual. Even if this utopian model were achieved, there would still be a problem about substituting one tradition for another, women's names for men's (although this may be a necessary short-term strategy); as bell hooks writes, 'for the oppressed, the colonised, the exploited', the movement from silence to speech is not merely an attempt to insert a selfhood into a history.[11] It is part of a political strategy for liberation, and therefore must break beyond the subject of individual speech and individual authorship, must do more than add another 'self' to the autobiographical tradition's necrophiliac collection.

The uses of autobiography – the conference

It was a conference held at Homerton College in the summer of 1994 that generated the work for this book. In planning a conference on the uses of autobiography, it was important, whether we were going to attack, broaden, jettison, or reinvent the tradition of autobiography, that the conference would address how autobiography articulates the relationship between individual consciousness and the social world. It seems that the growing acceptance of this tenet is one of the reasons why autobiography, now, is being put to such a wide range of different purposes and uses. It also seemed important that not only the content, but also the structure and process of the conference day, should be conceived, within its own constraints, in consciously political, egalitarian terms, to bear the freight of the ideological and critical issues which surround a discussion of the uses of autobiography.

The choice of guest speakers was intended to place focus on a selection of key issues: Barbara Castle on the writing and reception of published autobiography in relation to a public, political life; Kate and Edward Fullbrook on the subject of the literary and biographical uses of autobiography; and Stella Dadzie and Joan Scanlon as authors and editors of published works which draw heavily and explicitly on autobiography and oral testimony for the purposes of giving voice to the experience of oppression or powerlessness.[12]

Invitations to submit ideas for workshops and seminars went to groups and individuals both outside and inside the academic community. It is in the very nature of the issue, though, that it has been difficult to bring about equal access for all individuals, and to bridge the gap between groups identifying themselves in differently intersecting, and sometimes mutually exclusive terms: between writers and critics, between students and teachers, practitioners and theorists, town and gown, black people and non-black people, working-class and middle-class, and perhaps most tellingly, between political activists and academics. The venue of a higher educational establishment perhaps already signals elite forms of knowledge in inescapable ways, but the problem goes beyond that to all those big and little assumptions and practices which exclude that access to literacy and education of which, as this account will attempt to show, the autobiographical act can be so importantly indicative.

Responses were in the end gratifyingly large in number and wide-ranging in relation to many of the above issues and concerns. They were from research students, often in marginal and even beleaguered relations with their departments or colleges, from 'freelance' writers and performers, from staff working in adult and continuing education and in teacher education, the most under-funded areas of the post-compulsory curriculum, from teachers with little or no experience of published research, from undergraduates with a commitment to research and/or political ideas; and nearly all from people for whom auto-biography formed either part of a significant way of working with and for others, or a reflection of their commitment to interdisciplinary work, or political critique, or more often than not, all three.

For, alongside the attempt to establish a Western European autobiographical tradition, and perhaps in the teeth of it, autobiography is now often the mode that people turn to when they want their voice to be heard, when they speak for themselves, and sometimes politically for others. Autobiography now has the potential to be the text of the oppressed and the culturally displaced, forging a right to speak both for and beyond the individual. People in a position of powerlessness – women, black people, working-class people – have more than begun to insert themselves into the culture via autobiography, via the assertion of a 'personal' voice, which speaks beyond itself. In making a claim to a political voice, the autobiographer is often also in the process of contesting, explicitly or implicitly, what the authority of the 'educated' account has to offer. Certain experiences, particularly those associated with systematic oppression, have not been recorded, or have been represented partially, in stereotype or with flagrant bias.[13] In this context, autobiography can appear the most direct and accessible way of countering silence and misrepresentation.

This issue of claiming a political voice whilst setting the record straight also raises questions about literacy, and thus goes to the heart of one of the dilemmas about autobiography, for it may be that lack of access to literacy is the very reason why the registering of the experience of oppression, or the claiming of a political voice, have not been available strategies. And yet, in order to make good or challenge the educated account, it may be that literacy is important, or even a prerequisite. Oral forms can, of course, be very powerful ways of articulating first-person accounts, as in the public oratory of Martin Luther King, the performances of Caribbean poets, and in many other political and artistic domains. However, oracy is frequently symptomatic of a position of subordination, and in most cultures, is now bound by a relationship of dependence on literacy. Whilst the power dimensions of this are clear in the context of a culture which has been colonized or dominated, where the imposition of a certain kind of literacy is part of a colonial strategy (and some conference contributions would explore this as an issue of racial dominance), the relationship between oracy and literacy is an issue in all cultures. The questions then are about who controls that relationship, and who takes responsibility for it, and for what purpose.

One of the key contexts in which the conference promised to address some of these issues is that of education, where the use of autobiography is on the increase in a variety of contexts – in relation to access policies and strategies as well as curricular content. Explicitly or implicitly, the educational establishment has a position here in that, in relation to any curriculum, judgments have been made about what value is attached to literacy and in what form. Whether education is perceived by the autobiographer as a problem (because it is responsible for those very accounts which have excluded her or his experience), or as a solution (because it is a potential source of access to literacy and to the production of an authoritative account), will depend on whether the educational establishment can respond to the dilemma.

Those working on autobiography in adult and higher education perceive a tension inherent in a post-compulsory education system which remains designed primarily for a minority of the population. The emphasis on individualism, which comes with a process of competitive selection for entry, is liable to mean that only certain motivations for valuing education can be recognized, such as that of seeking social mobility through personal advancement.[14] In this context, the attempt to gain access to literacy for the purpose of articulating a different kind of politics, to represent group interests through the struggle for individual rights, may go against the dominant ideology of the educational establishment.[15] Ironically, literacy skills, or the absence of these, may become the very grounds for judging the student's inadequacy, rather than part of a legitimate claim to the resources of the educated account. The conference would take up these issues in a range of ways; in relation to access to literacy and education (and the resources of a 'higher' education) for students who have been prevented from taking conventional routes into education, in relation to past and present curricula and the ways in which authoritative accounts are enshrined in subject disciplines and modes of teaching, and in relation to the negotiation of radical forms of knowledge and learning process with students.

In another apparent paradox, a different kind of autobiography may find easy access to literacy and publication, being altogether more comfortably ensconced in prevailing forms of literacy and authoritative account. Published autobiography is often the mark of fame or individual success, applauding the achievements of the great writer, film star, politician or other public figure, and documenting the course of events which chart that fame. However, even in this context, and perhaps particularly so, it soon becomes apparent that, however much autobiography is supposed to be about personal life, 'the personal' nearly always stands for something additional to itself. As in John Major's notorious 'back to basics' campaign, the private lives of the great and famous are closely bound up with accountability in the public sphere. The personal *account* provides both the record of the life, and also the means by which that life can be held to account.[16] It is because of this accountability that autobiography and biography, probably more than any other written form, have a volatile relationship to censorship and to laws of defamation. Journalism thrives on this possibility of public accountability (revelation, sensation) whilst it gives editors headaches!

As well as revealing these apparently contradictory uses of autobiography, the conference addressed issues related to work on autobiography in the context of particular subject disciplines, that is, the *study* of autobiography, the increasing inclusion of autobiography in courses, and the purposes of that study. Literature students may find that autobiography is not recognized as one of the important genres of literature, and even that it is not recognized as a genre at all, where poetry, the novel and even drama are easily distinguished in terms of 'literary' categories. A genre which can appear in many guises, including diaries, letters, interviews, criticism, and indeed poetry, the novel and even drama, may indeed escape identification as a genre. For literature students who have an interest in autobiography, the obvious strategy is to focus on *literary* autobiography, the autobiographies of published writers. Although there is undoubtedly a place for this, it runs the risk of reproducing exclusively the one model of autobiography, the life of the famous person, and overlooking the ways in which, whether autobiography is a genre or not, distinctive textual features operate.

Empirical history and oral history draw on autobiography as 'evidence', but there has been unease and debate around this, which has drawn attention not only to arguments about the subjectivity and unreliability of evidence, but also to questions about the inherent conservatism of memory and personal testimony.[17] Cultural history may have been less dismissive of personal testimony on grounds relating to any innate properties, but may register a similar dilemma in rather different terms – that there are problems about the extent to which a testimony may conceal, say, its class origins in the very process of the attempt to claim textual authority, by leaning heavily on more 'distinguished' forms such as The Novel and poetic imagery and vocabulary.[18] Among historians, women's history appears to have had the most commitment to autobiography, whether in adding women's names to or challenging the Western European autobiographical tradition, or out of a feminist belief in the movement from silence to speech – retrieving silenced voices of the past.

Social anthropologists and ethnographers also systematically turn to first-person oral and written testimonies, in the process of observing and interpreting cultures and experiences not their own. Latterly, focus has centred upon the role of the interpreter in this context, and whether the interpreter's claims to authority should fall under greater critical scrutiny.[19] Also, as some conference papers promised to show, this is an obvious instance of where the language of the interpreter creates a relationship of dependence of the autobiographical subject on the interpreter, further complicated by the need for translation (even where the autobiographical subject is literate).

In education and particularly in drama method, the use of autobiography has been invited and promoted as part of 'child-centred' philosophy, in an attempt to utilize personal testimony to give value to each individual's experience. Again, though, a tension exists around individualism, for, if this project remains untheorized as an intended means of furthering the educational advance of the individual child, that very focus on her or his experience can become the grounds for judgments about personal inadequacy and educational failure.[20] If, however, that model of individualism is resisted, performance and theatre, and by extension any educational experience of a group, can generate a collective use of autobiography, which can also form the grounds for group coherence, for exploring and defining group experience in new ways.[21]

The concerns of the conference were in autobiographical use both in and beyond subject disciplines in the academic context, and both in and beyond the more directly politicized context. Much of professional practice, not to mention personal and public survival, relies heavily on the autobiographical mode, whether in the form of personal testimony, case history or confession (from police station to church). Psychoanalysis and other medical practices clearly depend on the process by which patients and clients are invited to offer an account drawing on memory and personal history, as part of the means by which professional definition and diagnosis of a clinical state take place. First-person testimony is also a fundamental feature of the courtroom and related judicial practices. Witnesses and 'suspects' are required to give a first-hand account, and in very direct ways this forms the grounds of legal judgment.

*

This commentary on the uses of autobiography is not intended to be exhaustive. Nor is it intended to define autobiography as either a genre or a subject specialism in itself (to be colonized by experts). Rather, its purpose is to indicate the range of concerns which conference papers addressed, and ways in which an understanding of the social, educational and political uses of autobiography can help to critique subject specialisms and authoritative accounts, where these rely on particular kinds of social and individual exclusion. The overarching aim is to identify and change educational and cultural processes, where these operate against oppressed and powerless groups. The crucial and intriguing dependence of most kinds of educational and professional process on the account of a personal life, or aspect of it, signifies a need for a detailed study of that dependence, with a view to enabling us to understand and activate autobiography around the political and educational intervention of our choice.

Notes

1 James Olney, in *Metaphors of Self: The Meaning of Autobiography* (1972) Princeton University Press, is one who constructs the tradition in this way.
2 *roland BARTHES par roland barthes* (1975) Paris: Editions du Seuil.
3 Sidonie Smith (1987) *A Poetics of Women's Autobiography: Marginality and the Fictions of Self-Representation*, Indiana University Press, p. 48, quoting Mikhail Bakhtin.
4 Olney 1972.
5 Celeste Schenck (1988) 'All of a Piece: Women's Poetry and Autobiography', in Bella Brodzki and Celeste Schenck (Eds) *Life/Lines: Theorizing Women's Autobiography*, Cornell University Press, pp. 281–305: 'Certain forms of women's poetry and autobiography can be read coextensively, in a manner that profitably destabilizes theory of mainstream autobiography and calls into question the patriarchal determination of genre theory more generally. . . . The law of genre, the enforcement of generic purity, the policing of borders, has remained since the classical period a preoccupation of *homo* (properly understood man) *taxonomicus*'.
6 See Joan Wallach Scott (1988) *Gender and the Politics of History*, New York: Columbia University Press, for much illumination on this issue.
7 Olney 1972, p. 36.
8 George Orwell (1938) *Homage to Catalonia*, 1984 edition, Harmondsworth: Penguin, p. 236.
9 Smith 1987, p. 51.
10 Estelle C. Jelinek (1986) *The Tradition of Women's Autobiography: From Antiquity to the Present*, Boston: Twayne Publishers, pp. ix–x.
11 bell hooks (1989) *Talking Back: Thinking Feminist, Thinking Black*, London: Sheba.
12 Barbara Castle (1993) *Fighting All the Way*, London: Macmillan. Kate and Edward Fullbrook (1993) *Simone de Beauvoir and Jean-Paul Sartre: The Remaking of a Twentieth Century Legend*, Hemel Hempstead: Harvester Wheatsheaf. Beverley Bryan, Stella Dadzie and Suzanne Scafe (1985) *The Heart of the Race: Black Women's Lives in Britain*, London: Virago.
   Joan Scanlon (Ed.) (1990) *Surviving the Blues: Growing Up in the Thatcher Decade*, London: Virago.
13 The 'distinguished' voices of the English literary canon have, for instance, deafened us to women's political activism, as Angela Ingram and Daphne Patai (Eds) and others show us in (1993) *Rediscovering Forgotten Radicals: British Women Writers 1889–1939*, Chapel Hill and London: University of North Carolina Press; see also Joan Scanlon, *Improper Readings, Liberalism, Sexuality and the Novel*, forthcoming with Polity Press, for a persuasive version of how this has happened; Maya Angelou,

Merle Collins, Bessie Head, Toni Morrison and many others are showing us the racial dimension.

14 One version of the pressure experienced in relation to the expectation of social mobility through personal advancement is that of 'the scholarship boy', documented by Raymond Williams, Richard Hoggart and others. Lisa Jardine and I make reference to this in chapter 6 of our (1990) *What's Left? Women in Culture and the Labour Movement*, London: Routledge, where we cite Richard Hoggart and his depiction of the working-class boy entering the 'privileged' education of the grammar school only to find himself, later in life, 'uprooted and anxious'.

15 John Beck (26 April 1994) unpublished short paper on 'Institutional Democracy', Homerton College, Cambridge, documents the current political culture of higher education and the 'qualitative loss' experienced as democratic process diminishes.

16 Some OED definitions of 'account' are: 'to narrate ... to render an account for trust moneys; to explain; to answer for ... a reckoning in one's favour; advantage ... a statement as to responsibilities generally; answering for conduct'.

17 See Jerry White, 'Beyond Autobiography', in Raphael Samuel (Ed.) (1981) *People's History and Socialist Theory*, London: Routledge and Kegan Paul, for aspects of this debate.

18 This use of 'distinguished' comes from the particular context of Shirley Peterson's piece, 'The Politics of a Moral Crusade', in Ingram and Patai 1993. For examples of working-class women autobiographers who lean on 'distinguished' forms, see my own (1985) *Victorian Writing and Working Women: The Other Side of Silence*, Cambridge: Polity Press.

19 See The Personal Narratives Group (Eds) (1989) *Interpreting Women's Lives: Feminist Theory and Personal Narratives*, Indiana University Press, for attention to this debate.

20 Ken Robinson, Professor of Arts Education at University of Warwick, at a public lecture at the Cockpit, London, a number of years ago, pointed out with characteristic ironic wit how devastating it would be to find that one had failed a GSE (or even got a mere 3 at CSE) in being 'one's self'.

21 This observation was in part brought about by Shirley Brice Heath's lecture (March, 1994) 'Learning for Anything Everyday: The Language of Power and Mobility', at Homerton College, Cambridge.

Chapter 2

Theories of Autobiography

PART ONE

The face of autobiography

Laura Marcus

Memory is a topic that has, in recent years, become increasingly central to our culture, as we debate the relationships between personal memory and social or collective memory and explore the question of what it means for cultures to remember or to forget their histories. The 'democratization' of the autobiographical genre has arisen in large part because autobiography has become redefined as an aspect of 'memory-work', part of a spectrum of life-histories and oral histories. The question of memory and autobiography is also inseparable from the question of what it means to put a life into narrative, to make a story or stories out of a life, as well as the question of autobiography as a staging of memory.

My interest in autobiography is as much in what is said about it as in what it is or does 'in itself'. The title 'the face of autobiography' in part marks my concern with the face that autobiography, as a 'genre', has turned to the world. And this is inseparable from the question of what critics and theorists over the last two centuries, if not longer, have made of autobiography.

The second half of this essay takes up a number of different themes, including the memorializing aspects of autobiography, images of death and defacement in recent intellectual biography and autobiography, and the dispersal of the autobiographical so that it becomes an effect rather than a full narrative.

*

In my recent study of autobiography, *Auto/biographical Discourses: Theory, Criticism, Practice*,[1] I was primarily concerned with the perceived instability or hybridity of autobiography as a genre. On the one hand, this makes it a particularly valuable resource in a variety of argumentative strategies in relation to such topics as subject/object, self and identity, private and public, fact and fiction. Autobiography also plays a central role in discussions of a perceived crisis of nineteenth-century and early-twentieth-century culture, marked by such notions as alienation, reification, the decline of community and the rise of mass society. Autobiography appears in part as a microcosmic version of many of these concerns, serving to articulate them, and, for some critics, to offer at least a partial solution. Autobiographical consciousness, for example, has been held up as a mode of healthy self-awareness which could heal some of the wounds of the nineteenth-century spirit.

On the other hand, autobiography is itself a major source of concern because of its very instability in terms of the postulated opposites between self and world, literature and history, fact and fiction, subject and object. In an intellectual context in which these are seen as irreconcilably distinct, autobiography will appear either as a dangerous double agent, moving between these oppositions, or as a magical instrument of reconciliation.

The proliferation of classificatory and categorizing systems in autobiographical criticism testifies to the extent to which autobiography is seen as a problem which requires control and containment. In the variant in which autobiography is seen as offering a solution and not just presenting a problem, the identity of autobiography is seen as a precondition or guarantor of a remedy for the fractured identity of modernity. For some recent literary critics and theorists who oppose the application of generic classifications to autobiography, the rejection of categorizing systems can also stem from a perhaps exaggerated sense of autobiography's role in bridging traditional oppositions. Here, autobiography is seen as 'transcending' rather than transgressing categories, generic and cultural. In a different model, taken up primarily by deconstructionist critics, autobiography becomes a testimony to the artificiality of all generic classifications and the repudiation of a model of genres as natural kinds. Thus autobiography is important as the most conspicuous example of a 'genre' which exposes the heterogeneity of all literary productions – as in Mary Jacobus' description of autobiography as 'that mixed and transgressive genre'[2] and Barbara Johnson's reference to the 'monstrosity' of autobiographical writing.[3]

There has been very little discussion of the competing claims on autobiography made by, or raised on behalf of, the various human sciences, in particular sociology and psychology, and even the natural sciences, for example physiology and biology. It is here that a number of the most interesting issues arise. The emergence of autobiographical criticism runs parallel to the formation of the modern disciplines, including literary studies and sociology. The demand that autobiography be understood as a specifically literary form arises within the context of recent battles between the new disciplines over particular domains and definitions of language, truth and knowledge. These debates have their roots in the earlier formation of disciplines, and these disciplinary conflicts are of paramount importance in understanding what is at stake in the debates over the provenance of autobiography itself.

In tracing the history of discussions and theorizations of autobiography from the late eighteenth century onwards, I have also been concerned with the ways in which the potentially uncontrolled productivity of self-reflection and self-narration is contained by a regulatory structure whereby autobiographies become the right of a privileged few, an autobiographical elect. The paradox is that autobiographies are also used as the basis on which ostensibly universal laws of human nature are constructed. There is then a contradiction – revealed clearly in nineteenth-century discussions of autobiography – between the pursuit of 'general laws' and the desire to restrict the writing of autobiography to the 'better' sort of person. (Illiteracy, of course, entails the automatic exclusion of those who would be unable to write their memoirs from the 'general laws' of characterology; literacy, interiority and the self as property are closely allied formations.) In the early twentieth century, the overwhelming concern with genius and its auto/biographical expressions are, at least in part, a response to ethnographic research. The autobiographies of 'great men' become the authentic data which shore up cultural certainties and provide the points between which the map of Western civilization is drawn. They often come to embody the cultural value with which the primitive artefacts of 'savages' are contrasted. The discourses of biography and autobiography and those of eugenics converge in the conceptualization of 'genius', often understood, as it was by Francis Galton, in the broader sense of 'high ability', transmitted largely within the boundaries of the upper classes and legitimating their rule by means of a new 'scientific' sociodicy.

Although the German historian and philosopher Wilhelm Dilthey (1833–1911) was as concerned as any nineteenth-century critic with the biographies and autobiographies of historically significant individuals – his models are Augustine, Rousseau and Goethe – he also offers a broader conception of historicity as something common to all and auto/biography as a mode of understanding, of self and other, to which every individual has access. Biography and autobiography form one end of a spectrum running through to broader forms of history and to some extent providing their foundations. Secondly, one of the ways in which Dilthey's rather undifferentiated category of 'life' becomes concretized is through an essentially biographical concept of the life-course or life-as-lived. Unlike Henri Bergson, who opposed life to conceptual knowledge, Dilthey stresses the interrelation between the two. We live out our lives in a temporal frame which integrates each experience into a broader context. This inclusive concept of historical consciousness has been central to popular and women's history and life-histories.

There remains a tension between inclusive and exclusive models of autobiography which is in large part responsible for the genuine perplexity that has existed between theorists of the autobiographical form in different disciplines. Sociologists and oral historians are bemused by the fact that discussions of a form of life-writing potentially open to everyone – each of us, after all, having the raw materials of an autobiography – should impel the literary theorist towards yet another discussion of St Augustine. Literary critics will vary in their responses to the autobiographical genre as democratic or elitist but are unlikely to wish to do without a finite set of autobiographical models or exemplars, and these have retained a remarkable consistency.

Such disciplinary differences may not be capable of or need resolution. We may want to accept that different disciplines constitute their objects of study in very different ways. We may feel that there is a distinct literary category of 'autobiography', to be distinguished from the broader category of life-writing. Or we may welcome, as I would wish to, the fact that current work in the field of autobiography is pushing towards an interdisciplinary synthesis, turning away from generic history towards a more conceptual approach to the history of culture, marked by recent works on, for example, self-fashioning, subjectivities, collective memory, confession and the social construction of childhood. In these diverse projects, autobiographies are figured in new and challenging ways, as material through which these social forms are constituted. But autobiography loses its singular and privileged status as a distinct genre and form of knowledge and we can no longer construct a history and a cultural field upon a select *Weltliteratur* plucked from the contexts of two millennia.

I am critical of many of the attempts to claim autobiography as a specifically literary form. These attempts often construct the historical approach to autobiography as a straw positivism which fixates on referentiality and fails to understand the necessary role of fictionality and autobiographical representation. On the other hand, we need to pay more attention to the relationship between autobiography and authorship: the way in which autobiography serves to secure or guarantee authorship. Philippe Lejeune's work on autobiography has explored this aspect of the genre in detail. As so often, pathology is the key to anatomy: inauthentic or ghost-written autobiographies and the anxieties they arouse shed light on the construction of autobiography itself. These texts indicate the existence of a convention, or what Lejeune calls a pact: 'what the public consumes is the personal form of a discourse assumed by a real person, responsible for his writing as he is for his life'.[4]

Autobiographies and biographies have played a key role in organizing the literary system and maintaining the value attached to the category of the literary and to authorship. In an article on the Enlightenment's invention of a 'public image' for its writers, Jean-Claude Bonnet looks at the ways in which the 'phantasm' of the writer, created in the imaginary or fictional space of the identification between writer and reader, has made 'biographical space' a necessary complement to 'literary space'.[5] This process of institutionalization is illustrated when a reader becomes witness to a writer's life: Boswell's biography of Johnson, Eckermann's conversations with Goethe. These 'executive figures' become guardians of the writer's public image. In a different context, biographies, autobiographies and memoirs, contemporary and retrospective, have been crucial in orchestrating literary or artistic groupings, such as the pre-Raphaelites or the Bloomsbury group, confirming the individual identity of the writer or the artist while consolidating an image of group identity.[6]

We see, in the autobiographies of writers in particular, that the autobiography contains various and, at times, competing definitions of 'literature'. The autobiography becomes a way of defining what literature is or should be and of charting the course of the writer's relationship to the literary – as, for example, in Sartre's autobiographical account of his childhood reading, the literary taste of the older generation and his own earlier misconceptions about literature, or in Anthony Trollope's representations of the writer as artisan. Autobiographical, authorial and literary spaces exist in complex interdependence with each other. Now that the question of authorship is receiving renewed attention – particularly with recent critiques of the debates of the 1970s and, in particular, of the so-called 'death of the author' – an examination of the institutional determinants of autobiography and authorship becomes particularly timely.

*

One of my main interests in autobiographical theory has been not so much the 'death of the author' as the discourses of death and monumentalization in both the theory and the practice of biography and autobiography. The conventions of posthumous publication, as well as the uneasy relationship between biography and autobiography, whereby biography as extended obituary notice colours the perception of autobiography as life-writing, have meant that autobiography has always been shaped by the funereal. The majority of twentieth-century theorists have rejected the Victorian notion of autobiography as an epitaph or a monument to a past life and a memento mori for future generations in favour of a stress on the communication of life and 'lived experience'. Deconstructionist theories, however, with their suspicion of the categories of subjectivity and experience, seem to point back to an image of autobiography as funerary architecture.

There are a number of aspects to the focus on autobiography and, or as, death in deconstructionist criticism: a romantic legacy in which self-consciousness is allied to self-dissection and even self-murder; a focus on mourning, melancholia and memory, particularly in Derrida's work; a desire for autobiography to speak the impossible phrase 'je suis mort'; a theory of writing as neither an expression of or supplement to the self, but a substitution for the autobiographical subject, so that the self 'dies' to the letter; a concept of autobiography as the tomb from which the subject speaks, in a further denial of voice as presence.

At this point it may be helpful to bring in Paul de Man's essay of 1979, 'Autobiography as De-facement', an article whose conclusions seem to me to be ambiguous but which I think still has something to offer. Highly critical of speech-act theories of autobiography, and of the contractual and legal metaphors employed by Lejeune and others – pact, contract, promise – de Man focuses on the rhetorical dimensions of autobiographical discourse. To summarize, necessarily inadequately, his complex arguments – de Man uses Wordsworth's 'Essays on Epitaphs' to argue for the role of 'prosopopeia' as the trope of autobiography; he defines it as the 'fiction of an apostrophe to an absent, decreased or voiceless entity which posits the possibility of the latter's reply and confers upon it the power of speech'.[7] The aspect of personification in prosopopeia is also tied into its literal definition as 'conferring a mask or a face' (*prosopon poiein*), and it is significant that the difference between face and mask is not remarked upon. What speaks in autobiography is a dead man – though the dead man speaking, addressing the living, also petrifies the living and produces an uncanny reversal of the living and the dead. Voice implies mouth and finally face. But the giving of face is also a de-facement; the textual subject is stabilized and given identity through its assumption of face, but to the extent that this is a false front, a face for the faceless, it de-faces. In order for the face, in its facelessness, to be recognized, it must be undone, de-faced. This is the second level of de-facement. Hence, de Man argues, Wordsworth's repudiation, his undoing, of the very trope – the prosopopeic – which gives voice and face, and which, it could be argued, allows Wordsworth himself to construct an image of true authorship and naturalized poetic identity in his autobiographical representations. The last point refers us back to the question of autobiography's role in constructing a coherent corpus for the author, held together by an image of authorial voice and face, the imaginary identifications by which words are transformed in the act of reading into the emanations of persons.

De Man's arguments uncannily anticipate his own 'unmasking' with the discovery of his journalistic writings in occupied Belgium. One crucial issue, for both de Man's accusers and his defenders, is the break or continuity between the de Man who wrote the wartime journalism and the de Man of later autobiographical theory – in the terms of autobiographical discourse, between past 'I' and present 'I'. Secondly, his writings contain very substantial reflections on the modes of autobiography, confession and apologia – reflections which assert their generic 'impossibility' or the bad faith they manifest. These elements in de Man's writing now tend to be read either as veiled confessions or as dissimulations – a special pleading by one for whom autobiography had indeed become an impossible act. Autobiography is, de Man suggested, a 'figure of reading' rather than writing. It is certainly the case that, rightly or wrongly, it is now difficult not to read de Man 'autobiographically'.

More generally, these questions of death and defacement seem to haunt other theorists' lives, so that intellectual biography and autobiography have become in recent years the sites of scandal and pathology. The issues of face and of name recur throughout, for example, James Miller's *The Passion of Michel Foucault*[8] and Louis Althusser's *The Future Lasts a Long Time*.[9]

Foucault had of course himself referred in *The Order of Things* to the effacement of 'man' 'like a face drawn in sand at the edge of the sea';[10] and only three years later he wrote: 'Do not ask who I am and do not ask me to remain the same.... More than one person, doubtless like me, writes in order to have no face'.[11] As Miller notes, Foucault claims in the same essay that the 'travesties' of theoretical innovations 'inevitably provoke a return to the work – *and* life – of the author'.[12] Questions of identity are imaged through the metaphors of face, effacement and defacement. For Miller, death re-emphasizes the face: Foucault 'was inexorably acquiring through the peculiar circumstances of his own death what he had for so long avoided through the labyrinthine style of his writing' – in Foucault's words, 'a face that cannot be exchanged'. The face returns in the mode of memorial. Miller's narrative – explaining the life through the death – begins with Foucault's funeral and ends with his deathbed scene, in which the biographical subject 'confesses' to the other (not Miller, but Hervé Guibert who is also French and gay and will die of AIDS) that all his work has been 'autobiographical'. As with de Man, who witnessed his mother's suicide by hanging, this can be explained, it is suggested, by a 'primal scene' of horror and brutality, with Foucault as child the witness to his father's surgery/butchery. The biographical form uncovers the autobiographical in the life-work, makes of the work (of philosophy and history) a working-through. In Nietzsche's words, 'Gradually it has become clear to me what every great philosophy so far has been: namely, the personal confession of its author and a kind of involuntary and unnoticed memoir'.[13] We need to think further about the reasons underlying this return of the previously discredited problematic of subjectivity, as well as the ways in which autobiography serves to frame the subject.

Louis Althusser wrote his life-story twice, the first time as farce and the second time as tragedy. 'The Facts' was written before Althusser killed his wife; *The Future Lasts a Long Time* was written afterwards, and it opens with 'the scene of the murder, just as I experienced it'[14] and indeed with the dead face of his wife Hélène. Death structures the whole of *The Future Lasts a Long Time*, and Althusser recounts his own life as one lived as if by a dead person. Named after his father's brother, Louis Althusser, to whom his mother was engaged until his death, Althusser tells us 'I bore the name of a man who still lived and was loved in my mother's thought: it was *a dead man's name*'.[15]

Hélène is also described as enduring death in life:

> I cannot tell you how much I was struck by Hélène's face the first time I saw it, and how it haunts me still. A friend who knew her well told me he came to understand her when he read a line of Trakl's: 'Schmerz versteinert die Schwelle' (pain petrifies the threshold), adding that in Hélène's case it ought to read 'Schmerz versteinert das Gesicht' (pain petrifies her face).... Her face bore the marks of death and despair: her own appalling past had become petrified. What was it that brought that

physical look of horror to her face ... doubtless it, too, was caused by feelings of extreme anguish that she did not exist, that she was already dead and buried beneath a great sepulchral slab of incomprehension. She was what she had been; Wesen ist, was gewesen ist (essence is what has been).[16]

(This really is special pleading: Althusser is claiming that the wife he killed was in essence already dead and buried.)

The last image is taken up by Althusser when he gives his reasons for writing the autobiography or, more accurately perhaps, the testimony. Like Judge Schreber, Althusser claims that he writes to regain his identity, to cease to be a missing person, 'to remove the weight of the tombstone which lies over me'. As de Man wrote, autobiography is the discourse of self-restoration. Althusser uses his autobiography both to restore and to entomb himself.

It is striking that the late twentieth century has seen such a return of themes of crime and reparation, notably those arising from the Second World War and the Holocaust, and that issues of memory and autobiography are now dominated by these themes. For reasons that merit further investigation, a great deal of intellectual work at the moment appears to be concerned with 'speaking out' or 'remaining silent'. Shoshana Felman writes about the ways in which 'testimony has become a crucial mode of our relation to events of our times ... our era can precisely be defined as the age of testimony'.[17] This shift, if that is what it is, from the self-consciousness of autobiography (which may conceal a cultural demand for confession) and the ethical responsibility to testify, has important implications for conceptions of the status and value of self-writings and for concepts of experience and our relationship to it. It would seem to entail a move away from self-reflection towards a sense that we are all witnesses of history's tragedies and may be summoned to testify to our knowledge of them.

In Shoshana Felman's most recent book, *What Does a Woman Want?*, the issue of testimony and witness returns in a specifically feminist context, as Felman insists upon the urgency of the autobiographical project for women.[18] The context of her discussion is the move in feminist and cultural theory towards 'personal criticism'. In personal criticism, what Nancy Miller calls 'an explicitly autobio-graphical performance' is made central to the activity of criticism, thus both foregrounding the identity of the critic and reconceptualizing the nature of criticism itself.[19] But Felman suggests that 'we have settled into the notion of autobiography a little too impatiently and self-complacently', and argues that 'none of us as women has, as yet, precisely, an autobiography'. Where de Man, as we have seen, referred to autobiography as the discourse of self-restoration, Felman argues that we need to understand women's autobiography, at this point in history, as missing. Contentiously, she claims that 'unlike men, who write autobiography from memory, women's autobiography is what their memory cannot contain or hold together as a whole, although their writing inadvertently inscribes it'. Felman suggests that telling the story of the self may be a way of killing aspects of that self or part selves, rather than preserving or maintaining them, while women's alienation from a totalized life-story means that they find the autobiographical in others' stories. The autobiographical is mediated, displaced – 'people tell their stories, which they do not know, or cannot speak, through others' stories'. Autobiography, that is, makes a detour through theory, through fiction, and through literature. And women's autobiography may be marked as much by a resistance to the autobiographical as by an embracing of it.

These and similar debates in current autobiographical theory suggest that new forms of autobiography are not simply a question of replacing one face with another or others. Hence the focus on mediation, obliqueness and the autobiographical as shock or surprise, the sudden eruption of subjectivity, often imaged as a face, through the surface of the text, as in Charlotte Brontë's novels. Hence also the complexity of mirroring imagery – the distorted mirrors, the anamorphic vision – and the uneasy mirrors of 'race' and identity, with their distorting reflections, masks and mimicry.

One example will have to serve here: an episode in the legal theorist Patricia Williams' *The Alchemy of Race and Rights: Diary of a Law Professor* – a work in which Williams brings the autobiographical into her theoretical discussions. Williams describes the occasion on which she was refused entry into Benetton's, by means of the buzzers which New York stores have now introduced as screening devices.

> If the face at the door looks desirable, the buzzer is pressed and the door is unlocked. If the face is that of an undesirable, the door stays locked. Predictably, the issue of undesirability has revealed itself to be a racial determination....
>
> I was shopping in Soho, and saw in a store window a sweater that I wanted to buy for my mother. I pressed my round brown face to the window and my finger to the buzzer, seeking admittance. A narrow-eyed, white teenager wearing running shoes and feasting on bubble gum glared out, evaluating me for signs that would pit me against the limits of his social understanding. After about five seconds, he mouthed 'we're closed,' and blew pink rubber at me. It was two Saturdays before Christmas, at one o'clock in the afternoon; there were several white people in the store who appeared to be shopping for things for *their* mothers....
>
> The violence of my desire to burst into Benetton's is probably quite apparent. I often wonder if the violence, the exclusionary hatred, is equally apparent in the repeated public urgings that blacks understand the buzzer system by putting themselves in the shoes of white storeowners – that, in effect, blacks look into the mirrors of frightened white faces for the reality of their undesirability.[20]

The ideology of race, that is, distorts the 'face to face' encounter.

Williams recounts her tellings of this story.[21] The first time 'I typed up as much of the story as I have just told, made a big poster of it, put a nice colorful border round it, and, after Bennetton's was truly closed, stuck it to their big sweater-filled window'. The second telling came when she wrote an essay for a symposium on 'Excluded Voices', sponsored by a law review. It was returned to her in proof form heavily edited, with all references to Bennetton's deleted, and with the elimination of 'all reference to my race ... because it was against "editorial policy" to permit descriptions of physiognomy'. The 'round brown face' at the window of Bennetton's is also the unacceptable face of the 'autobiographical' intervention into legal discourse – as unacceptable to her editors as her face was to the white teenager who refused her entry into the shop. The editors' further anxiety about the 'unverifiability' of Williams' story recalls the familiar anxieties over the status of autobiographical testimony and truth.

The metaphor of the 'face', then, brings together a number of my concerns: first, the ways in which the constructions of an autobiographical tradition have served to fashion a composite face of European culture; second, the concept of self-presentation as, in the sociologist Erving Goffman's terms, 'face-work' and hence the performances of identity; this has recently been emphasized in personal criticism; third, the uses of visual metaphors – of mirroring, of portraiture – in autobiographical theories, where autobiography is identified with self-portraiture. The themes of portraiture and self-portraiture often play on the concept of the face as the surface on which the lines of time, experience, character are etched, so that surface takes on depth and the face becomes a text which can be read, and is held to be a man's truest autobiography. (I say 'man's deliberately, recalling Oscar Wilde's aphorism that 'a man's face is his autobiography, a woman's face is her work of fiction'.) And finally, as I have noted, there are the eruptions of subjectivity, the return of the repressed, into the text, whether in the form of a face, a mask or a death's head.

Notes

1 L. Marcus (1994) *Auto/biographical Discourses: Theory, Criticism, Practice*, Manchester: University of Manchester Press.
2 M. Jacobus (1984) 'The Law of/and Gender: Genre Theory and *The Prelude*', *Diacritics*, Winter.
3 B. Johnson (1989) 'My Monster/My Self', in B. Johnson *A World of Difference*, Baltimore and London: Johns Hopkins University Press.
4 P. Lejeune (1989) *On Autobiography*, ed. Paul John Eakin, tr. Katherine Leary, Minneapolis: University of Minnesota Press, p. 194.
5 J-C. Bonnet (1985) 'Le fantasme de l'écrivain', *Poétique*, 63, September, pp. 259–77.

6   L. Marcus (1989) 'Brothers in their Anecdotage: Holman Hunt's Pre-Raphaelitism and the Pre-Raphaelite Brotherhood', in M. Pointon (Ed.) *Pre-Raphaelites Re-viewed*, Manchester: University of Manchester Press.

7   P. de Man (1979) 'Autobiography as De-facement', *Modern Language Notes*, vol. 94, no. 5, December, pp. 919–30, reprinted in *The Rhetoric of Romanticism*, New York: Columbia University Press, 1984, pp. 67–81.

8   J. Miller (1993) *The Passion of Michel Foucault*, London: HarperCollins.

9   L. Althusser (1992; tr. 1993) *The Future Lasts a Long Time*, tr. Richard Veasey, London: Chatto and Windus.

10 M. Foucault (1966, tr. 1970) *The Order of Things*, New York: Vintage Books.

11 M. Foucault (1969) 'What Is an Author?', in D.F. Bouchard (Ed.) *Language, Counter-Memory, Practice*, Oxford: Blackwell.

12 Miller 1993, p. 394 n. 9.

13 Quoted in Miller 1993, p. 372.

14 Althusser 1992, p. 15.

15 *Ibid.*, p. 54.

16 *Ibid.*, p. 159.

17 S. Felman and D. Laub (1992) *Testimony: Crises of Witnessing in Literature, Psychoanalysis and History*, New York and London: Routledge, p. 5.

18 S. Felman (1994) *What Does a Woman Want?*, New York and London: Routledge.

19 N. Miller (1991) *Getting Personal*, New York and London: Routledge, p. 1.

20 P. Williams (1991) *The Alchemy of Race and Rights: Diary of a Law Professor*, Cambridge, Mass., and London: Harvard University Press, pp. 44–6.

21 *Ibid.*, pp. 47–8.

PART TWO

Why does an author who apparently draws so much on autobiography seem committed to 'alienating' the reader?
A reflection on theories of autobiography with reference to the work of Janet Frame

Jane Unsworth

In this account I do not attempt any kind of theoretical overview but rather seek to elaborate a particular issue about the claims of autobiography to represent 'reality'. I am concerned to examine why we seek to identify a piece of work as autobiographical – that is, why we assume that it represents reality as opposed to fiction – and how we consequently value that work in terms of its artistic and intellectual content. Indeed, I question whether it is at all useful or possible to define any writing as 'autobiographical' in the sense I describe above, especially when that writing is not one's own. I will explore these issues with reference to my reading of the novels of Janet Frame.

In the context of this short account it is not appropriate to give an exhaustive reading of Frame's texts. What I would like to do here is to introduce Janet Frame's work and the way in which she and it are perceived. Through my close reading of Frame's novels I have identified issues relating to theories of autobiography, both in terms of the way Frame's writing has been received and what I understand to be the concerns of her work. I will extract the conclusions I have drawn from my reading of Frame's novels and present them as general theories which I believe may be applied to other fiction, particularly that which is deemed to be autobiography and by implication 'real' or 'true' and particularly that written by women.

My primary interest in Frame's public profile is the importance apparently placed on perceptions of her own experience in relation to the value accorded to her work. I suggest that possible origins of this form of criticism may have implications for other writers. Western traditions of Realism and the way in which women's writing has often been read in the light of their personal experience rather than intellect have been well documented. However, the implications of an emphasis on personal experience for feminist publishing in possibly placing it above the intellectual concerns of the writer are, I would suggest, cause for some anxiety. The label 'autobiographical', whether overt or implicit in readings of texts, reduces the impact of the intellectual content of Frame's work and may serve merely to perpetuate her marginal status by emphasizing her experience rather than her ideas. This interpretation is particularly inappropriate with regard to Frame, the primary focus of whose work is, I would argue, a critique of notions of objective reality.

Janet Frame is a woman writer, a novelist and poet. She was born in Dunedin, New Zealand in 1924 to a family of working-class British origin. She trained as a teacher but during this time suffered some form of breakdown which was diagnosed as schizophrenia (a diagnosis later found to be incorrect) and subsequently spent eight years in psychiatric institutions. Her first novel *Owls Do Cry* was published in New Zealand in 1957 and since then she has written ten more novels, three volumes of autobiography and collections of sketches and short stories and poems. She has won many literary awards and is seen as a major talent in her native New Zealand.

In the UK she remained largely unknown until 1980. The marginal position she held can be explained not only in terms of gender and her origins in an ex-colonial 'outpost', but also by the challenging form of her fiction which is characterized by shifts in perceptual position and form often employing apparently autobiographical elements and described by Jeanne Delbaere as 'difficult, even by contemporary standards'.[1] However, in 1980 The Women's Press published her second novel *Faces in the Water*[2] followed by other works throughout the decade. During this period Janet Frame began to receive acclaim in the British context. It was also during the 1980s that Frame wrote and published three volumes of autobiography, *To the Is-Land*, *An Angel At My Table* and *The Envoy from Mirror City* which have been transformed by her compatriot Jane Campion into the internationally successful film *An Angel At My Table*, released in 1991.

Thus Janet Frame has become an increasingly recognized figure in the UK. However, I use the term 'figure' rather than artist deliberately. It seems to me that Frame occupies a place in popular consciousness which is largely dependent upon her own life experience as opposed to her work. In conversation I have found that she is most easily identified as 'that woman who was in psychiatric hospital in the 1950s'. Interestingly I have also found that many people respond very positively to the mention of Frame without necessarily having read any of her work. They assume the quality and integrity of her writing because they respond personally to representations of her autobiography. The woman and her work seem to have become integrally linked in popular readings. The fact that Frame does indeed employ events, characters, narrative viewpoints and contexts which are similar to elements of her own life experience (particularly in earlier work) serves to further the interpretation of her writing as an almost therapeutic process. With this understanding the results of the process cannot be separated from the experiences they apparently portray. I would suggest that the origins of these assumptions are various and that they may have serious implications for the value accorded to the work of authors from marginal groups in society.

Janet Frame was first published in the UK in 1980 by The Women's Press, a feminist publishing house. It is a feature of the ideology of the women's movement to deem that personal experience is political, that personal difficulties are symptomatic of wider social problems and that in sharing individual

25

experiences and identifying with one another we raise consciousness. A feminist perspective on Frame's work may be to identify with the marginality and alienation apparent in her own life experience and relate this to her writing. Thus details of her autobiography become essentially linked with her creativity. As a first choice to be published, Frame's second novel *Faces in the Water*, which describes the experiences of a young woman hospitalized in psychiatric institutions apparently mirroring her own history, clearly introduced Frame as 'the writer who was in psychiatric hospital' as mentioned in my assessment of her UK profile. It seems that her life experience and the integrity and value of her work were linked with each other in the choice by The Women's Press to introduce Frame to the UK via her 'case history' novel, even though she had written eight more novels in the nineteen years since it was originally published in New Zealand.

A further explanation for these realistic readings may be the tradition of Realism in Western literary culture: that the writing should be approached and responded to as though it portrays reality. A Western reader may seek to identify those elements of Frame's fiction which correspond to events in her own life as autobiographical accounts, that is, as 'real', and thus interpret her work in close relation to her personal experience. This is a form of criticism which is often applied to the work of women writers: for example, the Brontë sisters' creation of characters such as the 'masculine and threatening' Heathcliff (*Wuthering Heights*, 1847) and the 'wild, bestial' mad woman Bertha Mason (*Jane Eyre*, 1847) has been viewed as symptomatic of their own sexual repression. Thus a British reader may be accustomed to view particularly the writing of women as a form of expressing their emotional state almost without control or awareness.[3] In the case of Frame's work the highly emotive content of her own experience of psychiatric illness and hospitalization may serve to reinforce this therapeutic interpretation of her writing. It is also true that there is a historical connection between creative women and psychiatric illness as a definition of their behaviours. Showalter identifies many examples such as Virginia Woolf and Florence Nightingale. However, though this issue is of undeniable importance in any critique of the way in which normality and deviance are defined it seems to me to be furthering the paradox identified in my question to discuss what I perceive to be Frame's personal experiences in relation to what is in fact a central theme of her work. Showalter reads the novel *Faces in the Water* as events 'recounted'.[4] Is it not possible that in this emphasis on the personal there is a danger of denying the control and intellect of the artist? Though personal experience is undeniably of political importance, it seems to me that to place it as the primary concern when considering an artist is possibly to deny or render secondary the intellectual content of her work. This could be seen as simply furthering the historical readings of women's writing as emotional and somehow uncontrolled rather than the intellectual response of the artist.

Upon even the most cursory reading of Janet Frame's novels it seems evident that far from intending the reader to become emotionally involved with the action or to identify with herself as apparently represented, she employs a variety of techniques to ensure that the awareness that one is reading a deliberately created fiction is never lost. It is this intentional diversion of the attention of the reader from the action or story of the text and towards the art form itself as an intellectual communication which I have defined as 'alienation' in my title. (I use this term in the sense employed by proponents of 'Epic Theatre' such as Bertolt Brecht who aimed to deliberately put the audience in the position of observer rather than involve them in the action as though it were 'real', in order to promote political thought.) I have already referred to the 'difficult' nature of her writing. She blurs the boundaries of genre and style and shifts the form of narrative perception thus constantly changing what the reader may consider to be the reality of the action. This represents a direct challenge to the Realism of Western literary traditions within which the reader becomes involved with the 'story' as though it were true, approaching analysis of the text with a psychological understanding of characters and actions and a clear view of the objective reality of the narrative. In fact Frame seems committed to deliberately alienating the reader in order to prevent this involvement with the text as though it represents reality. The repeated use of elements of autobiography in her fiction as well as the writing of an autobiography and agreement to the making of the film version would appear to be directly at odds with this anti-Realist aim of Frame's writing.

I would suggest that the way in which Frame employs autobiography in her writing actually extends the force of her examination of notions of fiction and reality and the way in which these are communicated. She challenges the idea of fixed truth, drawing attention to subjectivity in interpretation of events; themes running throughout her work. This is expressed using a concept she refers to as 'point-of-view' which can be defined as the essence of being. Each person exists in their own perceived version of reality, by definition partial and subjective, and to be without this is to be without identity. Thus her characters exist within their own points-of-view, action is created and re-created within complex webs of perceptions, fictions within fictions. The presence of authors and creators is constant, truth does not exist independently but rather as versions perceived and manufactured by individuals. It seems to me that in Frame's manipulation of events from her own experience she highlights her ownership of them. They exist as the creations of her imagination as much as her other fictions.

I would suggest that Frame's critique of the notion of an objective reality is an existentialist concern. In his analysis of psychotic disorders R.D. Laing writes: 'The art of understanding those aspects of an individual's being which we can observe, as expressive of his mode of being-in-the-world, requires us to relate his actions to his way of experiencing the situation he is in with us'.[5] For Laing's 'being-in-the-world' I suggest one could read Frame's notion of 'point-of-view'. R.D. Laing was profoundly influenced by existentialist thinkers, in his work with those members of society defined as deviant. His thoughts on the way in which people respond as their essential selves to their own perception of reality and in turn the way in which this is interpreted and labelled seems to correspond to the central theme of Frame's fictions which I have identified in this study. These notions of personal responsibility and the position of self (point-of-view) as opposed to a more comfortable acceptance of illusory social truths are present in Frame's examination of notions of reality and truth in her novels. Images of the conforming cover-up which the 'real' world requires are prevalent in her work. Frame presents a world in which interpretation of events and therefore the reality of individuals is entirely dependent on point-of-view and consequently cannot be seen as objective. Indeed the world, and its occupants who consider themselves to be the guardians of 'reality' as an objective absolute, stand on a ground of dishonesty and untruth. In employing elements of the supposed reality of her own experience in her fiction Frame is able to control and manipulate her narrative in order to force the reader to confront preconceived notions of objective reality very effectively.

Related to this existentialist thinking is Frame's examination of the role of language in perpetuating false notions of reality. She uses the term 'imposture' to describe the way in which language is actually used to conceal meaning and restrict understanding, affording a comfortable protection for those living, to use Heidegger's term, an inauthentic life. For Frame, language promotes false notions of the predominant vision of an objective reality. Characters in her novels are divided, unable to reach one another or communicate their essential actual selves, with apocalyptic consequences in several novels. Frame's writing suggests that if language is the only means available by which we are able to express our perceptions from our point-of-view, but in employing it we enter the false world of objective reality, then the way forward is the birth of a new language from a new way of thought. This view of the role of language may seem a paradoxical one when held by a writer yet in fact much of Frame's work is engaged in examining the impulse to write and the role of writing and the writer. I would suggest that in manipulating and re-using elements of her personal experience, Frame draws attention to the writer as creator and controller working from her own point-of-view rather than as neutral chronicler of events, real or imagined. She is attempting to create a new way of using language arising out of a new way of thought.

Finally, perhaps most directly relevant to a consideration of autobiography is the way in which Frame interprets the concept of memory. To her, memory is dictated by point-of-view. From the moment they occur, all events, thoughts and perceptions exist only in memory. They are therefore entirely dependent on the point-of-view of the present, perception existing as a dynamic rather than a fixed absolute. Thus even for the individual there is no fixed reality but rather a personal fiction, created and re-created according to the knowledge and concerns of the present. In the light of this, Frame's employment of details of her own experience in works of fiction serves to emphasize their created, fictional quality and thus offer a critique of notions of autobiography as personal reality as opposed to being the straightforward 'recounting' of her case-history as some form of therapy.

Janet Frame's work brings into question the whole notion that personal experience exists in any objective and fixed way and thus whether it can be written or recorded as such. I read Frame's fictions as a highly intellectual existentialist examination of the notion of objective reality. Her conclusion would seem to be that all writing, whether employing personal experience or not, must be seen as subjective and fictional, created in the intellectual and emotional context of time in its new setting. For such a writer's work to be read merely as an expression of her experiences can only reduce its impact.

Notes

1   Jeanne Delbaere (1992) 'Introduction', in Jeanne Delbaere (Ed.) *The Ring of Fire: Essays on Janet Frame*, Sydney: Dangeroo Press.
2   Janet Frame (1980) *Faces in the Water*, London: The Women's Press.
3   Elaine Showalter (1987) *The Female Malady: Women, Madness and English Culture, 1830–1980*, London: Virago.
4   *Ibid.*, p. 216.
5   R.D. Laing (1960) *The Divided Self: An Existentialist Study of Sanity and Madness*, London: Tavistock, p. 33.

Further Reading

W.S. Broughton (1992) '"With Myself as Myself": A Reading Of Janet Frame's Autobiography', in J. Delbaere (Ed.) *The Ring of Fire: Essays on Janet Frame*, Sydney: Dangeroo Press.

J. Delbaere (1992) '*The Carpathians*: Memory as Survival in the Global Village', in J. Delbaere (Ed.) *The Ring of Fire: Essays on Janet Frame*, Sydney: Dangeroo Press.

J. Delbaere (1992) 'Beyond the Word: *Scented Gardens for the Blind*', in J. Delbaere (Ed.) *The Ring of Fire: Essays on Janet Frame*, Sydney: Dangeroo Press.

P. Evans (1977) *Janet Frame*, Boston: Twayne's World Author Series 415.

J. Frame (1985) *Owls Do Cry*, London: The Women's Press.

J. Frame (1982) *Scented Gardens for the Blind*, London: The Women's Press.

J. Frame (1981) *Living in the Maniototo*, London: The Women's Press.

J. Frame (1989) *The Carpathians*, London: Pandora Press.

J. Frame (1990) *An Autobiography*, London: The Women's Press.

D.W. Hannah (1992) *Faces in the Water*: Case-History or Work of Fiction, in J. Delbaere (Ed.) *The Ring of Fire: Essays on Janet Frame*, Sydney: Dangeroo Press.

V. O'Sullivan (1992) 'Exiles of the Mind: The Fictions of Janet Frame', in J. Delbaere

(Ed.) *The Ring of Fire: Essays on Janet Frame*, Sydney: Dangeroo Press.

A. Rutherford (1992) 'Janet Frame's Divided and Distinguished Worlds', in J. Delbaere (Ed.) *The Ring of Fire: Essays on Janet Frame*, Sydney: Dangeroo Press.

Chapter 3

Gender, Militancy and Wartime

PART ONE

'She who would be politically free herself must strike the blow':
Suffragette autobiography and suffragette militancy

Maroula Joannou

In his autobiography *The Unexpected Years*, Laurence Housman recounts how
he was dining with a rich businessman and suffragette militancy was being
discussed. A local letter-box had been set on fire and the hope was expressed that
the perpetrators of the damage would be suitably punished. His host's daughter
was sitting next to him. 'I did it,' she said.[1] Like much in the autobiographies
of suffragettes and their sympathizers this anecdote subverts that which is taken
for granted about gender and class; the notions that well-brought-up young
women must be modest and ladylike and that criminal acts are perpetrated by
nameless deviants and not those seated around the middle-class dinner table.

This essay is concerned with twentieth-century autobiographies whose
authors were involved in suffragette militancy. I am interested in how women's
personal narratives help us to understand the construction of gendered identity
in a specific historical context and in the relationship between individual agency
and membership of social movements. The autobiographies in question are by
Mary Gawthorpe, Cicely Hamilton, Annie Kenney, Hannah Mitchell, Christabel,
Emmeline and Sylvia Pankhurst, Emmeline Pethick-Lawrence, Mary Richardson, Margaret, Lady Rhondda, Evelyn Sharp and Ethel Smyth.[2]

Suffragette autobiography is in some senses a misnomer for these texts.
Because militant suffragette activity lasted for only ten years, and was suspended
in 1914, enfranchisement, although of immense importance to their lives, was
not the raison d'être for any of these women. All these autobiographical subjects
were members of the Women's Social and Political Union, founded by
Emmeline and Christabel Pankhurst in Manchester in 1903, although Mary
Gawthorpe, Hannah Mitchell, Sylvia Pankhurst, Emmeline Pethick-Lawrence,

and Evelyn Sharp eventually became disenchanted with the policies of the leadership and left. For all but Cicely Hamilton, militancy resulted in imprisonment. In so far as militancy was dangerous, 'unfeminine' and often involved breaking the law, these autobiographical narratives set up the individual in opposition to the political expectations of family, friends and state.

Much recent theory of autobiography has been strenuously opposed to the idea of a recoverable self or history and has excised referentiality from its concerns. In *Autobiographics*, Leigh Gilmore writes that 'one of the crucial insights of feminist theory is that politics is conceivable without a foundational subject (i.e. "women"), in fact, the condition of political agency lies in this conceptual refusal ... When "women" is only a record of wrongs, only the grounds of either immersed oppression or transcendent "womanhood", then being able *not* to identify with the category as the grid of self-knowing and self-representation makes agency possible.'[3]

The autobiographical 'I' names the historical person, the textual construction, and the author, who is usually writing at some distance from the events she describes. To borrow Barthes' useful distinction, the autobiographical 'I' is the self who writes, the self who was, and the self who is.[4] Although the self may only exist as a story that can be told about the self, what is told about the self is not always the same story, and much will depend upon how it is told and by whom. The woman who writes her life, particularly if that life is a record of the political struggles of the marginalized, as in the suffragette autobiographies, is, by the very nature of the exercise, revising and questioning the pre-existing narratives about her, resisting and reformulating what is already known. For her, autobiography exists as an *alternative* site of self-definition and affirmation, an attempt to break patriarchal silences. The woman who wrote may be unknowable but what matters is that she was striving to be known.

As autobiography always involves some attempt by the writer to reproduce a remembered past in a lived present, autobiographical narratives clearly are not, and never can be, referential in any unproblematic way. But to reduce the lives of female autobiographical subjects merely to a 'record of wrongs', to 'immersed oppression' or 'transcendent womanhood', is to privilege the hypothesized absences over the real historical presences in women's personal narratives; to substitute *his*tory (or even *hys*teria) for *her*story. It is to efface the *active* record of women intervening in history and making history – and the possibility of understanding that which interposes itself between subjectivity and history helping to constitute both – leaving us with culturally constituted notions of femininity as silence and passivity.

However unreliable or selective the autobiographical 'I' may be, that autobiographical 'I' is not merely a textual construction, but the textual double of a woman in history who has been produced by the material differences in men and women's lives, and has selected, from the totality of her experiences, those which retrospectively appear to her to be the more significant. The place from which she writes, her place within history, is produced by difference and reproduces difference, and because the past comes to us as a series of contested, mediated and negotiated versions of events, the denotative and referential aspects of personal narratives are crucial in helping the feminist reader to understand much about the forms of women's resistance to patriarchal values.

While many autobiographical subjects have been less than fully aware of the importance of gender to their personal development, this cannot be said of the suffragette autobiographers, who were caught up in the main currents of feminism of their day. Ethel Smyth's pioneering work for women artists led Virginia Woolf to describe her as 'among the ice-breakers, the window-smashers, the indomitable and irresistible armoured tanks who climbed the rough ground; went first; drew the enemy's fire; and left a pathway for those who came after her'.[5] Dame Ethel, a successful composer when she met Emmeline Pankhurst, knew 'more than most people about the dire workings of prejudice',[6] but most autobiographical subjects had not achieved public prominence before joining the suffrage movement. The sense of agency with which their narratives are imbued is a direct outcome of participation in what was, in essence, a feminist consciousness-raising movement. As Emmeline Pethick-Lawrence, the energetic national Treasurer of the WSPU, observed in *My Part in a Changing World*, the suffrage campaign was 'our education in that living identification of the self with the corporate whole, which means an intensification and expansion of consciousness'.[7]

Women's relationships to each other and to the suffrage movement constitute the twinned thematics of their autobiographical self-representation. Moreover, these personal narratives affirm the importance of qualities such as 'identification, interdependence and community' not regarded as significant by male theorists of the autobiographical self.[8] Declaring oneself a militant meant the discovery of a wealth of hitherto unsuspected loyalty and affection, and a sense of gender solidarity at least as resolute as that engendered within any male community or institution. As Rachel Ferguson puts it, in *Victorian Bouquet*, the suffrage campaign 'was our Eton and Oxford, our regiment, our ship, our cricket-match'.[9] The focus on individual subjectivity in suffragette autobiography involves the construction of a personal identity in which investment in the communal is at least as strong as investment in the individualistic. Thus the autobiographies amply corroborate Mary Mason's well-known thesis that the grounding of personal identity in women's autobiography is frequently linked to a woman's identification of herself with a chosen 'other'.[10]

The authors of suffragette autobiography did not challenge heterosexuality explicitly but in the warmth of their friendships and commitment to other women.[11] The self, although in some ways unique, exists in a symbiotic relationship with the life of another, whose importance for the autobiographical subject is sometimes not diminished years after a formal separation. This is shown by the devotion of Ethel Smyth to Emmeline Pankhurst ('eleven years of deep mutual affection'),[12] and the adulation of Annie Kenney for Christabel

Pankhurst. Kenney effusively describes her idol as 'charming', 'cultured', 'brilliant', 'masterly', 'fearless' and 'courageous', and herself modestly as 'Christabel's blotting paper'.[13] The importance of female bonding is made clear in Liz Stanley's meticulously researched biography of Emily Wilding Davison, which establishes Davison's ties to a small group of women friends, particularly to Mary Leigh, who never forgot Emily Davison in the fifty or so years between the latter's death in 1913 and her own.[14]

The shared consciousness of the forms of male control of women, and of the unequal exchange involved in gender-based relationships, worked to equalize all within the movement, and to suspend, albeit temporarily, differences of class. Hannah Mitchell, who had grown up in rural poverty, spoke on suffrage platforms with women from privileged backgrounds like the author Violet Hunt.[15] In *The Hard Way Up*, Mitchell wrote that 'it was one of my compensations for the hard life I lived at that time to meet so many brilliant and gifted women, who did not seem to notice any defects in my intellectual equipment'.[16]

For most of our autobiographical subjects relationships with men were peripheral. Only Emmeline Pethick-Lawrence was married to a man who fully supported her political ideals – she writes of 'our intimate personal relationship, growing deeper every year'.[17] The difficulty of combining public work with the regular household chores imposed a particular strain on the marriages of working-class women. Hannah Mitchell observed that 'most of us who were married found that "Votes for Women" were of less interest to our husbands than their own dinners'[18] and as 'no cause can be won between dinner and tea', domestic unhappiness, 'the price many of us paid for our opinions and activities, was a very bitter thing'.[19]

I now wish to look at the discrepancy between how women who took part in militancy viewed their actions at the time and how militancy has since been viewed by professional historians. Militancy did not come easily to women and some WSPU supporters experienced a crisis of conscience when what the union required them to do was incompatible with deeply held pacifist convictions; Evelyn Sharp, for example, gives an account of one stone-throwing skirmish when to her surprise 'the War Office fell to my pacifist hand'.[20] But all the autobiographers justified militant action as a last resort after constitutional methods had been tried and failed. However, this is not the position of most historians. Indeed, the view that militancy after 1910 was politically counter-productive is shared by mainstream historians of every persuasion.[21]

In a seminal essay, 'The Value of Narrativity in the Representation of Reality', the historian Hayden White has argued that the writing of history in the form of narrative inevitably imposes a goal, a sense of an ending, on events. White suggests that historical discourse when narrativized tries to efface the presence of a narrator so that the story appears natural and not constructed by any form of ideology. Where narrativity is present, morality or a moralizing impulse is invariably present too.[22] Writing history involves epistemological choices about what is relevant to any given framework but although the selection of material is a function of the author's interpretive position the resultant narrative is usually presented to the reader as the objective truth.

As Jane Marcus has pointed out, the narrative into which women's militant struggle for the vote is often inserted within the mainstream histories is the narrative of the downfall of the Liberal Party for which the militant suffragettes are allocated some responsibility, along with the Irish question, the labour and trade union movement, and the First World War.[23] Moreover, a hierarchy of texts and discourses has been constructed in which the main function of women's personal narratives appears to be to lend support to male history's view of militancy in relation to the death of Liberal England. Thus a text written to be read *as* a particular history becomes a text subsumed *within* a particular history, and what is ultimately heard is not the voice of the autobiographer but that of the professional historian. If, as often happens, the historian and the autobiographer appear to offer radically differing accounts of the past, the resulting dissonances and disagreements are difficult to disentangle and demand careful recovery and evaluation.

However, the key question that the mainstream histories fail to address satisfactorily is the question that Annie Kenney asks in *Memories of a Militant*: 'Why were women Militant? ... What inspired women to suffer imprisonment, to lose friends, and to be exiled from family and home?'[24] Moreover, what is also often missing is any full sense of what participation in the suffrage struggles meant to the participants, any developed understanding of the culture of the suffrage movement from within, or of the implications for the self (and home and personal life) that militant action carried for women.

As Julia Swindells has argued, women's history must begin to produce a critique of the history 'which has ignored "personal" histories as inadequate evidence or else as the preserve of those who are "not quite" historians' and 'challenge what the "real" historians are doing and what they are failing to do with autobiography'.[25] It is, for example, impossible to believe that intelligent women displaying courage 'beyond the wildest imaginings of the Early Victorian'[26] did so in some lemming-like attachment to the infallible wisdom of the Pankhursts. Such courage only begins to make sense if we recognize the strength of the feminist ideas generated within the social and political network in which the subject located her life and work. It is only by diverting our attention from Andrew Rosen's scholarly (and mesmerizing) tables of the accelerating destruction for which the suffragettes were responsible that we can begin to see the women's suffrage movement as these women saw it, as a revolutionary, emancipatory movement which could give pointed expression to women's pent-up anger and end the accumulated centuries of women's wrongs.[27]

What matters for the purposes of this essay is not the role of militancy in the downfall of the Liberal government but its importance in the creation of new subjectivities for some women. If the prevailing metaphor in the histories is destructiveness, that in the autobiographies is the quest for personal freedom. Starting with the question 'why did women become militant?', a radical alteration in our vision takes place so it is possible to see meaning in what has previously been empty space. The orthodox plot recedes, and another plot, hitherto submerged in the anonymity of the background, stands out in bold relief like a thumbprint.[28]

In the first place, insufficient importance has been attached by mainstream historians to the crucial importance of feminist ideas within the WSPU. The suffragette autobiographies provide important insights into the culture of an organization financed, led and organized by women, in which, as we are reminded in *Memories of a Militant*, Mary Wollstonecraft was read and re-read.[29] Secondly, women's personal narratives answer Annie Kenney's question and provide us with many cogent explanations – such as opposition to child prostitution and the exploitation of women in factories – of why women were driven to militancy and ample evidence to show, as Constance Rover argued in 1970, how and why this dramatic consciousness-raising movement was organized and supported by many whose consciousness had already been raised.[30]

Thirdly, the autobiographies illustrate that the WSPU's tactics – another letter-box set alight here, another golf course dug up there – risked violence becoming a routine that brought little if any political capital. However, a high-risk strategy is different from no strategy at all. The suffragettes believed that militancy would pay dividends in any political settlement, an idea that was extraordinarily long-lived. Mary Richardson ends *Laugh a Defiance* (1953) on the triumphalist note that women were enfranchised because Mrs Pankhurst had threatened to recall her militants at the end of the war. 'It was, therefore, the Suffragette – or at least the threat of her return – who won, this eleventh hour victory.'[31]

Finally, what emerges from the autobiographers is deep-seated anger at the differential treatment afforded to men and women by the authorities and deep-rooted conviction that the full coercive machinery of the state – punishment vastly disproportionate to the seriousness of any offence – would not have been brought down to bear on them had they offended in the pursuance of some cause that was in the interests of men.

Not surprisingly, the view of suffragette militancy in the autobiographies differs from that of the histories in so far as the autobiographers articulate the emancipatory politics of women marginalized by history (and within most histories) and largely concerned with the affirmation of oppositional values and experiences. Strongly assertive, unapologetic and contentious, these autobiographies contest the claims that form the basis of domination and can be read as counter-narratives that oppose the dominant histories in telling us how and why women did not think, feel, or behave as women were supposed to do.

As Ethel Smyth observes, men had for fifty years 'complacently absorbed constitutionalist butter ("My dear Mr. Lloyd George," etc!)'[32] because the methods of the old suffrage societies had not antagonized them. What the autobiographies pinpoint is how the invasion of the male political arena by women pointedly refusing to 'suffer and be still' inaugurated a new political era in which impatience and anger increasingly came to replace the old certainties and continuities. For women who had grown up with Victorian standards of modesty, to violate the male symbolic order by raising their own voices and questioning the basis upon which men's claim to exert their control over women was made was, as Winifred Holtby explained in 1934, 'as if an emotional earthquake had shattered the intangible yet suffocating prison of decorum'.[33]

The iconography and language of the suffrage campaign in the autobiographies is one in which images of freedom and imprisonment are juxtaposed. For Margaret Haigh Thomas, imprisoned for setting fire to a letter-box, militant suffrage was 'the very salt of life', the knowledge of which had come 'like a draught of air into our padded, stifled lives'.[34] For Mary Richardson, who slashed the Velasquez Venus in the National Gallery 'to draw the parallel between the public's indifference to Mrs Pankhurst's slow destruction and the destruction of some financially valuable object'[35] what militancy demonstrated 'for the first time in history' was 'that women were capable of fighting their own battle for freedom's sake. We were breaking down old senseless barriers which had been the curse of our sex, exploding men's theories and ideas about us'.[36]

At times the rhetoric of the militant suffrage campaign is strongly reminiscent of the rhetoric used by the early utopian socialists. Annie Kenney, for example, recalls the conviction with which working women were told what would happen to them once women got the vote: 'Poverty would be practically swept away; washing would be done by municipal machinery! In fact, Paradise would be there once the Vote was won'.[37] But utopian or messianic elements in suffragette discourse are matched by a clear-headed ability to discriminate between the vote as a means of political influence and its greater importance as a symbol of freedom for the autobiographical subjects themselves. In the words of Emmeline Pethick-Lawrence, 'while working for the idea of political liberty, we were individually achieving liberty of a far more real and vital nature'.[38] As Evelyn Sharp explains, reforms can always wait a little longer, but 'freedom, directly you discover you haven't got it, will not wait another minute'.[39]

The picture that emerges from the autobiographies is of resourceful, decisive women organizing effectively on their own behalf. The autobiographer's awareness of 'intelligent discontents' is sometimes traced back to formative experiences in girlhood. Hannah Mitchell remembers darning all the stockings for the family at the age of 8; 'my first reactions to feminism began at this time when I was forced to darn my brothers' stockings while they read or played cards or dominoes'.[40]

The autobiographers are figures who relate as the textual 'I' to the organized struggle for the vote, combining factual information on the key landmarks of the suffrage movement with individual responses to the experiences of prison, hunger-striking, stone-throwing etc. Their books are not autobiography *rather* than history, but both autobiography *and* history, and because they tell of rebel women who collectively 'laugh a defiance', differ radically from the usual autobiography of a middle-class subject which presents itself as the record of an unusual but exemplary life.

In evaluating the relationship between the individual and the wider group it may be useful to analyse the suffrage movement with reference to what Rita Felski has defined as the feminist public sphere.[41] By this, Felski means a discursive space in which the shared experience of gender-based oppression unites all participants and provides the impetus for the development of a self-consciously oppositional identity. Internally, it generates a gender-specific identity grounded in a consciousness of community and solidarity among women. Externally, it seeks to convince society of the validity of feminist claims, challenging existing structures of authority through political activity and theoretical critique.[42]

The WSPU, to which the women autobiographers in this study, however briefly, belonged, is a dynamic example of a sphere of influence created by women for the articulation of their needs. Internally, it helped its members to develop a critique of male-defined society by contesting the dominant ideologies of the day in terms of a partisan and separatist truth. Externally, the WSPU disseminated its ideas through its bookshops, publications, bazaars, plays, exhibitions, processions, and meetings in which its supporters were given a chance to speak in public. In *Knight Errant* Cicely Hamilton explains that she came into 'the Movement' because it gave her a chance to write and speak against the secondary existence of women.[43] The organization also provided an internal network of support, hospitality and emotional sustenance for women suffering from 'suffragitis', the term Mary Gawthorpe used to describe sickness and exhaustion brought about by excesses of suffrage-related work.[44]

The autobiographies offer privileged insights into the culture of an organization which in its later years was predicated upon a distrust of all men and of all male organizations. Explaining her decision to found the WSPU, rather than to opt for co-operation with sympathetic men in the labour movement, Dame Christabel explained that 'mother and I arrived at the conclusion that who would be politically free herself must strike the blow'.[45] The suffragettes had practical as well as theoretical reasons for their suspicion of men. Sexual harassment was an occupational hazard encountered by any woman on a soap-box or selling papers in the street. Mary Richardson wrote: 'the sex filth which elderly men in particular seemed determined to inflict on us was the most hateful part of my daily experience'.[46] Her autobiography tells how the experience of verbal abuse from men accounted for her conversion to militancy: 'In a sense I was glad to hit back, to hit out at anything if I could in some way express my detestation of all the filthy remarks I had to listen to'.[47]

There is a strong element of selective self-presentation among the suffra-gette autobiographers whose texts present much more consistently positive images of women than does twentieth-century fiction by women writers of the time, feminist or not. But like all history 'from the inside', the autobiographies are not only privileged but also constricted by their inside position. To argue that they should be read carefully as important records of women's history is not, of course, to claim that they form a straightforward record, more or less reliable, of happenings in the past. Instead, they present us with partial, and often contradictory and competing, versions of what took place, and the silences and contradictions within the texts are crucial as it is here that the limits of historical understanding and consciousness will be revealed.

The suffragette militants were able to use the textual space of autobiography to express 'the culturally constructed and historically changing epistemology of the self'[48] and to reformulate their own relationship to dissidence. Their accounts are important primary documents which show women capable of political acumen, enabling us to see the autobiographical subjects as agents in their own destinies and not merely puppets ventriloquized by Emmeline and Christabel. In turn, they make clear that the policies adopted by the Pankhursts brought them into collisions with many dedicated women around them (including Emmeline Pethick-Lawrence and Sylvia Pankhurst) from which they had the good fortune to be saved, as Roger Fulford has put it, by the 'beacon lights of sense, friendship and loyalty to the cause, shown by those whom they hurled overboard'.[49]

Feminist objections to any concentration on the militant suffragettes are too well known to need rehearsing. The complaint that much is known about the national leadership and little about the working women who agitated for the vote is still justified despite much interesting work in the wake of Jill Liddington's and Jill Norris' study of the northern radical suffragists *One Hand Tied Behind Us*.[50] Further feminist criticisms of the WSPU centre on the autocracy of the Pankhursts, their indifference to the continual haemorrhaging within the membership and to the loss of working-class women from the rank-and-file, and on the lack of internal democracy. The latter was zealously defended by Dame Christabel: 'it was as though in the midst of battle the Army had begun to vote upon who should command it, and what the strategy should be'.[51] But it led to several damaging splits including the departure of an estimated one-seventh of all WSPU members to form the Women's Freedom League in 1907.[52]

Not only do the autobiographies provide an inside perspective on the tensions and disagreements rife within a complex and contradictory movement but also countless examples of generosity and sisterhood – not least the pointed refusal of those women with whom the WSPU leadership had fundamental disagreements to be drawn into public condemnation. As Sylvia Pankhurst wrote, 'I would not add one word to the chorus condemning those courageous girls who trusted implicitly in the wisdom of the union. I would not advocate secret militancy. I would take no part in it, but repudiation I would leave to others'.[53] Hannah Mitchell, too, disliked the use of arson but knowing the draconian punishments meted out to the suffragettes admits that she 'could not bring myself to blame them'.[54]

The earlier tendency to valorize individual militants has been contested by more recent tendencies to dismiss Emmeline and Christabel as incorrigible autocrats from whom feminism has nothing to learn; a charge always strongly denied by Dame Christabel ('mother and I were not the born autocrats we have been reported to be').[55] It is not my intention here to exonerate the Pankhursts from criticisms of their style of leadership with which I am fully in sympathy. However, I do believe that there is a danger of feminist historians throwing out the baby with the bathwater.

This may happen if we allow our own distaste for violent and hierarchical behaviour to depoliticize the militant women's suffrage movement, and to prevent us from seeing it as it was seen at the time; as a struggle for liberation inspired by important traditions of Scottish and English political radicalism, analogous to the parallel struggle for freedom of Britain's colonial subjects and of the Irish for self-rule. For those who participated in it, the struggle for the vote was predicated on the reclamation and affirmation of their full humanity and it is this which explains the extraordinary passion of the committed suffragette. As Evelyn Sharp reminds us, 'the mentality of the suffragettes cannot be properly understood unless present-day students of their agitation realise that it took place in another world in which . . . the denial of the franchise to a whole class implied the denial to that class of human rights'.[56]

Emmeline Pankhurst's autobiography repays careful attention as part of the wider initiative of recovering the meanings that the militant suffrage movement held at the time. Entitled *My Own Story*, published in 1914, and interspersed with loose transcripts of what was said on her own behalf in court, Mrs Pankhurst's personal narrative is a powerful tour de force which presents an eloquent case in her defence against her many critics. The last third of the book is entitled 'The Women's Revolution'.

The autobiography makes clear the militants' unswerving conviction that they were engaged in an epic battle for freedom: 'we of the WSPU, were women fighting in a woman's war'.[57] Much of *My Own Story* is an impassioned assault on men's double standards in condemning women for fighting for the very same objectives of liberty and democracy that men had taught them to think of as indispensable.[58] Emmeline Pankhurst argues that women had presented larger petitions in support of enfranchisement, and organized greater public meetings than ever before, in spite of the difficulties which women have had in throwing off their natural diffidence, but this had been to no avail and they had been driven to militancy.[59]

According to Mrs Pankhurst, women were justified in adopting the same methods men had done to win the vote. The militant men of 1832 did not burn down uninhabited buildings, but burned down historic residences over their owners' heads.[60] In contrast, the suffragettes had injured nobody and no blood had been shed, except on the part of women themselves to whom violence had been done. Moreover, precedents existed in English history of riots in which the authorities had judiciously decided that no punishments should be administered: 'Window-breaking, when English men do it, is regarded as an honest expression of political opinion. Window-breaking, when English women do it, is treated as a crime'.[61]

Although MPs had openly declared that if home-rule legislation were passed Ulster would take to arms ('we read in the papers every day reports of speeches a thousand times more incendiary than anything we had ever said'),[62] not one of the men responsible had been arrested. Furthermore, women's violent activity paled into insignificance by comparison with that of recent labour disputes: 'What the women had done was but a fleabite by comparison with the miners' violence'.[63] The labour leader, Tom Mann, had been sentenced to six months and released at the end of two for inciting the army not to fire on strikers.[64] John Burns had been acquitted for more dangerous behaviour.[65] But the national leaders of the suffragettes faced years of penal servitude on unproven charges of conspiracy or for the heinous offence of breaking a pane of glass worth just over two shillings.

The laws of inheritance, the laws of divorce, the laws of guardianship of children were scandalously unjust to women, Emmeline Pankhurst argued, adding that women of intelligence 'have for many years ceased to respect the laws of this country'.[66] Moreover, the suffragettes found themselves before the courts 'not because we are law-breakers' but 'in our efforts to become law-makers'.[67] She concluded emphatically that it was not the women who deserved to be brought to trial for their behaviour in relation to women's enfranchisement, it was the men.[68]

In responding to the personal narratives left us by women in the past we will wish to question some historical constructions of subjectivity and to identify with others, revisiting and revising our own life-stories in the process. Reading *My Own Story* – as a feminist and a socialist whose admiration for Sylvia Pankhurst dates back to my adolescence – I was at first reluctant to admit how deeply Emmeline Pankhurst's account had moved me. But analysing my responses to the autobiography (an autobiography which I had not expected to like) forced me to ask uncomfortable questions about my own feminism, to admit that my identification with Sylvia's politics had led me to make the same mistakes as the mainstream historians: to seriously underestimate the feminism of her mother and sister, and consequently that of the movement that the two have come to symbolize.

The ethical questions relating to militancy will create conflicting passions in feminists today as will the related questions of whether or not it is possible for feminist groups to avoid hierarchical ways of working which come to mind as we read these texts. The autobiographies show us precisely how and why their subjects chose between the different constructions of subjectivity and the political affiliations available to them at the time. And as the modern equivalents of these positions – militant, constitutional, rebel, conformist, heterosexual, woman-identified, sexually adventurous, celibate by choice, etc. – speak to the experience of the reader today, the autobiographies will test the constructions of our own subjectivities in much the same way as they have previously tested those of the autobiographical subject.

Notes

1   Laurence Housman (1937) *The Unexpected Years*, London: Jonathan Cape, p. 273. Housman was a leading member of the Men's League for Women's Suffrage. His sister Clemence was imprisoned for her refusal to pay the sum of four shillings and six pence to the Inland Revenue. A WSPU member, she was one of 1,000 women imprisoned during the militant suffrage campaign.

2   Mary Gawthorpe (1962) *Up Hill to Holloway*, Penobscot, Maine: Traversity Press; Cicely Hamilton (1935) *Knight Errant*, London: Dent; Annie Kenney (1924) *Memories of a Militant*, London: Edward Arnold; Hannah Mitchell (1968) *The Hard Way Up: The Autobiography of Hannah Mitchell, Suffragette and Rebel* (ed. Geoffrey Mitchell), London: Faber and Faber; Dame Christabel Pankhurst (1959) *Unshackled: The Story of How We Won the Vote* (ed. Lord Pethick-Lawrence), London: Hutchinson; Emmeline Pankhurst (1914) *My Own Story*, London: Eveleigh Nash; Sylvia Pankhurst (1931) *The Suffragette Movement: An Intimate Account of Persons and Ideals*, London: Longman; Emmeline Pethick-Lawrence (1938) *My Part in a Changing World*, London: Gollancz; Mary Richardson (1953) *Laugh a Defiance*, London: Weidenfeld and Nicolson; Viscountess Rhondda (1933) *This Was My World*, London: Macmillan; Evelyn Sharp (1933) *Unfinished Adventure: Selected Reminiscences from an Englishwoman's Life*, London: John Lane; Ethel Smyth (1934) *Female Pipings in Eden*, London: Peter Davies, 1934.

3   Leigh Gilmore (1994) *Autobiographics: A Feminist Theory of Women's Self-Representation*, Ithaca and London: Cornell University Press, p. 232.

4   Roland Barthes (1980) 'An Introduction to the Structural Analysis of Narrative', *New Literary History*, 6, pp. 237–72.

5   Jane Marcus (1981) 'Thinking Back Through Our Mothers', in Jane Marcus (Ed.) *New Feminist Essays on Virginia Woolf*, London and Basingstoke: Macmillan, pp. 1–30, p. 20.

6   Smyth 1934, p. 204.

7   Pethick-Lawrence 1938, p. 215.

8   Susan Stanford Friedman (1988) 'Women's Autobiographical Selves: Theory and Practice', in Shari Benstock (Ed.) *The Private Self: Theory and Practice of Women's Autobiographical Writings*, Chapel Hill: University of North Carolina Press, pp. 34–62, p. 38.

9   Rachel Ferguson (1934) *Victorian Bouquet: Lady X Looks On*, London: Ernest Benn, p. 21.

10   Mary Mason (1988) 'The Other Voice: Autobiographies of Women Writers', in Bella Brodzki and Celeste Schenck (Eds), *Life/Lines: Theorizing Women's Autobiography*, Ithaca and London: Cornell University Press, pp. 19–44.

11   This point is made in Johanna Alberti (1989) *Beyond Suffrage: Feminists in War and Peace, 1914–1928*, London and Basingstoke: Macmillan, p. 116.

12   Smyth 1934, p. 284.

13   Kenney 1924, pp. 229, 193.

14   Liz Stanley (1988) *The Life and Death of Emily Wilding Davison: A Biographical Detective Story*, London: The Women's Press.

15   Violet Hunt's autobiography (1956) includes an account of her suffragette experiences. See *I Have This to Say: The Story of My Flurried Years*, London: Boni and Liversight.

16   Mitchell 1968, p. 166.

17   Pethick-Lawrence 1938, p. 124.

18   Hannah Mitchell 1968, p. 149.

19   *Ibid.* p. 130.

20   Sharp 1933, p. 140.

21   See, for example, Arthur Marwick (1977) *Women at War 1914–1918*, London: Fontana, p. 25; Robert Ensor (1936) *England 1870–1914*, The Oxford History of England, Oxford: The Clarendon Press, p. 388; David Morgan (1975) *Suffragists and Liberals: The Politics of Women's Suffrage in Britain*, Oxford: Blackwell, p. 160; Andrew Rosen (1974) *Rise Up Women! The Militant Campaign of the Women's Social and Political Union 1903–1914*, London: Routledge and Kegan Paul, p. 243; Brian Harrison (1978) *Separate Spheres: The Opposition to Women's Suffrage*, London: Croom Helm, p. 196; Marwick gives WSPU militancy credit for making suffrage an issue between 1906 and 1910 but sees WSPU activity after 1910 as counter-productive; Ensor suggests that had militancy not been persisted in, a suffrage bill would probably have been passed between 1906 and 1914; Morgan speculates that after 1910 militancy probably defeated its objectives; Rosen sees the WSPU's policies in 1913 and 1914 as alienating the general public; Harrison discriminates between the milder forms of militancy between 1906 and 1909 and later militancy between 1912 and 1914 which was a hindrance.

22   Hayden White (1980) 'The Value of Narrativity in the Representation of Reality', *Critical Inquiry*, vol. 7, no. 1, Autumn, pp. 5–29.

23   Jane Marcus (1987) 'Introduction: Re-reading the Pankhursts and Women's Suffrage', in Jane Marcus (Ed.) *Suffrage and the Pankhursts*, London: Routledge and Kegan Paul, pp. 1–17, p. 2.

24   Kenney 1924, pp. 294–5.

25   Julia Swindells (1989) 'Liberating the Subject? Autobiography and "Women's History": A Reading of the Diaries of Hannah Cullwick', in The Personal Narratives Group (Eds) *Interpreting Women's Lives*, Bloomington: Indiana University Press, 1989, pp. 25–38, p. 24.

26   Richardson 1953, p. 103.

27   Rosen 1974, pp. 217, 221, 222, 229, 231, 238, 242.

28   Elaine Showalter (1975) 'Review Essay: Literary Criticism', *Signs: Journal of Women in Culture and Society*, vol. 1, no. 2, Winter, pp. 435–60, p. 435.

29   Kenney 1924, p. 299.
30   Constance Rover (1970) *Love, Morals and the Feminists*, London: Routledge and Kegan Paul.
31   Richardson 1953, p. 192.
32   Smyth 1934, p. 192.
33   Winifred Holtby (1934) *Women and a Changing Civilisation*, London: The Bodley Head, p. 53.
34   Viscountess Rhondda 1933, p. 120.
35   Richardson 1953, p. 165.
36   *Ibid.*, p. 103.
37   Kenney 1924, p. 59.
38   Pethick-Lawrence 1938, p. 215.
39   Sharp 1933, p. 128.
40   Mitchell 1968, p. 43.
41   Rita Felski (1989) *Beyond Feminist Aesthetics: Feminist Literature and Social Change*, London: Hutchinson Radius, pp. 166–7.
42   *Ibid.*, p. 167.
43   Hamilton 1935, p. 251.
44   Gawthorpe 1962, p. 232.
45   Christabel Pankhurst 1959, p. 43.
46   Richardson 1953, p. 12.
47   *Ibid.*
48   Gilmore 1994, p. 85.
49   Roger Fulford (1958) *Votes for Women*, London: Faber and Faber, p. 227.
50   Jill Liddington and Jill Norris (1978) *One Hand Tied Behind Us: The Rise of the Women's Suffrage Movement*, London: Virago.
51   Christabel Pankhurst 1959, p. 81.
52   See Rosen 1974 for a good account of what happened.
53   Sylvia Pankhurst 1931, p. 402.
54   Mitchell 1968, p. 246.
55   Christabel Pankhurst 1959, p. 247.
56   Sharp 1933, p. 132.
57   Emmeline Pankhurst 1914, p. 247.
58   *Ibid.*, p. 127.
59   *Ibid.*, p. 128.
60   *Ibid.*, pp. 214–5.
61   *Ibid.*, p. 119.
62   *Ibid.*, p. 267.
63   *Ibid.*, p. 219.
64   *Ibid.*, p. 249.
65   *Ibid.*, p. 125.
66   *Ibid.*, p. 291.
67   *Ibid.*, p. 129.
68   *Ibid.*, p. 246.

PART TWO

'Dear Laughing Motorbyke': Gender and genre in women's letters from the Second World War

Margaretta Jolly

In the history of literacy, the Second World War must count as an ironically progressive moment. Conscription, mobilization and evacuation provoked geographical displacement of massive proportions which suddenly forced people to sustain relationships with lovers, children, families and friends by writing, putting an end to the association of letter-writing with the upper classes.[1] Letters were everything: the news of life or death; the symbol of continuity when everything was changing.[2] But people wrote for pleasure as well as necessity, to express themselves as well as to communicate. Here I want to ask how this determines a critical approach to *reading* letters from the war. If it is obvious that letters are both communications and forms of self-expression, they have been peculiarly neglected by literary critics, despite the current interest in autobiographical forms. Furthermore, letters pose a particular challenge to critical reading informed by post-structuralist theory which can be said to question the possibility of recovering any communicative intent in texts in the first place.[3] Such a challenge only underlines our need to begin to read letters as more than simply historical evidence. There are important political implications here, since it displaces the traditional tendency to reserve the 'art' in letters for the 'leisured' classes, while seeing in working-class letters only their capacity as a technology of communication. With this in mind, I want to take a first step towards a more critical reading of such popular writing, by looking at some untypical wartime letters, letters between women friends who were not separated by war nor in danger, and who, I will argue, clearly exploited the peculiar attributes of the letter form as a genre of creative self-representation.

The 54 'Letters from Women Welders' rest at present in the Mass-Observation Archives at the University of Sussex, where they were sent by the woman to whom they were written, Valentine Pearson, in 1942.[4] The letters, dated between February and October 1942, are from two groups of young women,[5] Valentine Pearson's former pupils who were working as welders in tank production in Yorkshire.[6] They give us a very unusual record of working-class women's perspectives describing their escapades in the factory, the hazards of work and their attempts to get, give and sometimes avoid Cuddley Woodleys with men, especially visiting servicemen. Above all, they testify to the women's remarkable affection for Miss Pearson.[7] Agnes wrote to Valentine in 1942:

My Dear Laughing Motorbyke.,
I hope you are having no trouble in aquiring your petrel ration, because

should you have to garage your laugh, you would hardly be the same
person, at least to me. (Letter 44)[8]

If this wonderful metaphor must have surely activated Valentine's presumably
engine-like laugh, the letters themselves often seem to be metonyms of laughter;
social, spontaneous and full of these sort of baroque jokes at Valentine, each
other and the authorities. But at the same time, it is precisely these kinds of
constructions that make them neither simply history or literature; make them
more than the private texts they were originally intended to be.[9]

Bad girls

I didn't know you had some girls from Huddersfield learning welding,
it's to be hoped they behave better than we did, but by all accounts their
just as bad (Letter 1)

Helena's opening words, in the first letter of the collection, anticipate quite
uncannily the themes that run throughout the letters. The subjects of the
collection – indeed the heroines – are girl welders, and they are 'bad'.
Furthermore, it is the 'accounts' that circulate which make them 'bad'. In many
ways the pleasure of the narrative as a whole is precisely as a series of accounts
of 'bad girls'. Also significant as an inaugural statement is the move from 'I' to
'we' as the subject, midway through that first sentence. Helena writes for the
Penistone women as well as for herself. The collective narrative is initiated
almost at the same moment as the individual one. This sense of collective
identity is affirmed throughout the collection. The historian Penny Summerfield
draws on them as evidence of the particular camaraderie that women forged
during the special conditions of war work:

Belonging to a small group of comrades could be an enriching
experience, productive of life-long friendships ... [Valentine Pearson]
not only taught them the art of welding but also found them billets,
negotiated their pay and helped with family and love-life problems, as
well as sharing many a joke ... the correspondence records the support
they gave each other and the fun they had, through the ups and downs
of work, play, courtship and marriage during the war. They are still
friends today and two of them have continued to write regularly to 'Miss
Pearson' (or 'Dear Vagrant' as they affectionately call her on account
of her weekends in the country) ever since.[10]

Between women newly entering the heart of traditional men's work, the letters
sparkle with the sense of a shared adventure. At the same time, they are an

uncompromising record of the frustrations many women drafted into munitions felt, particularly earlier on in the war when the transition to war production was still uneven. Their motives for working were clearly primarily economic rather than patriotic or for self-fulfillment.[11] Nearly every letter complains about work conditions – being underemployed or overemployed; given cutting instead of welding to do; having to work alone or only with men; unfair tax deductions; unfair workloads; being patronized by the welfare officer, 'Grandmother Marflitt'; and enduring dreadful health hazards such as burns and eyestrain.[12] Jenny writes that 'We have a terrible time with the fellows they tease us awful. Enid has a new name now. Daphne Squeaker. because they say she squeaks when she gets mad.... Everything is so dull at work' (Letter 3). Amy tells Valentine one week that her hours are 7.30 a.m. to 7.00 p.m., and to 4.30 p.m. on a Saturday (Letter 15), and she does Air Raid Precaution duty on top of that. 'I wish Hitler was in bleeding Hell.... I will close now as I must get to the Pictures for seven because I have to be in bed for ten on account of that bleeder Hitler, you know you cannot burn the candle at both ends' (Letter 21). This typically perfunctory invocation of the war effort is in striking contrast to the real sense of solidarity between the women – and notably to the kinds of letter-collections published during the war which were predictably patriotic.[13] In another letter, Amy's reference to the war effort borders on sarcasm:

> I must thank you for a very enjoyable day Miss Pearson, its been lovely and I shall come again before long, don't worry, honest I will be thinking about you all night tucked in bed fast asleep and poor little me working like bleeding hell. if my letter seems all jumbled up you must excuse me because I have to keep breaking off, and doing a bit of work, to keep the production up, you know theres a war on. (Letter 30)

Parody of this sort is more than evidence of attitudes to the war, more even than a picture of the conditions under which women wrote to leave that evidence behind. As the representation of a typically satirical working-class humour, it is precisely what I want to argue is part of an *aesthetic* dimension fundamental to the experience of reading the letters. But this kind of play with the status of self and other goes beyond the question of the letters' aesthetic value. For in the ambiguous construction of Valentine as both confidante and patron that runs throughout the letters, we can come to see the way in which the letters leave us not so much objective records of experience but constructions of self. Read in this way, the collection as a whole represents a complex textual negotiation between the correspondents' identity as women, in which shared sexuality is the driving force of the letters, and their difference of class, age and professional status. This negotiation is most obvious in the address itself. Many of them refer to not presuming to call her by her first name at the same time as addressing her with all sorts of wild and wonderful nicknames, sometimes tinged with sexual innuendo. Shortly after addressing a letter 'Dear little glamour girl Hearthrob No 1', Amy writes:

> I must say one thing. I thank you very much for giving me permission
> to use your Christian name, but under circumstances I regret I could not,
> I would sooner give up writing to you altogether thank you all the same.
> (Letter 15)

The entrance of Ethel's boyfriend into the scene is particularly dramatic in this respect. There are three of his letters in the correspondence, prompted by his hopes that Valerie could secretly buy him a ring for his engagement to Ethel. John's second letter is addressed 'Dear Val', and in the third one starts off: 'Ethel headed this but thought Dear Val too familiar! and wouldn't go any further & so, well here I am' (Letters 34 and 35). At the same time, he disarmingly puts Valentine in the same provider position, confessing that he is 'a bit scared' of giving Ethel the ring. 'I never dreamed that one day I should be trying to ensnare a girl, I always thought that it was the other way round!', he tells her (Letter 34).

It is undoubtedly true that this sort of play with the construction of self and other was probably as much part of the welders' spoken as of their written relationship with Valentine. But this only underlines the fact that letters require terms for textual recognition that do not presuppose a strict divide between the oral and written, but are based on a notion of discourse that traverses both. At the same time, it is crucial that we do not simply read the letters as transcriptions or extensions of speech, however much the oral patterns present in the welders' letters and the communicative nature of the genre may tempt us to do so. Ponder the following quote from Agnes:

> I feel I could sit & write & write & better write, just as I loved to stand
> and talk to you, but although I have not told you all I should have liked,
> I really must make my Allenbury's Food, (builds bonny babies) and go
> to bed it is very very late. (Letter 45)

If it is clear that writing is like 'standing and talking' for Agnes, she also explores the distinctive pleasure of writing, which is generated as much by internal momentum ('write & write & better write'), as by the wish to 'tell all'. This double, and contradictory, aesthetic is a classic paradox of the epistolary genre. Critic Horowitz notes that 'the ideal vehicle for communication of the passions allowing for the greatest *vraisemblance* (with "I" and "you" linked directly), the letter, like the journal, is also the intense consciousness of writing'.[14] As Horowitz suggests, we must not read the letters' 'communication of the passions' or '*vraisemblance*' too literally. In many ways this is the crucial challenge of the epistolary genre, as it binds history and self-construction, relationship and text, even more tightly together than other autobiographical forms.

Agnes and Amy's correspondence

The coincidence of linguistic play and relationship is particularly impressive in the letters from Agnes[15] and Amy and I want to focus on them for the middle of this part. Agnes' ten letters consciously set up the correspondence as episodes of an on-going shared romantic comedy:

> My Dear Instigator of Laughs,
> I laughed untill I cried when I read your last description of the latest adventure, of the hero, & heroine of our most important love story. I wonder what the next breathtaking incident will be in the next installment. (Letter 45)

Note again the parody of official language, in her new version of the laughter motif. Agnes' narrative begins with a letter written on a journey to Glasgow, to visit her husband, Jack. Due to travel problems, she ends up staying in a hotel on the way, where she is approached by a handsome Canadian soldier, who calls her Blondie and admires how she scribbles away at her letter. The writing itself becomes part of the scenario she is describing. We imagine the soldier watching her writing as she describes him doing so, so that she flirts by writing as well as writing about flirting, in a classic epistolary synchronicity of narrative and event. This seems to draw Valentine too into the sexual tease, as the projected other, underlined by Agnes telling Valentine that she tells the soldier that she is writing to '*some* person':

> Eddie has just come downstairs and pulled a wry face when he saw me still writing, he said, 'Golly, it sure must be some letter, & some person to whom you are writing,' I said, 'How right you are – to both of them.' …if you could only hear the cracks he is making at this letter, … he just said if my pen was a horse he would back it, he has never seen a pen fly like mine does. (Letter 48)

A main event in the plot of Agnes' letters is the removal of her 'fangs', in a series of awful visits to the dentist. Evidence of women's health problems, particularly from their work, runs throughout the letters. But Agnes' fangs seem to have a symbolic significance. Not only are they a trademark of her appearance with the other woman, but in the letters become a comic offensive against sexual encounters with men:

> Speaking of your undesirable companion, I once suffered much the same sort of experience coming from Manchester to Penistone. He actually did pounce – in Woodhead tunnel, but my teeth served me well again. Jack [her husband] will be crowing when my fang does the dissapearing trick. (Letter 45)

The sub-plot of her traumas at the dentist, and the sexual overtones of her 'fangs', is her bigger worry that she is pregnant. She makes it quite clear that she hopes that she isn't, dosing herself with raw gin and 'little black pills'. In Letter 45, she describes going to Doctor Smythe:

> Jack is begging of me every letter to go to Scotland to recuperate, & I told the doctor tonight, he said 'by all means the change of air would work wonders. My God what with a sore head, lumps, teeth out, anticipated journeys, & er, and little bits o' things, you really are in a way.' I blushed & answered, 'Yes! but of all the complaints you have mentioned, the "little bits o' things" I don't want that to go any further.' He laughed & put his arm around my shoulders & told me I mustn't worry, all that happens is an act of God. Thats twice he has told me that. I suppose, and rightly so, you will be tired of hearing my complaints.

As 'little bits o' things', Agnes' pregnancy is never directly mentioned but recurs in veiled terms in other of the correspondences as well as her own. To contemporary historians, this is precious and unusually explicit evidence of women's sexual experiences and attitudes in an era when sex was still officially a taboo subject. But again, it is the writers' coded assertion between women of their sexual realities – both pleasurable and painful – that produces literary suspense and richness. Amy, for example, refers to some metonymic 'Nappies' in Letter 17: 'Good old Aggie getting her hand in, but it is as well she is learning how to wash things for a start, because she might be busy washing Nappies if things don't turn out for the better.' And in Letter 24:

> I am going to meet Chick tonight lovely, I have not seen him all week but I got a letter from him yesterday, an hour from now + I shall be (having it) (a cuddley Woodley) Ah ah you thought I meant a bit of Agnes's stuff didn't you. No I could not do to be like her or else there would trouble at this establishment.

Amy's parodic reference to 'this establishment' again gives us some idea of the 'accounts' the women give of each other's 'badness'. As in most of them, here Amy does not judge Agnes bad herself, but alludes to others' judgments, most likely parents', that force circumspection and caution. Agnes herself seems unclear as to whether it is Doctor Smythe who is tired of hearing her complaints, or Valentine, or really, that she herself is tired of Doctor Smythe. 'He laughed & put his arm around my shoulders & told me I mustn't worry, all that happens is an act of God. Thats twice he has told me that.'

Amy's letters form the core of the correspondence. They are remarkable for their buoyant, even flirtatious style. Of all the letters, these are the ones we can visualize flying back and forth, reminding us of that strange way that a letter is an object as well as text, potential fetish as well as communication. She says that Nellie, who is sick in bed, wants her to 'lay on the bed beside her, but I have refused, but tomorrow I will get in, and press your note into her bosom' (Letter 22). Her minimally punctuated associative rushes and her frank accounts about her love-life make fast-paced reading. In Letter 17 she says she realizes she was 'a naughty thing five-timing', before starting up with the desirable Chick:

> We have spent a marvellous evening together last Friday honestly speaking lots of love was not in the running he was lovely I bet he will be mad when he gets my letter putting him off tomorrow. He is still very much in love, it is his Birthday a week on Wednesday but I don't know what he wants there is one thing he does want more than anything (real love) ha ha I am going to give in though before long if things don't alter at Hopkinsons I am just in the mood maybe it is as well I am not seeing him tomorrow because I should not hesitate to let him (have it) I dont give a bugar what happens nowadays I absolutely loath Hopkinsons anyway as far as gas cutting is concerned I am definitely not stopping on that machine I AM GOING WELDING they have upset the applecart this week. (Letter 17)

The monologic flow from writing about being 'in the mood' to loathing Hopkinsons here poignantly underlines the sexual restrictions a woman faced then where the price of 'real love' was jeopardizing your job through risk of pregnancy. 'I AM GOING WELDING' contradicts 'I dont give a bugar what happens nowadays', a contradiction that makes it plain how little she enjoys that restriction. More often though, the effect of her associative style is of pleasure and intimacy, overflowing boundaries:

> I hope [Agnes'] Sweetheart gets some digs for her, and then maybe her will be able to finish the job off right, and bring forth fruits.
> Talking about fruit, I have just had some prunes for my sweet tonight and I was reading your letter at the same time, and did I laugh. I think mine would be much sweeter than yours, because the day I wet myself, with laughing, I had some Prunes up my knickers slop, and I threw them under the saw somewhere, but I am in good condition so you will not be poisoned. (Letter 17)

Her dry-humoured changes of register from the everyday 'job' of having a baby to the quasi-Biblical 'bringing forth fruits' and then to the prunes she had for her sweet, express the same casual critique of the powers that make babies, struggle and hard work, working women's lot. But although it certainly isn't clear to me what bacchanalian games the sweets, laughter, fruit, and wetting themselves are all about it is their excess and delight that remain.

War and the epistolary self

Much in the letters seems to me to represent the polar opposite to the realist model of writing asserted in the typical wartime advice on letter-writing which filled the popular press as millions of separated families and couples tried to keep relationships going by correspondence across often dramatic differences in experience. This advice was aimed largely at women and centred on boosting absent men's morale by keeping home alive in 'word-pictures.'[16] The circumstances of the welders' letters, in which writing was interspersed with frequent visits, and neither party was in danger, relieved them of this strain to make the letter impossibly transparent, literally a 'window' onto the other's experience. However, there is a more political implication in the freedom of the welders' letter-writing. This is that, while women writing to absent men typically faced an ironic double bind of simultaneously representing self-sufficiency and dependency, the welders' and Valentine's shared wartime adventure as women allows a much freer ranging between identification and difference. Similarly, at the level of the collection as a whole, the welders' epistolary drama gives us a much more open-ended narrative of women's wartime experiences than those maritally structured stories.

This poses an interesting challenge to potential editors of the letters. We have seen that the letters, written during just a few months, are structured around the group rather than the individual, around perspective rather than narrative development. I hope I have brought out how this is part of what makes them such a unique record of women's wartime experiences. But it also makes them more difficult to read than a more chronologically organized and individually focused collection. In my view, editing should 'complete' and 'end' the individual life-stories without imposing a heavy closure on the letters that would undermine the real sense of these women's will to self-determination, which, as an aesthetic effect, is precisely the will to an unfinished story.

However, there is a more general point here about the value of a relational versus autonomous model of self. For women, this has huge significance, and indeed determines the persistent connection between women and the epistolary genre. The autonomous versus relational self (while being perhaps an essential distinction in all cultures) is formulated around the public–private distinction that characterizes modern industrial (and post-industrial) society, and, with that, the structures of women's secondary status in the broadest senses. The public–private opposition had long provided the basis of the feminist conundrum: equality versus difference. The same ambivalence must characterize our reading of women's letters. On the one hand, the literary history of women's 'special' relationship to letter-writing shows that although – and perhaps because – women have tended to be seen as superior letter-writers to men, it also shows women as confined and limited. On the other hand, we can turn this around, and take it as evidence of precisely how far we have associated the representation of liberation with the structure of the narrativized and individualist history rather than the rhetorical, social address of the letter-writer. In other words, have we unwittingly naturalized the autobiographical model of liberal humanism as an inevitably superior form for representing women's autonomy? It would be interesting to weigh up the relative determinations of literary form and historical context here. For example, on the one hand, the New Right has strongly influenced people's memories of the war as about unity and collective national identity. On the other hand, the prerequisites of the autobiographical form itself may influence how people structure their war stories as tales of individual growth or autonomy.

Conclusion

With this in mind, I want to finish by panning back to what contemporary feminists are saying about women's consciousness during the war. Their general consensus is that many women did have radically new perspectives and experiences but that they kept them within a mental framework of 'for the duration'. But these women's testimonies can force us to rethink our own frameworks as feminists, suggesting that we shouldn't necessarily throw out family ties and domestic identities as criteria for fulfilment.[17] I have suggested that the personal nature of letter-writing involves questions of identity in relation to others (in contrast to autobiography which is structured around the origin of the self), in a way that makes letters an appropriate resource for this reassessment. They can offer versions of history that can be part of reclaiming what many women who lived through the war say it meant to them, as a celebration not of the independent self but of the self in context. Life-stories here are not solipsistic journeys, but circuitous, dialogic or even polylogic narratives. At the same time, the fascination of history through letters is that the structure of determination is always in dramatic tension with the moment of becoming. In that sense, the motorbyke is still laughing.

Notes

1 'There has never been such a need for letters as now. In a world rife with separations, with families parted, routines of a life-time broken, with men set down in strange climates and far-flung places, and the hope of reunion still far away, there is little beside mail to bind us together and preserve all-important ties': Margaret Cousins (1942) 'The Art of Writing a Good Letter', *House Beautiful*, November, p. 55.
2 'I almost cried when I got your...[letter] the other day – it reminded me so strongly of all I hold dear... I can't possibly hope to tell you all mail means here...': Lieutenant George Morrison, Egypt, 19 September 1942, in Annette Tapert (Ed.)

(1984) *Despatches from the Heart: An Anthology of Letters from the Front during the First and Second World Wars*, London: Hamish Hamilton, p. 77.

3 A classic example is Jacques Derrida's 'Signature, Event, Context' in which he in fact uses the letter as a metaphor for the way we misleadingly conceive of language as communicative: Jacques Derrida (1982) 'Signature, Event, Context', in *Margins of Philosophy*, Hertfordshire: Harvester, pp. 307–30.

4 Some of the writers were traced by Dorothy Sheridan, the Mass-Observation Archivist, and subsequently interviewed by Penny Summerfield in 1989 with a view to possible publication. At that time, the welders were pleased to hear that their letters were available to the public and indeed surprised that they had survived. On the advice of Dorothy Sheridan, and given the difficulties of re-tracing the welders, we have taken this as an indication that they would be happy to have extracts published in this article. In the meantime, Dorothy Sheridan is attempting to resume contact with the surviving welders to invite them to transfer formal copyright of the whole set of letters to the Mass-Observation Archive.

I wish to thank staff at the Mass-Observation Archive for their assistance in my research and also the welders for their inspiration. I look forward to any opportunity to discuss and negotiate both the status and the content of the letters more directly with them.

Valentine Pearson sent diary reports to Mass-Observation from January 1940 until July 1941 and responded to M-O directives throughout the war. Unfortunately her diary ends before the period of the letters.

5 The collection also includes three letters from a boyfriend of one of the women to Valentine Pearson.

6 The women had been sent by their employment exchanges in Penistone and Huddersfield to be trained by Miss Pearson at her father's firm in Sheffield in 1941–2.

7 I have taken some of the details of the welders' situation from the references to and extracts from the letters in Dorothy Sheridan (Ed.) (1991) *Wartime Women: A Mass-Observation Anthology, The Experiences of Women at War*, London: Mandarin Paperbacks, pp. 176–80, and Gail Braybon and Penny Summerfield (1987) *Out of the Cage: Women's Experiences in Two World Wars*, London and New York: Pandora Press, pp. 190–1, 204, 209, 217, 222, 229.

8 MOA Box Women In Wartime, 3F, letter 44. From now on all quotations are from this source (note that references follow the letters' original numbering by the earlier archivists). Quotations are taken from the original letters, without changing spelling or punctuation.

9 Here I attempt to meet that challenge. It is also a step towards a general revaluation of letters as a genre. Letters have been relatively neglected in the current wave of critical interest in autobiographical forms of writing, and the concurrent attempts to think through the complex relationships between discourse, form and history. This is despite the way that the genre raises interesting questions about reading–writing relations, the construction of self–other relationships in writing and the distinction between private and public forms of writing. It is a particulary surprising neglect in feminist theory of autobiography, since there is a strong historical connection between women and the epistolary form.

10 *Out of the Cage*, p. 204.
11 See *Out of the Cage*, p. 190.
12 Amy indeed during the course of the letters is advised to give up welding due to burns on her eyes, which she is very upset about – and that isn't only about the money.
13 A spate of letter-collections was published testifying to the British spirit particularly after the events of 1940. See, for example, Diana Forbes Robertson and Roger W. Straus (1941) *War Letters from Britain*, New York: Putnam.
14 Louise K. Horowitz (1981) 'The Correspondence of Madame de Sévigné: Letters or Belles-Lettres?', *French Forum*, vol. 6, pp. 13–27.
15 Agnes is sometimes referred to as Fanny.
16 See Judy Barrett Litoff and David. C. Smith (1990) '"Will He Get My Letter?": Popular Portrayals of Mail and Morale During World War II', *Journal of Popular Culture*, vol. 23, no. 4, pp. 21–44.
17 Indeed, Penny Summerfield is currently modifying her influential thesis that the war saw no profound change in women's status in the light of her interviews with older women who testify to its importance in their life-histories: Penny Summerfield (1993) 'Work, Horror, Maturation and Love: The Second World War in Women's Lives', presentation at Women's History Network Conference, London, September.

Chapter 4

Making Sense of the Self: Cultural Identities Under Pressure

PART ONE

A strategy for survival

Clare Blake

On 11 April 1986, Brian Keenan, a lecturer in English at the American University of Beirut, was kidnapped, while on his way to work. He was bundled into a green Mercedes and then for the next four and a half years kept hostage in the underground prisons of Lebanon. John McCarthy, a British journalist, was also taken captive, six days later. Their kidnap was a political retaliation – they were pawns in a war game between Britain and the Muslims in the Lebanon. They both experienced initial periods of isolation, but the two men were put in the same cell for their remaining captivity. Both men have gone on to write autobiographies which tell of their experience. Brian Keenan's autobiography, *An Evil Cradling*, is a deeply philosophical account of his experience – detailing his feelings, his growing understanding of himself, those around him, and their situation.

Keenan's imprisonment, and its translation from a tangible experience to a narrative form, is indeed remarkable. The very nature of this book demands that we do not read it thoughtlessly. It is a powerful and passionate portrayal of a man's deepening self-awareness through all that he had to endure. It challenges its readers to re-evaluate what they may view as the purposes and function of autobiography.

James Olney writes, 'A man's life-work is his fullest autobiography.'[1] What grounds do Keenan and the other hostages have for writing a book at this stage in their lives, barely middle-aged, and with much of life still ahead of them? The key to this lies in the understanding of their lives that they have reached, rather than the number of years they have been alive. One of the most prevalent things that emerges is that we read, in autobiography, an experience of the 'self' of the writer, whether or not we receive this view of 'self' in an ordered, logical format. Keenan, himself, is his own theorist, because he is committed to analysing his experience and to producing a meaning from it. Keenan has no time for what he calls the 'voyeuristic vulture'. In his preface he describes the reasons for writing his book, and also sets out to explain the processes that will unfold within the book. He writes, 'This book will be an attempt to reveal men "in extremis"' and he describes how the book is both a therapy and an exploration. It is so much more than simply a chronological catalogue of events, or a revelation of the horrors of imprisonment and torture. *An Evil Cradling* is an exploration into the very soul of one man, which, as James Saynor of the *Observer*, in his review of the book, says, 'plunges far deeper into a mind stripped to its essentials than one had a right to expect'. As one reads this book, it reveals itself most fully in two dimensions. On the one hand, its creation is a therapy. By the end of the book, we feel that some form of healing has indeed taken place, both for Keenan and, perhaps, even for us, as some readers may be touched by this work. As well as this, though, it is impossible not to be an awed spectator, captivated by his heroism, and appalled by his suffering. The effect that this book has on its readers is not to be underestimated. Keenan's preface seeks to prepare the reader for what will follow. In a sense it requires a purging of whatever preconceived attitudes one may try to bring to the book. It also warns what will follow – we are not spared the very frightening exposure to Keenan's insanity. Keenan 'imprisons it on paper' and, in so doing, has ultimate mastery over it, but the graphic details of his descent into madness are unflinchingly recorded. There is something haunting about the description of his madness, and the exposure of his mind as he battles to survive, which we as readers may find hard to ignore. Keenan has triumphed against these conditions, and I challenge anyone who reads this book not to marvel at the very small bridge which separates sanity from insanity, and thus be struck by the horror of what Keenan had to endure.

Highlighting a few extracts from the text will explain how Keenan came to survive his ordeal in the remarkable way that he did. This survival involved forming a strategy for coping, and this strategy crossed all aspects of his experience of life. An integral part of coping with his experience was the necessity for him to first come to terms with himself. His fellow captive, John McCarthy, found the same thing : 'Isolation' and 'seemingly endless amounts of time' were a recipe for long periods of introspection, and this involved dealing with the past – facing up to what they had done with their lives thus far, and also coping with the crushing feelings of failure and inadequacy that washed over them as they re-evaluated their lives. They found that a 're-birth' had to take place, a reassessment of both themselves and their role in the world, in order that they might then continue to survive and grow meaningfully, in their prison.

Perhaps we had learned much about ourselves in that long period of isolation, delving back into our history and stopping abruptly to confront the full meaning of a specific incident.... It seemed as I thought back over the poignancy and vividness of these memories that I had been more blind then than I was now even in the darkness with this piece of cloth perpetually confining my eyes.[2]

This reassessment of themselves enabled them to reach new levels of self-awareness, and it equipped them to cope with their ordeal. They found strength in their new understanding. It is as though their time away from the normalities of life had reopened their eyes to the possibilities life held, and they considered their own role and value in the world. This 'awakening' meant that they were able to find a meaning in their lives thus far, and a meaning in what they were enduring in their cells. Without this experience, they might not have come to have such a clear understanding of themselves. Keenan's background and personality were a vital key in helping him survive. A hot-headed and sometimes stubborn Irishman, he had been brought up in Northern Ireland, and was familiar with the threat of terrorists and the IRA. Therefore, from this background he had formulated a view of the terrorist mentality, and his attitude and response was already ingrained in his blood.

> I was brought up in that harsh, divided landscape of the Northern Irish working class and I came into captivity with all its attendant baggage, good and bad. John McCarthy, from the utterly different background of the English upper class, discovered his own 'people' and baggage. In the circumstances in which we found ourselves physically chained together we both realised an extraordinary capacity to unchain ourselves from what we had known and been – and to set free those trapped people and parts of ourselves. We came to understand that these trapped people included our own captors and we were able to incorporate them in our healing process. All these people that John and I discovered and shared in the deepest intimacy of our confinement spoke, I believe, of a world familiar to us all – a world laden with social, cultural, political and philosophical divisions which manifest themselves in their most extreme and confused forms on the streets of Belfast and Beirut.[3]

Accepting himself was a crucial aspect of coming to terms with his imprisonment. This cocooned him from being destroyed by the wider reality of his plight – of being a pawn in a political war game between the West and the East. In a way, the war, for Keenan, was not simply one that raged against his Islamic captors – although it is significant, and will be examined later – but it was also a battle for control of himself. The methods he used are a lesson for us all, and his bravery speaks volumes about his strength of character and his capacity for endurance.

Keenan describes how he used memories as a strategy for breaking free. One such memory flooded back to him, in his prison cell, and he used it as a motto for the rest of his imprisonment. These were the words of Homer which were carved in stone on the entrance to the American University of Beirut – 'To strive, to seek, to find and not to yield'. He would not give in to the crushing despair, or the creeping madness which threatened to consume him, as he had seen it do to others. He was and is, by nature, an extremely philosophical person, and so was able to use this to preserve a sense of himself amid the mental chaos that enveloped him. His use of this strategy was invaluable to him, because he planned to stand outside of himself in the greatest moments of his madness and observe himself travelling down this path to insanity, without yielding or submitting to it.

Keenan took this one step beyond simply observing. As a lecturer in English, he had a great fascination with words and narrative, and he used his gifts to further help him survive. In order to, as he describes, 'repossess himself', he embarked on writing down every minute of his madness and then he reviewed it every few days. The following extract embodies the very essence of why I consider this book to be so powerful. It concerns the recording of his madness on paper, but I think that its significance far exceeds this individual incident. It epitomizes what I have understood to be part of a definition of 'autobiography':

> I would record my feelings, never trying to work them into a structured language or comprehensible form, simply recording everything as it happened, how it happened... At intervals of three of four days I would read over what I had written and then deal with what confronted me: a rigmarole of confusing ideas, of abstract thinking, of religious mania, of longing, of grief for my family, so much of it incomprehensible to me but there in front of me, a witness to myself; I had thought this, believed this, written this. How could I make sense of it? In all its confusion, this surreal manuscript had become my magnum opus. How little a person knows what is in himself...
>
> Eventually it came to me that here in these pages there was something I could only dimly perceive, some threads running through and holding it together like the veins that carry blood to the living heart. Here in all this confusion some veins of life held everything together. I don't fully know what it was, yet remember feeling that in these strange pages was a whole human being.[4]

Keenan was able to glimpse the very essence of himself. Having preserved this sense of who he was, he was able to fortify himself with such knowledge, and steady himself for the onslaught of whatever was to come. Keenan's autobiography does not contain this original 'diary of madness'. It is important to recognize that it existed, though, because it serves as a strange but vital source on which Keenan seems to have built his autobiography. It is possible that Keenan recognized, then, the huge value of narrative in creating sense and in containing an experience, and that he then applied this knowledge to the writing of his autobiography. While the original 'magnum opus' is not present here, it is possible to acknowledge its existence as a strategy for living through and making sense of his insanity, and it succeeds in creating something positive from the horror of his experience. What seems interesting to question is whether the writing from within his moments of madness could be deemed as being 'autobiography' itself, or whether its reworking makes it 'autobiography', when he writes from the vantage point of a more removed, much clearer 'under-standing of self'? If portraying a 'sense of self' is an important goal of the autobiographer, it is important to recognize both of these stages in his writing, as autobiography. This means acknowledging the fevered scribblings of his insanity as an intrinsic part of his 'self', in his reactions to the experience as it sought to consume him, and to see it as a valid narrative offering. *An Evil Cradling*, the finished narrative, is a coherent reflection of his experiences, and portrays a wider sense of himself than the single instance of his madness. Both, I would argue are 'autobiography', and both reveal the 'self' of Keenan. Whether or not we will ever be able to have access to those initial writings does not detract from the fact that this 'magnum opus' is written from deep within Keenan's 'self'. Its creation, stemming from a particular need, during his hostage experience, is enough to point to the employed use of a strategy – irrespective of this manuscript's existence or widespread availability now. To an extent, I am suggesting that this book is still very much an important part of his hostage experience. He has been able to translate the meaning he made from his ordeal – from an experience that went beyond words, thoughts and feelings, into a comprehensive, literary form. It has enabled Keenan to have ultimate mastery over his ordeal, by facing it again, and by 'locking it up' in words that do not betray himself, or what happened to him.

It is also important to look at Keenan's relationships with his fellow prisoners – in particular, his cohabitant, John McCarthy, because this was a significant part of Keenan's coping strategy. During their time together, the two men formed an extremely close bond, having got to know each other so well. This involved learning to live with one another, and accepting their different qualities as equally valuable and worthwhile. They learned from each other, and taught one another. On his release, Frank Reed, an American hostage, met up with Jill Morrell, John McCarthy's girlfriend, and described the relationship that Brian and John had formed: 'the whole thing was about two men living together, how they communicated with each other, how they supported each other. . . . It's a beautiful story'.[5]

At the moment of his release, in the text of his autobiography, Keenan considers his friendship with McCarthy, and this extract explains, in some small way, the richness of their relationship, and the way that their understanding of each other was vital to their endurance and survival. He debates whether to refuse his offered freedom, in favour of not abandoning McCarthy.

> I remember every moment of my time alone, my time with John and with those other captives. . . . And as I review it all, all that wonder, I see his face stare at mine. I had watched this man grow, become full and in his fullness enrich me. And I know that if in my defiance I walk back into that room and have myself chained, refusing to go home, I will have diminished him, for he is a bigger man than to succumb to the needs that isolation breeds. I cannot do this, I cannot belittle him. I know that in going free I will free him. He will not surrender, he has gone beyond it. I know that the deep bond our captivity has given us will be shattered if I return. Our respect for each other demands of each that we take our freedom when it comes.[6]

Keenan also harnessed to himself other discoveries that he made about his relationships with all of the prisoners, as a way of coping with life in his underground prison. For example, he came to understand that no one was better than the others – despite their feeble attempts to assert their own importance. Sharing in each other's suffering was also necessary, and to deny this, or to despise that person, was tantamount to hating oneself. Keenan acknowledged that often what he saw in others was merely a reflection of himself, and he had to find a way of coping with this pain. He describes how important it was to care for those who were sick, because, as he writes, 'It struck home to me that when we participate in another person's suffering, we in part heal ourselves'.[7]

Keenan also used his subjection to the threat of death to strengthen and sustain him, rather than live in constant fear for his life. On more than one occasion, he met the threat of death. One such example was through the menacing tricks of his captors, as they pretended to have killed other prisoners, using fake gunshots, in nearby rooms. Similarly, there were times when Keenan's defiance would leave him uncertain as to the consequences of his actions. On other occasions, he faced crazed beatings from his captors – irrational and violent men, in those moments, whose moves could not be predicted. Keenan learned, that in those moments of extreme violence, it was he who emerged the victor. He discovered a strength in enduring the beatings, and he described this to Jill Morrell, who records his words in her autobiography, *Some Other Rainbow*:

> He had intellectualised what had happened to him, and sometimes it was difficult to follow his thoughts, thoughts that he must have had honed over the years. The beatings were endurable, he said, they weren't the worst thing. When it was over, all the guard had done was beaten you: at the end your spirit was still there, so while the guard had demeaned

himself you were in a much stronger position than before. I could just about rationalise that, but it was difficult. It was an effort to follow Brian's argument at times, especially given the softness of his voice. I had to strain forward and leap over philosophical fences to keep up and I wasn't sure if I altogether understood.[8]

Keenan's constant subjection to the threat of death enabled him to pass beyond the fear of death. He writes: 'My own thoughts of death were the reverse of gloomy. It was dazzling and light-filled. Death was only a moment of life bursting into life.'[9] Much of his reasoning bore some relation to his understanding of his captors, because he recognized that they were more dominated by death than himself. In the same passage where he explains his view of death, he writes: 'Here was a world and a people trapped in death's shadow. The eclipse of the sun at the moment of crucifixion had not passed for them.' Keenan was able to form an understanding of his captors that enabled him to pity them, rather than have a great hatred for them. His time living in Beirut before his capture also enabled him to experience their culture, both from his dealings with people and from the stories that he heard. He came to recognize that his captors were prisoners, and, in a sense, less free than the men they were guarding. His captors' violence was cruel and often childish, but they seemed to be as fearful of the consequences of their violence as were their hostages, because it would be reported to their superiors. Keenan and his fellow captives came to recognize the responsibility of the West in contributing to the situation. Their captors had formed a distorted view of Western culture, from their obsession with the violent and sexual American videos that they watched loudly and avidly. They would often work themselves up into a frenzy and then vent their violence on their prisoners. Their narrow-minded assumptions that Keenan and McCarthy would have sexual relations, if they were not tied beyond each other's reach, is a further indication of their ignorance. As Keenan noted, 'The poison was not in the locks but in mental chains of our captors'.[10] Keenan's growing pity for these men stemmed from a growing understanding of the parallels between his own nationality and theirs:

What was in a man that allowed him to lock up another human being for long periods of total darkness – a human being he did not know or understand, who had given him no offence, nor committed any crime against him. We could never answer the questions we asked ourselves. But as we talked and tried to understand how these men could ever justify their actions, I recall saying to John 'I understand it, I accept it, even though I do not condone it . . . . I think I understand it.' John looked back at me, puzzled, and quick as a flash I said to him, 'Well in another sense now you know what it is like to be Irish'.[11]

Despite the obvious cultural differences, there were some parallels to be drawn between the warring world of Northern Ireland and the streets of Beirut. What we may constantly be in awe of is the strength of character that enabled Keenan to possess this understanding of himself and his situation, and to emerge with the clarity and insight which he now possesses. He has walked away from the experience with a freedom that not only marks his release from the physical chains that bound him, but which has also emancipated his whole outlook on his life and its potential.

Notes

1   James Olney (1972) *Metaphors of Self: The Meaning of Autobiography*, Princeton University Press.
2   Brian Keenan (1992) *An Evil Cradling*, London: Vintage, pp. 127–8.
3   *Ibid.*, p. xvi.
4   *Ibid.*, pp. 80–1.
5   John McCarthy and Jill Morrell (1993) *Some Other Rainbow*, London: Bantam.
6   Keenan, 1992, p. 292.
7   *Ibid.*, p. 176.
8   McCarthy and Morrell, 1993.
9   Keenan, 1992, p. 251.
10 *Ibid.*, p. 286.
11 *Ibid.*, p. 183.

PART TWO

Cultural identities under pressure

David Whitley

The focus of this account, linking two apparently very different kinds of narrative, emerged in the process of preparing a session for the conference on *The Uses of Autobiography* in the summer of 1994 at Homerton College. I had intended to write something for the conference on an aspect of V.S. Naipaul's travel narratives and, as usual, I was late getting my thoughts committed to paper. Whilst I was still turning various possible approaches around in my mind, I had the good fortune to be able to work with Clare Blake who was, at that stage, well advanced in preparing the third-year dissertation topic on Brian Keenan which was to form the basis for her own conference paper. It was her enthusiasm for Keenan's narrative which inspired my own interest, and suggested the possibility of combining a slightly different approach to Keenan's work with what I wanted to say about Naipaul. In coupling these writers together I may have taken advantage of the gifts of Fortune, but the linkage is not, I hope, entirely arbitrary. For in both these accounts the presentation of the author's 'self' is offered in the context of powerful judgments of the *otherness* of the fundamentalist Shiite Muslim culture to which each writer is exposed. But it is only partly the overlap in terms of content – or, more precisely cultural and political context – which concerns me here. A more intriguing contrast can be drawn between the clarity with which each of these narratives shapes judgments about fundamentalist Shiite culture, and the more problematic sense which is made of the 'self' within which these judgments are formed. The coexistence of these two modes – a problematic, potentially confusing sense of self-identity developed in a context where the *otherness* of an alien culture must be sharply defined – is not simply interesting. I want to argue here that it marks a kind of limit to the projects within which each of these autobiographical narratives strives to attain its inner coherence.

The nature of these projects is rather different but each writer is keenly sensitive to ways in which national identities may be deployed in constituting a sense of self and other. In Brian Keenan's account of his experiences as a hostage in *An Evil Cradling*, for instance, 'Irishness' acquires a central significance. In the early stages of his narrative, Keenan's Irish identity is construed mainly as a site of political neutrality in relation to the conflicts raging in the Lebanon. He comes across as an outsider, concerned but also detached from the situation. In the period immediately following his capture Keenan draws on this identity to shore up his optimism and strength with the hope of an early release. This hope, partly willed, is founded on the view that Ireland (unlike Britain) is not implicated in the Anglo-American axis of power around which the hostage campaign is primarily focused.

But as the time spent in captivity lengthens, the chimerical nature of this view becomes more apparent, and it is gradually replaced by a more powerful and engaged construct of Irish identity. This emerges in particularly complex forms in the developing relationship with John McCarthy, but it is also involved in the way Keenan articulates his relationship to his captors. Here his 'Irishness' is seen as a fundamental resource in defining a stance of resistance to the oppressive, dehumanizing conditions in which he finds himself. But it is also a way of establishing connectedness, of laying claim to an understanding of his captors and the way they think. This assertion of cultural identity both to resist and to comprehend is sustained through the notion of historical parallels between the culture and history which sustains terrorism in Northern Ireland and that which pertains to Palestine and the Lebanon. Knowing the culture which engenders terrorism in Ireland, it is implied, provides a route to understanding the basis of all terrorism – even that which emanates from apparently very different cultures. The basis of this understanding is more psychological than historical, though it includes an awareness of cultural identity and the way this is shaped. It results most characteristically (although there are eddies of sympathy within the main current) in an assertion of disdain for the attitudes and motivations of the Lebanese guards. This is often couched in terms of a universal psychological explanation for their conduct. The following passage is fairly representative of this aspect of the writing.

> Allah, the God of retribution and judgement, dominated their minds. How can a man love the thing he fears? When fear commands the mind then the heart is imprisoned. In time I came to understand the greater and more profound prison that held our captors. For years we were chained to a wall or radiator, but they were chained to their guns; futile symbols of power, not power itself: real power embraces; it cannot destroy.[1]

The emotionally uplifting notion that 'real power' is positive and essentially loving (it 'embraces') derives, I would suggest, from a therapeutic perspective on human consciousness and development. It is the psychology of personal growth which is invoked here, made more powerful, perhaps, by the rhetorical form, which is nuanced with an alternative language of religion and faith. The authority to pronounce judgment in this form derives from a particular inflection of the author's Irish identity, though. Brian Keenan's individual suffering makes it necessary – indeed essential for his psychological survival – to forge a strong view of his captors and their relation to him. This view inverts the demeaning aspects of the ritual humiliations which are daily enacted on the prisoners, so that it is the guards who, in the narrative, come to be seen as less than human, alienated, imprisoned. But for the writer's individual suffering to become meaningful, it needs a reference point which is larger than the individual. Here the authority of the writer's voice is enlarged through the association of Keenan's individual suffering with the whole history of oppression and resistance sustained by the Irish people. This association becomes most explicit in the record of conversations between Keenan and John McCarthy. Here, for instance, they consider how their captors could justify what they were doing:

> we found ourselves talking of how men could do such things as had been done to us.... We could never answer the questions we asked ourselves. But as we talked and tried to understand how these men could ever justify their actions, I recall saying to John 'I understand it, I accept it, even though I do not condone it ... I think I understand it.' John looked back at me puzzled, and quick as a flash I said to him 'Well in another sense now you know what it is like to be Irish.' He knew what I was hinting at, for so many people in the history of Ireland had lost their lives or liberty and now here was this English man undergoing something of the agony that people were still suffering in English jails.[2]

Here the ambiguities and tensions that inform Keenan's selected memories of life in Belfast before leaving for the Lebanon appear to be resolved in a moment that is seized on as an instance of illuminating clarity. Both here and within the wider context of Keenan's relationship to Irish history there is a strongly expressed need to find a horizon beyond the immediate confusions of pain and violence that will enable strong, clear judgments to be formed.

Yet this assertion of 'Irishness' is not simple, for it is itself born out of significant gaps, silences and elisions. In the bulk of the text, relating events from the years of incarceration, Keenan lays claim to a kind of pan-Irish identity: a romantic amalgamation of the qualities of creativity, stubbornness and passionate resistance that together constitute a literary appropriation of Irish history. But this literary typology succeeds precisely because it runs together sharp divisions of class, religious and political affiliation from the actual history. Brian Keenan's own background, as he acknowledges in the early sections of his narrative, is more specific than the pan-Irish identity that provides such powerful moral and emotional underpinning for the later part of the book. His family and roots are in Protestant, working-class Belfast. This provides a strong, particular kind of cultural identity in its own right, of course, but the strongest emotional and political affiliations point towards mainland Britain rather than to a more purely Irish identity within which sharp historical divisions might be dissolved. The early part of the autobiography glosses – tantalizingly – over what one assumes must have been a profound shift in allegiances.

What emerges from this silence is a desire to move outside the framework of the political in constructing meaning for events. In this context the curiously inconsequential story of Keenan's defiance of the union strike action while a student at Belfast University becomes a strange parable for a more general attempt to chart a path towards an arena for action and thought that transcends politics in a dogged, rather isolated, heroic and individual way. One wonders, indeed, whether the initial attraction of Beirut was that it represented a displacement – different, less personally implicating – of that nexus of political forces that had proved so painfully intransigent and irresolvable in Ireland. Certainly the specific form in which Keenan attempts to make 'sense of the self' – his coming to terms with the significance of the historical moment within which the years of torture and imprisonment were embedded – involves a denial of the determining power of the political that seems to have both conscious and unconscious components. The movement of the narrative is insistently (and perhaps understandably) inwards; the language of analysis has most impact where it draws on therapeutic and, ultimately, in an odd inchoate way, spiritual perspectives which equate political force with impotence.

In a sense, V.S. Naipaul's travel narrative *Among the Believers* moves in the opposite direction. The terms of reference for travel narrative writing do not attempt, in the first instance, to evaluate inner experience, and the impulse towards understanding and explaining the cultural *other* encountered on the journey has more natural roots in this genre. Nevertheless, Naipaul's writing also turns on the intellectual power which accrues from not only describing but also placing, questioning and, at certain key moments, shaping strong critical judgments in relation to cultural difference. Subtly, almost incrementally, the lineaments of the cultural identity and values of the author's self are threaded into the narrative process that shapes these judgments. 'Making sense of the self' is not a strategy for survival as it is in Keenan's narrative. But a keenly discriminating awareness of the different strands of cultural experience and identity that inform the writer's judging self is very much part of the dialectical movement of the narrative. The complex cultural identity of the author's self is represented with just sufficient cogency and force to provide a clear, evaluative basis for the critique of the *other* – Islamic fundamentalist culture – which is the primary focus here. Yet the clarity of exposition depends, as I hope to show, to an extraordinary degree on equivocation in terms of the way the author's self can be represented in the process of communicating with others on the journey. To put it more crudely, Naipaul keeps having to lie about himself to keep the lines of communication open and stay afloat. It is some of the implications of this enforced misrepresentation of self that I want to test out.

The first part of Naipaul's book, on which I wish to concentrate, relates events primarily centred on interviews conducted with editors and journalists in Tehran and on a journey to the holy city of Qom, where a further interview has been set up with the Ayatollah Khalkhalli. The latter has acquired the nickname of the 'hanging judge' because of his role in speedily expediting a large number of executions in the immediate aftermath of Iran's revolution. The narrative begins seemingly innocently, almost arbitrarily, in the middle of events. Naipaul finds himself let down by one guide and having to engage another – Behzad, a politically active communist with whom he strikes up a much more sympathetic alliance – in order to make the journey to Qom successfully. But as events progress it becomes clear that, although sequences appear to follow on naturally, there has been a careful selection of key incidents and images whose collective force underpins central passages of cultural judgment and analysis. The narrative itself is not perfunctory: it has its own momentum, interest and vitality; but in the larger structures of the novel its representative functions are subordinated, unobtrusively and with great craft, to the requirements of the cultural analysis. As with Keenan, the cultural identity of the author plays a crucial part in producing a particular kind of authority for the voice articulating these judgments. Cultural identity here, though, does not rely on affiliation to a single national set of characteristics, but rather asserts a plurality of associations. Naipaul's childhood home was in Trinidad; his family history relates him to upper-caste Hindu culture in India, his education and early adult life to Britain; he has lived for long periods in the United States and South America and owes much in terms of intellectual development and range of cultural sympathies to these countries; and, of course, his professional reputation rests in perhaps equal parts on his identity as both novelist and travel writer. The point here is not only the sheer range of cultural allegiances and perspectives that are potentially in play, although the dominant authorial tone – urbane, self-possessed, highly attuned to the nuances of cultural difference, yet not tied to a specific cultural field – is obviously dependent on this. But the perhaps more significant point is that this plurality of cultural identities creates not only opportunities for the travel writer – the range of sympathies and understandings being correspondingly vast – but also a crucial problem. Which of these cultural identities should be allowed to dominate in creating meaning from the experience on which the writer works? If more than one, how will an overall sense of coherence be established? Or should this cultural pluralism be allowed to establish itself in a mode where relative values have freer play – a post-modern refusal to locate meaning within a single coherent viewpoint?

It is my contention that Naipaul resolves – rather than solves – this problem by adopting two main strategies. The first of these is deeply rooted in the culture of his intellectual training. I take this to be grounded on the Anglo-American empiricist tradition in terms of cultural and historical analysis. The basis of this tradition is embedded in humanist principles and presuppositions. By 'humanist principles' I am referring to the long tradition of scholarship and debate which is predicated on the view that careful, discriminating and scrupulous weighing of evidence is sufficient to establish authoritative judgments that can be substantiated with some objectivity. The analysis that is offered as an integral part of Naipaul's narrative partakes of this humanist project both in terms of its scrupulous weighing of evidence and in the confident assertion of judgments which ensue. This is a rationalist tradition, originating in the Renaissance, sharpened in focus and philosophical orientation during the Enlightenment.

The humanist element in Naipaul's intellectual training, then, provides him with an identity as a writer more attuned to scholarship than to journalism. The clear, unforced eloquence of the prose style is likewise in key with humanist values relating to expression: it is the style early humanists identified as classical. But the humanist principles underlying this style of analysis also mean that a plurality of potential viewpoints must be subordinated to the demands of a single coherent value system. Otherwise objectivity falls prey to cultural relativism. Here a second strategy comes into play. Certain cultural perspectives must be given much higher profile than others in shaping judgments, so that the coherence of the evaluating voice rather than plurality of viewpoints will hold sway. In fact, the axis upon which the most central judgments are located is that which relates Iran to the United States. At the time the narrative was written, 1980, this was also the axis along which the most powerful and significant political tensions were developing. In this approach, then, judgments which might be formed from a British Trinidadian or South American perspective are made less relevant. An Indian cultural identity is invoked in making understandable conversations that develop in modes characterized as 'Eastern', but it is the civilization of the United States which is the litmus test for evaluating the kind of culture Iran appears poised to become.

One of the most complete – and succinct – articulations of the kind of judgments that are developed along this line occurs at the end of a passage summarizing the plot of an 'accomplished' Iranian novel, written just before the fall of the Shah, which Naipaul construes as symptomatic of a fundamental fault line developing in Iranian culture. The novel, written in English by a young Iranian woman, Nahid Rachlin, tells the story of Feri, an Iranian research biologist who has married an American and initially lives and works in Boston. Returning to Iran on a holiday and falling ill there, she gradually becomes more and more alienated from her American life. A doctor who treats her leads her to feel that she should give up her life in the United States and return to Iran permanently. It is worth quoting the latter part of Naipaul's summary and the judgment he draws from this in full:

> Feri's American husband, previously summoned, arrives to take her back. He is seen as a stranger, but fairly (and this fairness is part of the novel's virtue): a man of work and intellect, private rather than solitary, self-sufficient, a man made by another civilisation, his marriage to an Iranian his single unconventional act. It is impossible for Feri to go back with someone so remote to the American emptiness. She will lose her research job. But she doesn't mind. She will, in fact, lay down that anxious, all-external life of work and the intellect. She will do as the doctor did; she will visit mosques and shrines, and to do that she will put on the 'chador'. She feels she has never really been happy. Tranquillity comes to her with her renunciation (and oddly – a good

stroke of the novelist's – ideas for research which she will never now carry out).

And – though the novelist doesn't make the point – it is as if Feri and the doctor, turning away from the life of the intellect and endeavour, have come together in an Iranian death pact. In the emotions of their Shia religion, so particular to them, they will rediscover their self esteem and wholeness, and be inviolate. They will no longer simply have to follow after others, not knowing where the rails are taking them. They will no longer have to be last, or even second. And life will go on. Other people in spiritually barren lands will continue to produce the equipment the doctor is proud of possessing and the medical journals he is proud of reading.

That expectation – of others continuing to create, of the alien, necessary civilisation going on – is implicit in the act of renunciation, and is its great flaw.[3]

The judgment here – and it is central to Naipaul's account – is clear. Feri's and the doctor's choice is representative. Iran has rejected what America is here represented as standing for: the 'life of the intellect and endeavour'. What the characters in the novel perceive as peace, spiritual tranquillity, Naipaul interprets roundly as a 'death pact'. And the path which Iran has chosen, implied in Feri's act of renunciation, is seen as fundamentally flawed – the fierce rejection of Western values locked into a complacent and unacknowledged dependence on the material and intellectual productivity of the West.

Whether this judgment is as just as it purports to be is not a question I want to pursue here. Although it begs many questions about post-colonial independence, it is clear and, within its own terms of reference, coherent. This coherence is achieved, I have suggested, by bringing potentially contradictory strands of cultural identity into focus within the compass of a single country's representative function. Although it could obviously be seen in other ways, America here stands for Western creativity and productive energy generally. But the coherent viewpoint that is achieved here at a level of general analysis is counterpointed, even threatened, by the potential fragmentation of cultural identity in the autobiographical narrative. Here – particularly where the chosen narrative form is directly reported dialogue – the cool, firm judgments that are offered in general perspective give way to the most convoluted twisting as different options for the author's representation of his own cultural identity are assessed, screened and complexly evaluated in terms of the response they are likely to engender. Here, for instance, is an extract relating a conversation with an Iranian physician on the plane flying out to Iran which is initiated through Naipaul's mistaking the identity of his wife:

He . . . said in English that his family were in the seats across the aisle:

his son and daughter, and his handsome wife, who couldn't speak English but who smiled forgivingly at my error. He was a physician. He and his family had just been to the United States to see their eighteen-year-old son.

I recognised that we were beginning to fall into an eastern, Indian kind of conversation, and I responded as I thought I should. I said, 'But that must have been expensive.'

'It was expensive. For the fare alone, 800 pounds per person. Except for the girl. She's under twelve. Over twelve you pay full fare. Have you been to the United States?'

'I've just spent a year there.'

'Are you a physician?'

I didn't feel, going to Iran, I should say I was a writer. I said, 'I am a teacher'. Then I felt I had pitched it too low, so I added, 'A professor'.

'That's good.' And, as though he drew courage from my calling and my time in America, he said. 'The revolution is terrible.'[4]

Later in the narrative these hesitations over an acceptable choice of professional identity will be made to appear simple beside the writhings that occur in relation to religious and national affiliation in an interview with the Ayatollah Shirazi. Here Behzad translates Shirazi's questions for the beleaguered Naipaul:

'He wants to know what your religion is.'

'What can I say?'

'You must tell me.'

I said, 'I am still a seeker.'

Shirazi, his face calm, his large eyes smiling, assessing, spoke at length. His enunciation was clear, deliberate, full of rhythm. His full lipped mouth opened wide, his clean teeth showed.

Behzad said, 'He wants to know what you were before you became a seeker. You must have been born into some kind of belief.'

It was of the Pakistani students that I was nervous. They had been told – with some truth, but more for the sake of simplicity – that I came from America but was not an American. For them to hear now that my ancestry was Hindu would, I thought, be unsettling to them; the Hindu–Muslim antagonisms of the Indo-Pakistani subcontinent went deep. They would feel fooled; and they had been so welcoming, so open. They had arranged this meeting with their great teacher, and even now never took their gaze – beatific rather than obedient or even awed – off Shirazi.

I said to Behzad, 'Can you tell him I never had any belief? Tell him I was born far away, in the Americas, and wasn't brought up to any faith.'

'You can't tell him that. Say you are a Christian.'

'Tell him that.'

And as soon as Behzad began to talk, I regretted what I had asked him to say. Shirazi hadn't been taken in by my equivocations, he knew that something was wrong.[5]

Such passages convey an acute sense of cultural identity not as expressive of existential roots but rather as a kind of social semiotic. It is the way cultural tags are read as signs by others that is the issue at stake here; the possibility of offending, disturbing or creating dangerous antagonisms is ever present and the conversation develops in a kind of vertiginous spiral, the gulf in terms of what is communicable becoming more and more apparent. The author, of course, seeks to maintain purposeful clarity in terms of meaning offered to the reader. Though they demonstrate confusion, the limits of what can be known and shared with others, such passages do so in an exemplary way. They illustrate the anxiety, the restrictions, at the heart of this culture and the resulting tensions. This is another dimension to the cultural analysis on offer, and as such it is quite consistent. But it is also another way of telling; it creates an authorial presence made manifest not through exquisitely controlled, lucid exposition but rather through anxiety – defensive, exposed. And this anxiety springs from the coexistence of such multiple possibilities for cultural identity and the forms in which this may be expressed. Here we witness the return of that plurality of cultural perspectives and meanings that has elsewhere been crafted into a single coherent focus. Just as the therapeutic project which underlies Keenan's writing is driven by the force of the political which it seeks to negate or transcend, so in Naipaul's narrative the desire to shape a clear view, informed by broad, humanist values, is worked through in a context in which cultural identities are represented as polarized, precarious and fragmented. Both narratives show cultural identities under intense pressure; both shape themselves around contradictions inherent in these pressures.

Notes

1 Brian Keenan (1992) *An Evil Cradling*, London: Vintage, p. 147.

2 *Ibid.*, p. 183.

3 V.S. Naipaul (1981) *Among the Believers*, New York: Alfred A. Knopf, p. 15.

4 *Ibid.*, p. 17.

5 *Ibid.*, p. 50.

Chapter 5

Constructing the Self, Inventing Africa

PART ONE

Gender and iconography in auto/biographies of Nelson and Winnie Mandela

Cheryl-Ann Michael

> [In] iconographic representation ... specific individual realities are ...
> given mythic extension through association with the qualities of a class.
> ... [T]he myth of difference from the rest of humanity, is thus, to an
> extent, composed of fragments of the real world, perceived through the
> ideological bias of the observer.[1]

Two images of Nelson and Winnie Mandela dominate the envisioning of the
New South Africa. The first is of the couple walking hand-in-hand through the
gates of Victor Verster prison on the day of Mandela's release – emblems of the
promise of a free nation. The second image is of the couple, now estranged,
seated together at the first opening of parliament, gazing uncomfortably away
from each other – an unhappy portent for the birth of the new nation.[2] Here I look
at auto/biographical representations of Nelson and Winnie Mandela as icons of
a future nation. I suggest that their 'specific individual realities' are given
'mythic extension' through an association with an ideal of nation which is
imagined through the metaphor of the family. The conflation of the family and
nation is seductive because it allows a projection of both the ordinary (we the
people) and the ideal onto a real family. They are at once of the people and
exemplary. As Gilman suggests, they are icons because they embody both
difference and familiarity.

The autobiographical writings of the Mandelas are constructed by editors out
of interviews and/or collections of largely political writings (in the case of Nelson
Mandela), and include profiles of the subjects by other people. To what extent, and

to what end do the subjects collude with or resist constructed images? How do gendered constructions of family influence an envisaging of nation? What are the *uses* of political autobiography? Lives in biography as well as autobiography are often structured retrospectively, seemingly tracing the subject's development to the present. It has been argued, however, that past events are selected and narrated to accord with the self-image of present 'I'.[3] In political autobiographies, I argue, what is presented is an illusion of a linear development of political consciousness which cloaks an erasure of differences between past selves and the present 'I' or subject, thereby enhancing his/her iconic stature.

In auto/biographies of Nelson Mandela, the man is clearly the father of the child. His biographers stress the importance of his royal background in shaping his leadership qualities. Mary Benson reads Mandela's running away from an arranged marriage as 'symboliz[ing] a deeper rejection [of] chieftainship ... he had made up his mind never to rule over an oppressed people'.[4] A youthful decision made prior to his entry into politics is recast from the vantage point of his present role. Mandela's rejection of communism is explained, not in terms of the political debates of his adult years, but as originating in 'his strongly traditional background [and] his religious upbringing [which] had taught him that communists were anti-Christ'.[5] The emphasis on Mandela's traditional background serves a dual purpose. It presents his abilities as a leader as inherent and essential, and at the same time soothes the fears of Western powers, offering Mandela as a sympathetic figure, a bulwark against communism. Mandela himself emphasizes his traditional background, offering an idyllic version of pre-colonial history:

> Then our people lived peacefully, under the democratic rule of their kings.... All men were free and equal and this was the foundation of government ... in such a society are contained the seeds of revolutionary democracy, in which ... poverty, want and insecurity shall be no more.[6]

The shift from the past to the future tense signals a post-colonial fusion of a Western concept of nation with the egalitarian values of the pre-colonial African past. Caroline Neale argues that historical writing in the decade following decolonization in Africa was dominated by the need to prove that equality between black and white was possible, and by 'the idea of progress'.

> 'Achievements' were still defined in Western terms, in the context of an evolution from more primitive forms toward the modern nation-state, which was seen as the culmination of mankind's progress to date. The creation of African self-respect was felt to rest upon repeated demonstrations that Africans, too, had participated in and contributed to this development.[7]

Mandela's vision of the future nation, therefore, does not mark a radical departure from Western concepts, but offers conciliation. It is significant that during the treason trials sympathetic newspapers abroad such as the *New York Times* cast the Rivonia men as 'the George Washingtons and Ben Franklins of South Africa', and did not draw the more obvious comparison with black American leaders such as Malcolm X and Martin Luther King.[8] Such portrayals remove the disruptive threat of resistance, allowing the leaders to be incorporated into an acceptable 'Western democratic' paradigm of freedom.

Imprisoned, Mandela's image as the future leader took on iconic dimensions. This was reinforced through profiles by fellow prisoners such as Mac Maharaj and Michael Dingake. We learn that Mandela never engaged in small talk, but conducted himself as if he were already in office, meeting people by appointment, and devising strategies to challenge prison conditions. He 'is a very friendly and warm person, but ... he maintains a distance', and 'has had the confidence of all prisoners whatever their political persuasion'.[9] His daughter Zindzi, recalling her first visit to Robben Island, proudly relates that among the prisoners, 'Mandela is considered the father, the leader'.[10] During prison visits, conversation being restricted to family concerns, Mandela used the term 'my people' to fool the warders and convey and receive political information.[11]

The combination of austerity and approachability, of benevolent father and flawless leader, created a potent icon of a free nation, and it is Mandela's absence from the everyday world which made possible the impossible perfection of this figuration. It is significant that in *Higher than Hope*, written in anticipation of his imminent release, Fatima Meer seeks to show Mandela as an ordinary person, to bring him closer to the people for most of whom he had been a faceless symbol. She chooses the family as a means of dispelling the alienating distance of the icon, dwelling on ordinary activities such as watching videos and playing with grandchildren.[12]

While Nelson Mandela's image conflates 'father' with 'leader', Winnie Mandela's identity fluctuates ambivalently between that of Mother of the Nation and African Warrior Queen. Meer establishes her descendence from Madikezela, 'a marauding chieftain',[13] and in her introduction, Benjamin compares Winnie Mandela to Ma Nthatisi, the widow of an influential Sotho Chief, a 'woman of great intelligence, beauty and political talent' who had once ruled the area to which Mrs Mandela was banned.[14] However, what is stressed is her nurturing image, her beauty and vulnerability: '[S]he had not become a single-minded political fighter, tough and immune, but has remained vulnerable'.[15] 'In twenty years she had become a leader in her own right; and she had become more beautiful'.[16] Benson mentions Winnie Mandela's initial attraction to The Unity Movement in the context of Nelson Mandela's joke of having rescued her from a rival organization.[17] Winnie Mandela herself, however, rewrites this period of her history in her auto/biography, claiming to have 'drifted to the ANC' with friends, prior to her meeting Mandela.[18] If, as I argue below, Winnie Mandela bases and justifies her own power on her husband's symbolic status, then she must show their political views to be identical. Divergent political views (even those of the past) may disrupt the emotional force of the metaphor of family as a unified nation. Profiles by friends emphasize her interest in politics as manifest in concern for less fortunate people, even before her marriage.[19] She appears destined to fulfill the role of Mother of the Nation. When Nelson Mandela is sentenced to imprisonment Benson does not quote what she describes as Winnie's 'typically powerful and brave statement', but lingers instead on the private spectacle of grief: 'When she reached her home in Orlando, after putting the children to bed, she broke down and wept'.[20] In shaping an appeal, the picture of the bereft wife and mother offers greater opportunities for sympathy than the strong statement of resistance.

Winnie Mandela herself describes the experience of living under bans in terms of its preventing her fulfilling a mother's role: 'I was never there as a mother to hold my little girls' hands, take them to school'.[21] Her recognition of the potential of the image of motherhood for gaining sympathy does not, however, lead her to political inertia. While Nelson Mandela saw politics as involving separation from his family,[22] she redefines 'each black home [as] a political institution' where the mother is a political mentor to her children.[23] While Mandela sees violence as a last resort, she argues that 'you have to use the language they understand: to have peace, you must be violent'.[24] However, although she rejects the admonishments of Mandela and the family lawyer George Bizos that she is 'completely and utterly undisciplined' and behaves like 'an Amazon', her denial is couched in the form of justifying her behaviour as self-defence. She emphasizes, too, her esteem for Bizos: 'I would listen to him as I would listen to my father. He treats me in the same way Nelson does'.[25] Her declaration : 'I came to believe that my own struggle is to be won by means of blood and iron' is framed by an amusing anecdote about an eccentric teacher's obsession with Bismarck.[26] Interestingly, Benjamin, who otherwise presents taped interviews as a series of seamless first-person narrations by Winnie Mandela, erasing her own participation, inserts '(*Laughs*)' in parentheses at the end of this anecdote, drawing a heavy-handed emphasis on her presence, verifying that this was not meant seriously. Here the awareness both of Winnie Mandela and of Benjamin, as editor, of the importance of presenting self and subject in a mode of appeal, manifests itself in a concern to play down the element of threat, of the uncontrollable inherent in the image of the Warrior Queen. Winnie Mandela's repeated invocation of Mandela as father-figure may be understood in this light, but I suggest that her references to the 'father–daughter' elements of their relationship – 'I sometimes think, for him I am just a continuation of his children'[27] reveal her ambiguous perspectives on gender and political action. She declares that her mother's longing for a son instils in her a determination to 'prove to her that a girl is as much of value to a parent as a son', but she associates her mother with a doomed Christian fatalism, a passivity which she rejects in favour of the ardour of her father's stories of Xhosa warriors and leaders.[28] The development of her political consciousness is male-centred – '[w]hen my father taught me history, I began to understand'.[29] She expresses her admiration of prominent women in the ANC and acknowledges their influence upon her, but adds: 'they were just a continuation of Nelson . . . . When I was with them, I felt I was with Nelson'.[30] This, of course, is not meant to be a devaluation of women's political roles. Her conflation of the cult of the political personality with a male figurehead, in this instance her husband, may reflect a deliberate presentation which wins her a space centre-stage. Yet, at the same time, it might reveal, too, the contours of her relationship with Mandela as being shaped to some degree by the esteem of a pupil for a mentor. What is clear is that Winnie Mandela's *recognition*, if not acceptance, that the political arena is male-dominated, leads her to present her own political role as developing under the aegis of the father/leader.

Her seeming self-effacement may be read as a strategy which allows her to establish a power-base during the period of her banning. She ascribes the support of black people in Brandfort to their reverence of Nelson,[31] and refers to her husband as the personification of the struggle: 'I knew when I married him, that I married the struggle'.[32] As his wife, she is able to make use of the aura of his power without appearing to be seeking power for herself, thus avoiding the censure of the Left. Equating Nelson with the struggle allows her to claim a symbolic role for herself: 'I have ceased a long time ago to exist as an individual . . . . My private self does not exist. Whatever they do to me, they do to the people in this country . . . . I am a living symbol of whatever is happening in the country'.[33] Doris Sommer reads the construction of the self in Latin American women's *testimonios* in terms of '*metonymy*, a lateral identification through relationship, which acknowledges the possible differences among "us" as components of a whole' in opposition to 'the *metaphor* of autobiography . . . which substitutes one (superior) signifier for another . . . I for we'.[34] Although Winnie Mandela's declaration above is presented as metonymic, an identity understood through community – 'I am one of the people' – it is in fact a metaphoric assertion of a singular personality who claims the mantle of representativeness. Personal trials and activities then assume a larger political significance.

She challenges petty apartheid in Brandfort, entering whites-only shops, using white entrances, encouraging the black population to follow her example. But she also sets up soup kitchens, sewing circles, and creches with financial aid from sympathetic organizations abroad: activities which conform with the conventional role of political leaders' wives.[35] Brandfort, the site of banishment in the on-going present, is transformed by Winnie Mandela into the locus of the free nation to be. The iconic images of Warrior Queen and Mother of the Nation enable her to refuse the boundaries of the marginal space of exile, recasting it as the centre, where the political struggle is symbolically played out in her victories over the authorities and white inhabitants. But although she insists that her presence forced white people in Brandfort to think about social issues,[36] the mayor of Brandfort's comment, 'We accept her now. She is clean and well-behaved .... I've spoken to her, and she's well-educated', reveals a reception which hinges upon her difference from the black people she claims to represent.[37] Her presence, rather than dismantling racial stereotype, simply wins her the grudging recognition of the exception.

When she does openly claim an individual political identity, she is careful to present this in terms of the people's recognition of her achievements:

> In the earlier years I was just a carbon copy of Nelson. I was no individual. If I said something, it was Nelson's wife who said so. When he was no longer in the picture (I so hate talking about myself!), the public began to say, I wasn't just a carbon copy as such; I had ideas and views of my own. I had my own commitment and I wasn't just a political ornament.[38]

Winnie Mandela's carefully negotiated self-presentation is necessitated by the conflicting images of Warrior Queen and Mother of the Nation which surround her identity. While the former image signifies the explicit power of a strong personality, the latter carries connotations of selflessness. The nuclear family, when invoked as a metaphor of the nation, inscribes male power as central, and female roles as supportive. This gendered concept of nation constrains womens' political engagement, marking activities which exceed or disrupt supportive roles as unnatural. Since Winnie Mandela herself had often used the iconic image of motherhood to establish a political role, she is caught between the polarities of Good Mother and Unnatural Mother when she becomes embroiled in the scandal of Stompie Moeketsi's murder. Exploiting the concept of the 'normal' family, she justifies her removal of the boy from the home of the Rev. Paul Verryn, accusing him of being a homosexual which she defines as an illness: 'My responsibility as a mother is to draw attention to this problem'.[39]

Emma Gilbey's biography of Winnie Mandela written following the trial, although purporting to account for her fall from grace, offers as its structuring argument a portrait of Mrs Mandela as unfit to be The Mother Of the Nation. The very title, *The Lady – The Life and Times of Winnie Mandela*, is reminiscent of the salacious revelations of picaresque novels. Gilbey inverts the laudatory paradigms of previous auto/biographical accounts which champion Winnie Mandela as ideally and inherently suited for her future role. Instead she presents her as a vicious bully during her childhood, power-hungry, using her 'feline sensuality' to keep Nelson Mandela under her spell, and a snob who saw herself as superior to ordinary people.[40] We are told that black people in Brandfort were 'anxious about ... her influence over their children [and] were frightened of her'.[41] Gilbey dispels the myth of the ideal family, quoting rumours of a plot to assassinate Nelson Mandela which implicated his wife.[42] She ends the biography with Winnie Mandela having gained election into the Women's League of the ANC, ranged against her husband:

> As she increased her power base and positioned herself for the future, Winnie had one indisputable advantage over her seventy-five year old husband.
>
> She was nearly twenty years younger than him.[43]

Gilbey, as much as sympathetic biographers, works within a paradigm of political biography which renders the identity of the subject static, while claiming to delineate development. As a genre, political auto/biography itself appears confined to producing either hagiographies or character assassinations. Such a paradigm obscures the complexities of personal histories and the political arena. It at once constrains and inflates identity into one-dimensional stereotypes. These extremes may be explained in light of the use of political auto/ biographies as 'religious' texts or icons of conversion. Winnie Mandela relates how a young Afrikaner policeman, horrified by the shooting of children during the Soweto uprising in 1976, seeks her out. She gives the conflict-ridden young man a copy of Nelson Mandela's *The Struggle Is My Life*.[44] Nelson Mandela himself, commenting on a proposed family biography, advocates self-censorship while stressing the importance of portraying personalities 'not as angels, but as real men of flesh and blood with virtues and weaknesses'. He is appalled by sensational revelations, referring to the autobiography of Margaret Trudeau as damaging to Premier Trudeau's political career: 'A happy family life is an important pillar to any public man'. It is, however, this very association of good leadership with an ideal of family as a metaphor of nation which produces the extreme stereotypes which he rejects as unreal.

Notes

1 Sander L. Gilman (1985) 'Black Bodies, White Bodies: Toward an Iconography of Female Sexuality in Late Nineteenth Century Art, Medicine and Literature', *Critical Inquiry*, vol. 12, no. 1, Autumn, p. 204.
2 See the *Guardian*, Tuesday 10 May 1994, front page.
3 See, for example, Jean Starobinski and Seymour Chatman (1980) 'The Style of Autobiography', in James Olney (Ed.) *Autobiography: Essays Theoretical and Critical*, New Jersey: Princeton University Press.
4 Mary Benson (1986) *Nelson Mandela*, Harmondsworth: Penguin, p. 21.
5 *Ibid.*, p. 31.
6 Winnie Mandela and Ann Benjamin (Eds) (1984) *Part of My Soul Went with Him*, New York and London: W.W. Norton and Co., p. 53.
7 Caroline Neale (1986) 'The Idea of Progress in the Revision of African History, 1960–1970', in Bogumil Jewsiewicki and David Newbury (Eds) *African Historiographies*, London: Sage Publications, pp. 112–13.

8   Benson. 1986, p. 162.
9   Nelson Mandela (1990) *The Struggle Is My Life*, New York: Pathfinder, pp. 249–58.
10 Mandela and Benjamin 1984, p. 137.
11 *Ibid.*, pp. 131–4.
12 Fatima Meer (1988) *Higher than Hope*. Harmondsworth: Penguin, pp. 328–9.
13 *Ibid.*, p. 97.
14 Mandela and Benjamin 1984, p. x.
15 *Ibid.*, pp. xvii–xviii.
16 Benson 1986, p. 214.
17 *Ibid.*, p. 75.
18 Mandela and Benjamin 1984, p. 34.
19 *Ibid.*, pp. 34–66.
20 Benson 1986, p. 163.
21 *Ibid.*, p. 170.
22 Mandela 1990, p. 121.
23 Benson 1986, p. 172.
24 Mandela and Benjamin 1984, p. 79.
25 *Ibid.*
26 *Ibid.*, p. 32.
27 *Ibid.*, p. 134.
28 *Ibid.*, p. 29.
29 *Ibid.*, pp. 30–1.
30 *Ibid.*, pp. 51–2.
31 *Ibid.*, p. 5.
32 *Ibid.*, p. 51.
33 *Ibid.*, p. 5.
34 Doris Sommer (1988) ‘’’Not Just a Personal Story’’: Women’s Testimonios and the Plural Self’, in Bella Brodzki and Celeste Schenck (Eds) *Life/Lines: Theorizing Women’s Autobiography*, Ithaca and London: Cornell University Press, p. 108.
35 Mandela and Benjamin 1984, pp. 6–14.
36 *Ibid.*, p. 6.
37 Benson 1986, p. 212.
38 Mandela and Benjamin 1984, p. 73.
39 Emma Gilbey (1994) *The Lady – The Life and Times of Winnie Mandela*, London: Vintage, pp. 205–6.
40 *Ibid.*, pp. 13, 45, 68.
41 *Ibid.*, p. 128.
42 *Ibid.*, p. 279.
43 *Ibid.*, pp. 298–9.
44 Mandela and Benjamin 1984, p. 116.

PART TWO

Memory, history and 'faction' in Wole Soyinka's *Aké* and *Isara*

Ato Quayson

Susan Friedman offers an interesting critique of general theories of autobiography that postulate it as having to do solely with a growth of individualism.[1] She is right in arguing counter to Gusdorf and others that the autobiographical self depends on *identification*, *interdependence* and *community* as means of enablement. Though her critique is raised mainly in the context of women's autobiography, hers is an interesting way of considering questions of minority auto/biographies in general. Yet her proposition, though useful, requires qualification. I would like to suggest that selfhood or individualism must also take account of the social and other institutions with which the self enters into adversarial and/or non-contradictory relationships. In a discussion of the development of the *bildgungsroman* in the West, Franco Moretti notes that whereas, in the nineteenth century, novels tended to 'personalize social relations among individuals', in the *bildgungsroman* of the early twentieth century, social institutions began appearing as such: church, school, business bureaucracy and the law were all shown as institutional articulations with which the individual had to deal, often problematically.[2] Taking a leaf from the *bildgungsroman* into an analysis of auto/biography, we may argue that the individual's growing awareness of selfhood emerges at the conjuncture of relations between the self and others as well as in the relationships between the self and social institutions.

In the context of African literature and auto/biography, however, it is fair to say that the most significant institution is that of the nation-state in all its dispersed expression. As Neil Lazarus and others have shown, African literary writing is best explored within the context of attitudes to the evolving nation-state itself, both in its colonial and post-colonial dimensions.[3] And yet it is not always that this concern with the nation-state as an institution is revealed explicitly. Sometimes, it can only be discerned in terms of the discursive position given to publicly sanctioned history within the space of literary or auto/biographical discourse. Wole Soyinka's auto/biographies are particularly useful for a discussion of these issues because of the often self-conscious fusion of fact and fiction to which he is predisposed in writing them. I wish to explore Soyinka's *Aké*[4] and *Isara*[5] in relation to how 'private' and 'public' history appear in the two works and how they relate to his growing awareness of the post-colonial state as an *institution*.

Aké is the earlier of the two works. Published in 1981, it attempts to reconstruct childhood memories. In the general tradition of autobiographies, it tells of Soyinka's growing awareness of the social mores of his culture. But it also tells of his awareness of contradictions at all levels of society and culture.

Scepticism is the dominant mode of growing awareness in the work. In fact, this scepticism is a major determinant of how public history, in the sense of events that occur outside his small family circuit and which have wide consequences for his society, enters the text. The two major public events that enter the text are the Second World War and a women's riot over taxation. The war enters the frame of the text partly through a radio box, a new addition to the household and considered capable of producing oracular wonders. Every hour, it delivers THE NEWS and this completely enchants Soyinka's father and a number of his friends who congregate without fail to listen to the box (p. 108).

Later on in the narrative, Soyinka reports how 'Hitler monopolized the box' with his own special programme and he details the names that people made out of the war situation. 'Win-de-Woh' became a form of greeting between his father and friends and new women's hair-dos were named after war jingles. For the young Soyinka, the War seems to be a thing of great amusement. At no time is the sense of potential tragedy involved in the War allowed to disturb the essential humour and lightheartedness of the narrative. In fact, the humour with which the War is treated is further extended later on when he describes the antics of a local lunatic who vows to face Hitler and his men squarely if they ever attempt to set foot on Aké soil. Paa Adatan, the brave lunatic, uses his self-proclaimed bravery to get favours of food and money from the market women of Aké. When he is handed a few pennies by Wole's mother, he draws a straight line in front of her shop and explains: 'Dat na in case they come while I dey chop eba for buka. If they try cross this line, guns go turn to broom for dem hand. Dem go begin dey sweeping dis very ground till I come back. Make dem try am make I see' (pp. 110–11). Later on he has to prove his mettle against some soldiers who come to buy groceries at Wole's mother's shop but after a brave struggle he is overpowered and tied up. The point of all this, it seems, is to parody the War and to show how little it meant at the level of local existence in spite of its world-historical significance. The War does not loom large in Aké, something quite different from how it features in *Isara*. The thing to note is how Soyinka parodies public history such that it cannot disrupt the essential humour of his childhood memoirs.

The parodic treatment of the Second World War has a counterpart in the second event of public significance that enters the frame of the narrative. It is an uprising of women in Abeokuta against an oppressive poll tax which was introduced in the early 1940s by the colonial authorities and supported by local chiefs. The event has major significance for Wole's definition of an appropriate social role especially as it comes directly after a trope of manhood training in the text. The manhood training itself is dispersed among experiences he has at his father's village on a visit there. The dispersed experiences involve all the classic rituals of manhood training: he is taught how to work on the farm; to kill, cook and eat a snake; how to react when confronted by a hive of wild bees and how to decode the nature of forest sounds (pp. 131–8). And late one night, his grandfather puts him through a major set of rituals involving painful incisions on his ankles as well as lessons on courage in the face of adversity. The initiation is carried out because his grandfather feels Wole needs protection before he goes off to boarding school to mix with older men. It is interesting, therefore, that the next segment of the narrative is the women's organization and the young Wole's role in it as an errand boy. This seems to be as important in the text as his first experiences at boarding school and his first trip alone to the big city to sit for an entry exam for secondary school.

The text moves backwards and forwards between his first days at boarding school and the events of the women's uprising. It is the only time the text adopts such a method of moving backwards and forwards between the same set of events. It is as if to suggest that after manhood training the text disperses the mode by which the young Wole is to define an appropriate mode of social existence between two highly charged gendered positions. The description of the women's organization along with their riots takes forty-three pages of text, while the matters about school take twenty.

The women initially start protesting against the tax by sending delegations but they are galvanized into direct action when an old woman comes to report the heartlessness with which she is treated by the tax-collectors. The anger of the gathered women is almost palpable as they resolve to march on the chief's palace. A martial trope is in evidence:

> The women rose in one body. Hands flew to heads and off came the head-ties, unfurling in the air like hundreds of banners. The head-ties flew downwards, turned into sashes and arced round the waists to be secured with a grim decisiveness. Kemberi leading the way, they poured out of the grammar school compound, filled the streets and marched towards the palace at Aké. (*Aké*, p. 202)

The women go to camp outside the palace of the Chief and stay there for several weeks in support of their demands. Soyinka describes how they terrorize some members of the masculine *Osogbo* cult (Council of Elders), and how the uprising turns not only into a critique of colonial rule but also of traditional patriarchal authority.

There are aspects of the uprising that Soyinka does not mention but which it is important to draw attention to. Raymond Prince reports that when policemen were sent to disperse the women, they waited till the policemen were close enough and chased them away by brandishing menstrual cloths at them.[6] This might well be taken as apocryphal, but there is no doubt that the women strategically deployed feminine stereotypes to prosecute their struggle against the hegemonic order. Part of a song that Nina Mba sets down as having been sung by the women has a devastating reference to women's bodies as a means of cursing and restating their determination not to pay the tax:[7]

O you men, vagina's head will seek vengeance;
You men, vagina's head will seek vengeance
Even if it is one penny. If it is only a penny
Ademola, we are not paying tax in Egbaland
If even it is one penny.

The predatory quality of the metaphor of vengeance-seeking vaginas shows the uncompromising stance the women had taken and their preparedness to shock the patriarchal structures into paying rapt attention to their demands.

We can only speculate as to the reasons for Soyinka's silence about these details. Perhaps it was one which he felt too clumsy to handle. It seems, however, that though Soyinka did not report this fact, it had a significant impression on him. The description of the uprising itself reveals the oppressive lineaments of the institution of Yoruba kingship and Soyinka's growing awareness of its problematic exercise of power as it articulated colonial interests at this time. The uprising not only put the status of Yoruba kingship to question, it also displayed subversion against this supremely masculine institution as a gendered moment in which all patriarchal taboos and social codes propping up the institution of kingship were repudiated in the cause of a higher ideal of justice. The uprising helped to inscribe women in his mind as a challenge to received codes of authority as well as being potentially chaotic. Soyinka reproduces their mode of subversion time and again both in his literary writings and in his political activities.

In his writings, the most memorable women are frequently figured as *femmes fatales*. Segi in *Kongi's Harvest*[8] is such a one, as is Madame Tortoise in *A Dance of the Forests*.[9] But there is a direct, if lighter return to the women's historic threat to masculine authority in *Death and the King's Horseman*.[10] A policeman is sent by the colonial authorities to go and arrest the King's Horseman who is supposed to commit ritual suicide on a certain night. He is accosted by a group of young girls and women who refuse him passage and begin to tease him. He tries to make his authority firmly felt but things take an uncomfortable turn for him when the girls threaten to pull down his shorts to see what 'authority' he carries in them. The whole of the encounter is filled with sexual innuendoes, and it is ultimately a fear of castration that sends the policeman running away. It is difficult not to think that this is a comic replay of the colourful details left out of the description of the women's uprising in *Aké*. The point is that the charge of the details is not completely lost but is transferred into the characterization of women in his literary writings and the relationships they have with masculine authority.

The public history that enters the frame of *Aké* is reported either parodically, as is the case with the Second War, or as a means of social critique, as in the women's uprising. And in both cases public history is significant for what it reveals about the subversion of received notions of authority. In the case of the details surrounding the Second World War, it is Soyinka himself who renders it in his text parodically, while in the case of the women's uprising, the uprising represents a subversion of received forms of authority. The two are closely related in terms of the mode of general questioning that goes on throughout the narrative. The important thing is not the historicality of specific details, something we largely take for granted, but the discursive position they have within the autobiography. The ways in which history enters the text is linked to a general tendency towards deflating or subverting the space of received truths. This figures an attitude not only towards history as such but also towards the post-colonial nation-state. This point cannot be fully appreciated unless set against the ways in which public history enters the frame of *Isara*, the second work.

Isara, published in 1990, is set in his father's hometown. The purpose for working on *Isara* is made explicit from the Author's Note to the novel. As Soyinka says:

> I have not only taken liberties with chronology, I have deliberately ruptured it. After all, the period covered here actively is no more than fifteen years, and its significance for me is that it represents the period when a pattern in their lives was set – for better or worse – under the compelling impact of the major events in their times, both local and global, the uneasy love-hate relationship with the colonial presence, and its own ambiguous attitudes to the Western-educated elite of the Nigerian protectorate.
>
> Life, it would appear, was lived robustly, but was marked also by an intense quest for a place in the new order, and one of a far more soul-searching dimension than the generation they spawned would later undertake. (Author's Note to *Isara*)

We should note that he says here he is taking liberties with facts. He calls this biography a work of 'faction'. It is a mixture of fact and fiction. It seems, though, that this book is a much more serious work in terms of the discursive position of history than the earlier work. This seems not only to be a function of Soyinka's stated intention but also that of the dominant archive on which he draws for the work. Whereas the reconstruction of *Aké* was drawn mainly from memory, this work is drawn from written documents. The initial impulse to write *Isara* came when he chanced upon an old metallic box of his father's which contained 'a handful of letters, old journals with marked pages and annotations, notebook jottings, tax and other levy receipts, minutes of meetings and school reports, programme notes of special events, and so on'. With these fragments from a documentary archive, Soyinka is closer to the stuff from which publicly sanctioned history is recorded than in *Aké*.

There is a decidedly different texture to public events in this work from that in *Aké*. The narrative even centralizes writing as a trope around which events are recalled and organized. The book opens with his father trying to reply to a letter from a fellow teacher from Canada. His mind analyses the letter while going ahead to sketch his own reply. What is interesting about this is that Akinyode is shown defining Nigeria to the outside world. This immediately gives the history of the country a different status from that of the first work. There is an interest in showing the country as an equal partner in the global socio-cultural economy. The text returns several times to Akinyode's letters and also to entries in his journals so that writing becomes inscribed as the arena within which significant history is rehearsed.

Another important thing is that all the characters in this work have a knowledge of world-historical events. Akinyode and his friends take account of the worldwide depression of the 1930s when planning their business ventures. The Second World War looms large in the consciousness of the characters. In one of the letters that feature in the text, there is a careful analysis of the demand for raw materials that the war machinery would require and how it would be useful for the friends to enter into rubber production or soap manufacturing. The writer of the letter takes note of the fact that one issue of *The Nigerian Teacher* makes reference to the soap-making industry and this is taken as a sure sign of the times (p. 49). Again, Akinyode and his friends are shown to write about the Second World War in certain West African journals. Writing and documentation are central to the lives of the characters. There is an impression of robust action, as Soyinka points out, and the upwardly mobile elite of his father's group all display their qualities for leadership. The upshot of all this is that public history has a more serious place than private or domestic history, which was not the case in *Aké*. Furthermore, there is a sense in which the biography is written so as to show his father's life and those of his friends as the articulation of the essential lineaments of a whole epoch. In this sense, there is a suggestion of epic scale to the characterization here which was absent from *Aké*.

We may argue that the epic scale of the characters relates indirectly to the attitude to the colonial state held not only by those of whom he is writing, but by Soyinka himself. Both works are written by him from the vantage point of distance in time. *Aké* is about his own childhood and *Isara* is about an era in the past. However, the dominant archive of the one is memory while that of the other is documents. In both cases, Soyinka is inscribing his views about his past and what has gone into making him who he is. The mode by which facts, in the form of public history, enter the two texts differs precisely because Soyinka is plotting his differing attitudes to different moments of the post-colonial state from the present position of his own selfhood and political praxis. Thus, *Isara* represents a notion of potential epic status for the nation-state in the period before the disillusionment of post-Independence set in. What he describes of the characters of his father's era is the potential that the African nation-state had in the moment just prior to Independence and its insertion into the global political and cultural economy. In *Aké*, on the other hand, there is a bent towards irony, satire and the deflation of received categories. Whereas *Isara* is aligned to what we may assume was his father's consciousness of the potential sources of social action, *Aké* is firmly tied to Soyinka's own understanding of how the possibility for meaningful action is configurated within a highly problematic African post-colonial space. It is instructive to note, then, that *Ibadan*, published thirteen years after *Aké* and continuing the autobiographical trajectory of the childhood memoirs into adolescence, early adulthood and post-Independence Nigeria, adopts a much more acerbic and openly sceptical tone about the politics of his country.[11] And, significantly, he writes in the introduction to *Ibadan* of his strenuous resistance towards the writing of a sequel to *Aké* until the present political crisis in Nigeria[12] brings it uncannily to him that there is a cyclicality in the affairs of his country that conceptually aligns the present happenings to those in the early 1960s. It is only then that he manages the sequel. Thus, the parodic tone of *Aké* cannot be read except as revealing the silhouette of disillusionment and scepticism about history, the state and received categories all held gingerly within the form of childhood memoirs. It represents a moment of masking, falling between the bitterness of *The Man Died*,[13] which is his notes from prison, and *Ibadan*, whose plot ends just at the point where events are to lead to his imprisonment.

Taken together, the mode by which public history enters the frame of *Aké* and *Isara* traces the attitudes towards the African nation-state in its colonial and post-colonial manifestations. Soyinka's auto/biographies reveal that an analysis of the form as an expression of selfhood has to take into account how selfhood grows out of its problematic relationships not just with others, but with institutions too, some of which, like the African nation-state, take on a problematic mode of signification for all selves.

Notes

1 Susan Stanford Friedman (1988) 'Women's Autobiographical Selves: Theory and Practice', in Shari Benstock (Ed.) *The Private Self: Theory and Practice of Women's Autobiographical Writings*, London: Routledge, pp. 34–45.
2 Franco Moretti (1992) '"A Useless Longing for Myself": The Crisis of the European *Bildgungsroman*, 1898–1914', in Ralph Cohen (Ed.) *Studies in Historical Change*, Charlottesville and London: University Press of Virginia, pp. 430–59.
3 Neil Lazarus (1986) 'Great Expectations and After: The Politics of Postcolonialism in African Fiction', *Social Text*, 13/14, Winter/Spring, pp. 49–63.
4 Wole Soyinka (1981) *Aké: The Years of Childhood*, London: Rex Collings.
5 Wole Soyinka (1990) *Isara: A Voyage around Essay*, London: Minerva.
6 Raymond Prince (1961) 'The Yoruba Image of the Witch', *Journal of Mental Science*, 107, pp. 795–805.
7 Nina Mba (1982) *Nigerian Women Mobilized: Women's Political Activity in*

Southern Nigeria, 1900–1965, Berkeley: University of California Press, p. 150.

8 Wole Soyinka (1974) *Kongi's Harvest*, in *Collected Plays 2*, Oxford: Oxford University Press.

9 Wole Soyinka (1973) *A Dance of the Forests*, in *Collected Plays 1*, Oxford: Oxford University Press.

10 Wole Soyinka (1975) *Death and the King's Horseman*, London: Methuen.

11 Wole Soyinka (1994) *Ibadan: The Penkelemes Years, 1946–1965*, London: Methuen.

12 The present political crisis in Nigeria was initially generated by the cancellation of the results of the 1993 presidential polls, seen by international observers to have been free and fair, but considered by the military authorities to have changed the balance of power too sharply in favour of one of the contestants thought to be generally beyond their control. Violent riots, mayhem and general suspicions of the military government's motives have characterized Nigeria's politics since then.

13 Wole Soyinka (1972) *The Man Died*, London: Rex Collings.

Chapter 6

Autobiography, Authenticity and Nineteenth-century Ideas of Race

PART ONE

Sentimentality and the slave narrative: Frederick Douglass' *My Bondage and My Freedom*

Sarah Meer

The fugitive slave, Frederick Douglass, wrote his first autobiography, now regarded as the classic slave narrative, the *Narrative of the Life of Frederick Douglass, An American Slave*, in 1845.[1] By the time he wrote his second autobiography, *My Bondage and My Freedom*, ten years later, he had a substantially new story to tell.[2]

Douglass' first autobiography was written with the encouragement of the Massachusetts Anti-Slavery Society for whom he had worked as an abolitionist lecturer from 1841. His *Narrative* set down in print a story he had by then told many times on anti-slavery platforms around the States, and it clearly shows his commitment to the brand of abolitionist politics espoused by William Lloyd Garrison. Like many nineteenth-century slave narratives it was driven by a commitment to what may be called a 'historical' and also to a 'rhetorical' purpose.[3] Douglass' narrative related the facts of his life, and also aimed to persuade its readers of the iniquities of slavery and the validity of the abolitionist cause.

The second autobiography was published after a traumatic split with Garrison and the American Anti-Slavery Society but Douglass was still trying to expose the wrongs of slavery by writing his life.[4] Covering the intervening years of freedom, whereas the first book dealt mainly with Douglass' life in slavery, *My Bondage and My Freedom* charts his growing political independence over these years, and the eventual break with the Garrisonians. Most interestingly for students of autobiography, it also goes over some of the ground covered ten years earlier, and by filling in certain details and adding particular emphases, produces a significantly different sense of places and events. The second time round Douglass was still drawing on the same material and still trying to produce an anti-slavery text, but the result was a rather different story.

The first autobiography revolved around Douglass alone, with his quest for freedom pushed insistently to centre-stage, but in the second Douglass recalls important relationships with his own kin, with other slaves on the plantation, and with the family of his former master. There is a new sense of affection and even nostalgia for the Southern society and for his fellow slaves, left behind in his escape; and a new criticism of racial prejudice and patronizing attitudes in the North, tarnishing the simple picture of the haven for fugitive slaves that Douglass had produced in his *Narrative*.

This change of emphasis goes with a change of style. The critic William Andrews has noticed what he calls a more 'novelistic' approach in *My Bondage*, consisting of more detailed descriptions of events, more attention to dialogue and a willingness to play up the comic potential of some episodes, even at the expense of sacrificing their polemical and symbolic power.[5] I would like to expand on Andrews' observation by pointing to the special influence of the sentimental novel on Douglass' text, and in particular that of Harriet Beecher Stowe's *Uncle Tom's Cabin*.[6]

The mid-nineteenth-century sentimental novel in America concerned itself with the domestic milieu, placing an emphasis on the family and assuming that women's main importance lay in their role in the home. Written and read primarily by women, such novels glorified motherhood as the hope of the next generation and the entire nation. Their hallmarks were melodramatic scenes designed to provoke laughter and tears, as well as the emphases on the mother/child bond, other familial relations and the home environment. Although its theme of slavery is unusual among such novels, for many critics *Uncle Tom's Cabin* is a classic example.[7]

Stowe's novel was serialized in the *National Era* in 1851, and published as a novel the following year. It was *the* publishing success of the nineteenth century, selling 10,000 copies within the first week, and 300,000 within the year, and was also reviewed respectfully in Frederick Douglass' newspaper.[8] The novel concerns a pious and longsuffering black slave, Tom, who is separated from his family and sold down South, where in a famous scene he dies at the hands of his brutal owner. In another well-known episode, the white slave-holder's angelic daughter Eva also perishes; her consumptive demise, it is hinted, mysteriously caused by her exposure to the cruelties of the slave system.[9] The novel uses the sanctity of motherhood as its most powerful argument against slavery, the mark of true humanity that the slave woman Eliza, who runs away to the North to avoid being separated from her child, possesses, while the slave-owner Marie St Clare does not. At the end of the book Stowe appeals to the 'mothers of America' who, she says, if they had exerted themselves earlier, could have trained their sons out of their slave-holding habits.[10]

In 1853, the following year, Stowe published a factual book on slavery, *The Key to Uncle Tom's Cabin*, which supposedly consisted of the documentary evidence out of which she had woven her story.[11] Some of this evidence came from unpublished slave narratives which she included, along with extracts from published narratives, including Douglass' own. In 1851 she had written to Douglass asking for help in providing authentic details for *Uncle Tom's Cabin*; now she was using his *Narrative* to verify the emotional truth of her novel.[12] In the course of defending *Uncle Tom's Cabin* Stowe also came to comment on the material she selected from the slave narratives. In so doing she brought the agenda of her sentimental novel to bear on Douglass' first autobiography.

Just as *Uncle Tom's Cabin* had been especially concerned with slavery's constraints on motherhood, so in the *Key* Stowe selected for discussion the part of Douglass' *Narrative* that had touched on his relationship with his mother. In the original the passage is actually very brief but Stowe retells it lingeringly and with added emphasis. In the *Narrative* Douglass notes that Maryland slaves are often separated from their children, and wonders if this is a deliberate attempt to prevent familial bonds. Stowe relates this as fact:

> An incident which Douglass related of his mother is touching; he states that it is customary at an early age to separate mothers from their children, for the purpose of blunting and deadening natural affection.[13]

In fact Douglass states that his mother was hired out during this period, which suggests that the separation was for motives of profit, as much as of psychological engineering. Stowe continues the sad story, and adds her own interpretive comment:

> When he was three years old his mother was sent to work on a plantation eight or ten miles distant, and after that he never saw her except in the night. After her day's toil she would occasionally walk over to her child, lie down with him in her arms, hush him to sleep in her bosom, then rise up and walk back again to be ready for her field-work by daylight. Now, we ask the highest born lady in England or America, who is a mother, whether this does not show that this poor field-labourer had in her bosom, beneath her dirt and rags, a true mother's heart?

The Douglass text does not stress the point that slave women are true mothers like the rest of us; presumably Douglass takes that for granted. In his telling of it this is the end of the story, but Stowe continues to expatiate on the inhumanity of this system at great length:

> The last and bitterest indignity which had been heaped on the head of

the unhappy slaves has been the denial to them of those holy affections which God gives alike to all. We are told, in fine phrase, by languid ladies of fashion, that 'it is not to be supposed that those creatures have the same feelings that we have,' when, perhaps, the very speaker could not endure one tithe of the fatigue and suffering which the slave-mother often bears for her child. Every mother who has a mother's heart within her ought to know that this is blasphemy against nature, and, standing between the cradle of her living and the grave of her dead child, should indignantly reject such a slander on all motherhood.[14]

When Douglass rewrote his autobiography in *My Bondage and My Freedom*, he enlarged and expanded on the very passage that Stowe had picked out in his first *Narrative*, tightening his sentimental focus by selecting blighted family relationships to identify the true injustices of slavery. In so doing he was shifting the weight of his argument, which in his *Narrative* had centred on the primary problem of the institution, that one human being could own another. In *My Bondage and My Freedom*, he leans more heavily on the argument Stowe had reiterated in her novel, that the sanctity of family life could not be maintained under such a system of ownership. He writes of his separation from his mother at the time of her death:

The heartless and ghastly form of slavery rises between mother and child, even at the bed of death. The mother, at the verge of the grave, may not gather her children, to impart to them her holy admonitions, and invoke for them her dying benediction. The bond-woman lives as a slave, and is left to die as a beast; often with fewer attentions than are paid to a favorite horse.[15]

Douglass' writing here echoes Stowe's elaboration on his earlier narrative: he speaks of 'holy admonitions', and later of 'sacred tenderness'; she of 'holy affections'. He also evokes the peculiar image Stowe produces of a mother 'standing between the cradle of her living and the grave of her dead child'. This is the sentimental fascination with the deathbeds of the virtuous that Ann Douglas has observed in the mid nineteenth century: the literary variety tended to feature women and children, and was often accompanied by moral conversions by repentant family members grieving for the dying heroine.[16] Stowe turned the convention to good anti-slavery effect, using the death of Little Eva to stage an emotional appeal for freedom for St Clare's slaves. The golden-haired slave-holder's daughter triggers the emotions; Little Eva is made most emphatically white in the scenes where she is most powerfully the slaves' advocate.[17] Douglass too produces an image of the mother–child bond that is shadowed by the spectre of death, but in his narrative slavery is 'ghastly' for the way it impedes the usual sentimental conjunction of the mother, the child and the impending demise. He takes the model a stage further than Stowe, turning the trope into a polemical assertion that weepy deathbed scenes are one of the markers of living humanly which slavery denies the slave.

Anti-slavery writers frequently argued that all humans should be allowed family relationships, and that slavery's interference with such rights was a sin. A clear echo of these anti-slavery arguments is heard in Douglass' assertion that to be divested of the last attentions of one's family 'is to die like a beast': to have one's humanity denied. This differs from the standard abolitionist argument, however, in that Douglass is not just noting the absence of consistent familial relations under slavery, he is decrying the absence of the novelistic symbol of such relations, the deathbed scene. He has not only borrowed his model of normal family relations from the sentimental novel, but has used the most potent contemporary icon of those relations. Unlike Stowe, who had first used the sentimental trope for the anti-slavery argument, Douglass does not use the scene of death to provoke an emotional outpouring against slavery, and he does not produce a white focus for this emotion to act as an interventionist on the slaves' behalf. He invokes the sentimental tour de force, but as an absence, not as just another tear-jerker. He also thwarts the narrative expectations of his sentimental readers, warning that 'Scenes of sacred tenderness, around the death-bed, never forgotten, and which often arrest the vicious and confirm the virtuous during life, must be looked for amongst the free'.[18] Douglass makes the sentimental scene no longer the means of the text, but the desired end, and an end that is thwarted by slavery. The deathbed scene becomes in his text the 'holy' mark of proper, and in this case free, family.

Douglass' main concern in *My Bondage*, like Stowe's in *Uncle Tom's Cabin*, was the harm slave life did to what he posited as the natural structure for family relations. As in the novel, several of the most poignant moments in the text revolve around enforced family partings, particularly Douglass' from his grandmother and from his mother. Douglass extracted even more telling an argument, though, from an episode featuring a singular lack of feeling, and not only that, a reunion; for when he meets the brothers and sisters to whom he should feel as passionate an attachment as to his grandmother, he is almost as indifferent as if they were unrelated strangers. This passage, because it is structured around an absence of feeling, and even because it deals with a meeting and not a parting, reverses Stowe's sentimental tactic of loading with significance a tremendously emotional moment of separation.[19] Whereas Stowe used the parting scene to provoke in the readers strong feelings which were then supposed to lead them into specifically anti-slavery sentiments, Douglass made his point by thwarting any sentimental demands of the narrative.

> I had never seen my brother nor my sisters before; and, though I had sometimes heard of them, and felt a curious interest in them, I really did not understand what they were to me, or I to them . . . I heard the words

brother and sisters, and knew that they must mean something; but slavery had robbed these terms of their true meaning.... Think it not strange, dear reader, that so little sympathy of feeling existed between us. The conditions of brotherly and sisterly feeling were wanting – we had never nestled and played together.... 'Little children, love one another,' are words seldom heard in a slave cabin.[20]

Just as in the non-deathbed scene, *My Bondage* here cheats the reader of the convention of the emotional parting, by turning it into a meeting that has already been emptied of its appropriate emotional content by the slave system. Just as the slave had been deprived of the acquaintance of his own family, so is the reader denied the required sentimental scene, and Southern slavery is the culprit.

Stowe had picked out Douglass' writing about his mother for special attention in her *Key to Uncle Tom's Cabin*, and in his second narrative it is Douglass' mother who is made the focus of the lament for the absent home and family, although she is not actually present during the episode where it occurs at all, whereas Douglass' grandmother is. In the rhetoric of the sentimentalized slave narrative, families and hearths belong by rights to mothers, and there is no substitute for biological mothering. Douglass writes how he had lavished his first affections on his grandmother, but attacks the conditions which had made her his primary carer:

[T]he tenderest affection which a beneficent Father allows, as a partial compensation to the mother for the pains and lacerations of her heart, incident to the maternal relation, was, in my case, diverted from its true and natural object, by the envious, greedy, and treacherous hand of slavery.... I never think of this terrible interference of slavery with my infantile affections, and its diverting them from their natural course, without feelings to which I can give no adequate expression.[21]

In this further indictment of slavery for the harm it did families, the office of mother is treated as a divine appointment, and thus even for Douglass' grandmother to have taken on his care represented a major usurpation. Douglass' argument against slavery upholds a tightly nuclear family, defining it in precisely the terms valorized by Stowe and the sentimental novelists so enamoured of their mothers.

Yet there is also a sense of a wider slave community and a different kinship structure in *My Bondage*, which militates against the nuclear ideal of part of the novel. There is a conflict between the book's drive to excoriate slavery and that to remember a lost childhood with some regret; between bewailing the absence of one kind of family contact and mourning the loss of the less conventional one he did have.[22] The narrative shift from the 1845 autobiography was not wholeheartedly sentimental, nor did it only confirm Stowe's domestic ideal.

My Bondage also describes for the first time how the young Douglass met slaves who remembered being brought from Africa, and spoke the plantation dialect: 'a mixture of Guinea and everything else you please'. These slaves, and those who remembered their parents' stories of enslavement, taught Douglass 'a burning hatred of slavery'. Because they had been born free, they gave him a history in which slavery was exposed as an unnatural condition, encouraging him to identify himself with the whole slave community, not just his nuclear family, whose history could neither supply him with a birthdate nor a father. Douglass also delineates a rigid plantation 'etiquette' based on a respect for one's elders:

> A young slave must approach the company of the older with hat in hand, and woe betide him if he fails to acknowledge a favor, of any sort, with the accustomed '*tankee*' & co.

These manners are celebrated in contrast to white people's, both those of slave-holders and those of the North. Douglass affects to blame the South for patronizing treatment of black people, but he makes a strong point about the Northern instances of it too.[23]

Douglass manipulated the sentimental conventions to forge an anti-slavery argument that did not require a white mediator, or expressions of surprise that black people could feel familial love as passionately as did white, and at the same time he built into his narrative a sense of a black community with its own language, relationships and customs. In telling his life-story for the second time in print, he negotiated the expectations of the white Northern readers who had bought *Uncle Tom's Cabin* in such droves, but he also pointed to experiences and relationships for which the sentimental idiom could provide 'no adequate expression'. The historical drive was not totally subsumed in the rhetorical needs of his narrative, and perhaps its influence on *My Bondage and My Freedom* meant in some part a recovery of the slave community Douglass had lost, and that the abolitionist circuit had failed so dismally to replace.

Notes

1 Frederick Douglass (1982, first published 1845) *Narrative of the Life of Frederick Douglass, An American Slave*, London: Penguin.
2 Frederick Douglass (1969, first published 1855) *My Bondage and My Freedom*, New York: Dover.
3 These terms are adapted from William L. Andrews (1986) *To Tell a Free Story: The First Century of Afro-American Autobiography, 1760–1865*, Urbana and Chicago: University of Illinois Press. In borrowing them I do not mean to imply a necessary distinction between history and rhetorical writing, or that histories are ever merely factual without being persuasive, but to suggest how the documentary and the

polemical impulses that have been identified in slave narratives could produce more than one story.

4   Douglass parted political company with his mentors from about 1847 over his plan to start a weekly anti-slavery paper and his disagreement with some of the major tenets of Garrisonian doctrine. Unlike Garrison, Douglass came to believe that the Constitution did not in itself endorse slavery and that abolitionists who could, should use their vote against slavery, rather than boycotting political action. See Andrews 1986, p. 216.

5   Andrews 1986, pp. 280–9.

6   Harriet Beecher Stowe (1981, first published 1852) *Uncle Tom's Cabin, or Life Among the Lowly*, London: Penguin.

7   See, for instance, Ann Douglass (1987) *The Feminization of American Culture*, New York, Knopf.

8   Robert S. Levine (1992) '*Uncle Tom's Cabin* in *Frederick Douglass's Paper*: An Analysis of Reception', *American Literature*', vol. 64, no. 1, pp. 71–93; Joan D. Hedrick (1994) *Harriet Beecher Stowe: A Life*, New York and Oxford: Oxford University Press, p. 223.

9   The connection between Eva's death and the slave system in the novel is discussed in Philip Fisher (1985) *Hard Facts: Setting and Form in the American Novel*, New York: Oxford University Press, pp. 106–7.

10 Stowe 1852, pp. 623–4. Several critics have dealt with Stowe's valorization of motherhood in detail. See especially Elizabeth Ammons (1986) 'Stowe's Dream of the Mother-Savior: *Uncle Tom's Cabin* and American Women Writers Before the 1920s', in Eric J. Sundquist (Ed.) *New Essays on Uncle Tom's Cabin*, Cambridge: Cambridge University Press.

11 Harriet Beecher Stowe (n.d., probably 1853) *The Key to Uncle Tom's Cabin; presenting the original facts and documents upon which the story is founded together with corroborative statements verifying the truth of the work*, London: Clarke, Beeton & Co.

12 Hedrick 1994, p. 218.

13 Douglass 1845, p. 48; Stowe n.d., p. 24.

14 Stowe n.d., p. 24.

15 Douglass 1855, p. 57.

16 Douglas 1987, pp. 200–26.

17 Thus in the moment when she simultaneously converts Topsy to goodness and the eavesdropping Miss Ophelia into overcoming her prejudice, she is contrasted with the slave, 'one of the blackest of her race' sobbing in her lap 'while the beautiful child, bending over her, looked like the picture of some bright angel stooping to reclaim a sinner': Stowe 1852, pp. 351, 410.

18 Douglass 1855, p. 57.

19 Douglass 1855, pp. 49, 57. An exemplary, and extensive instance of such a parting scene in *Uncle Tom's Cabin* is Chapter 10, where Tom is parted with many tears not only from his family, but from his fond mistress and master's son as well: Stowe 1852, pp. 162–74.

20 Douglass 1855, p. 48.

21 *Ibid.*, p. 53.

22 The treatment of the Garrisonians is similarly complicated; they figure as both exploitative and admired benefactors.

23 Douglass 1855, pp. 76, 70. Douglass observes: 'so completely has the south shaped the manners of the north ... that even abolitionists make very little of the surname of the negro. The only improvement on the "Bills", "Jacks", "Jims", and "Neds" of the south, observable here is, that "William", "John", "James", "Edward", are substituted' (Douglass 1855, p. 70).

PART TWO

Speculating upon human feeling: evangelical writing and Anglo-Jewish women's autobiography

Nadia Valman

The two starting points for this paper are the Evangelical Revival of the late eighteenth and early nineteenth centuries and the publication of Sir Walter Scott's *Ivanhoe* in 1819. Following the enormous success of Scott's novel, and in particular his Jewish heroine Rebecca, there was a striking proliferation of fictive Jewesses in popular literature, and my particular interest here will be its conjunction in the mid nineteenth century with texts produced as a result of the Evangelical Revival. After the tradition of Shakespeare's Jessica and Marlowe's Abigail, the figure of the Jewess had always been noted for her eager willingness to renounce her own cultural heritage and embrace the dominant culture, and she now became the subject of a large number of evangelical tracts, narratives of conversion written in novel form. These novels, some historical and some contemporary in setting, were unremarkable to the extent that they were merely further reworkings of the formulaic evangelical story of the regeneration of the sinner for the edification of the unspecified reader. However, they also suggest a more particular context in that they coincided with a wide range of projects to convert English Jews to Protestant Christianity, a campaign which, as Mel Scult has shown in his study of conversionism in Britain, was spectacularly unsuccessful but no less spectacularly supported and invested-in by Victorian middle-class Evangelicals.[1]

This proliferation of activity produced a notable disproportion between the visibility of the Jew – and especially the Jewess – in the public sphere, and their visibility in literary discourse. Novel-readers and theatre-goers would have encountered many fictional versions of the Jew, most of them stereotypes, while conversionist societies, in particular the London Society for the Promotion of Christianity among the Jews, which sponsored nationwide meetings, lectures and publications on the subject, 'had little competition in molding attitudes and ideas about the Jews'.[2] Indeed, demographic statistics suggest that very few contemporary Britons would have ever actually encountered a Jew.[3] In 1756, a century after their readmission to England following the expulsion of 1290, the Jewish population was 8,000, rising to about 27,000 in 1828 and 40,000 in 1860, never more than 0.2 per cent of the population of Britain before the last third of the nineteenth century.[4] Only a very small number of British Jews achieved any kind of public status at this time, and even fewer were women. Thus the figure of the Jewess in literature is primarily a figment of discourse, produced by non-Jewish writers for non-Jewish readers, a figure of imagination, fantasy and desire.

And yet, surprisingly, the first published accounts of Jewish women written by themselves, and in their own voices, were produced within a few years of the publication of *Ivanhoe*. They are clearly products of the Evangelical literary boom, as they are all conversion narratives, stories of Jewish women who renounce family, religion and culture, and convert to Christianity. The first, *Sophia de Lissau, or, a Portraiture of the Jews of the Nineteenth Century: being an outline of the Religious and Domestic Habits of this most interesting nation, with explanatory notes*, was published anonymously in 1826. It turned very rapidly into a family saga, and was followed by the story of Sophia's sister in *Emma de Lissau* (1828) and an account of the previous generation in *The Orphans of Lissau* (1830). These novels tell the history of a middle-class Jewish family of Polish origin living in England. The family is austere, disciplinarian and pharisaical, and is dominated by a strictly religious Jewish matriarch, Anna de Lissau, who rails against Christians, and England, and torments her daughter Emma mercilessly. The beautiful and pious Sophia, meanwhile, is hopelessly adored by her father's non-Jewish ward, Sydney, and resists his efforts to introduce her to Christianity. Instead she agrees to marry a Jewish man, convinced that his religiosity signifies virtue. However, his fanaticism hides violence and infidelity, and Sophia becomes resigned to suffering, desiring only consolation. She eventually dies a martyr's death, continuing to resist the conversion that would allow narrative closure. However, in the sequel, her sister Emma, encouraged by a female teacher, fulfils her sister's potential and converts.

Madame Brendlah's bizarrely titled *Tales of a Jewess, illustrating the domestic manners and customs of the Jews. Interspersed with original anecdotes of Napoleon* was published in 1838. This is also a conversion story, narrated in the third person, about Judith, Jewish daughter of an eclectic foreigner, a German physician brought up in 'profligate' *ancien régime* France, who changes his religion (to marry a Jewish wife) and his political allegiance after the revolution. Judith begins her assimilation to the Protestant environment at an English boarding school, starts to read the New Testament in secret, and quickly becomes convinced of its truth. She resists an arranged marriage, endures the emotional blackmail of her mother and the persecutions of a rabbi who lives in the household, and is eventually reunited with her Christian childhood sweetheart, with whom she elopes.

The third autobiography I will be considering, *Leila Ada, the Jewish Convert. An Authentic Memoir*, was first published by Leila Ada's editor, Osborn W. Trenery Heighway, in the 1840s and followed by a second and third edition in the 1850s and various offshoots, *Select Extracts from the Diary, Correspondence, etc., of Leila Ada* (1854) and *The Relatives of Leila Ada: with some account of the present persecutions of the Jews* (1856). These posthumously published accounts of a Jewish woman's journey towards Christianity are narrated '*verbatim et literatim*', in her own voice, which debates and struggles with itself in diaries and letters dating from her early teens.[5]

The texts somewhat strenuously stress their authenticity. Leila Ada's editor is anxious to reassure the reader of the purity of the narrative: 'we have everywhere carefully abstained from mixing the language of our own thinkings with the words of that excellent young person who is now with God'.[6] Madame Brendlah states explicitly in *Tales of a Jewess* that the information contained in her narrative is taken from real life:

> Let not the reader expect to find in the following pages, feigned stories, nor tales from the visions of fancy. What is related is mostly founded on facts. If the names of the individuals concerned are altered, it is because it would be unjust to her friends for the Authoress to expose the frailties incidental to human nature; nor would it be decent in her to hold up to ridicule the religious tenets of the Jews, however erroneous she may *now* consider them.
>
> The Authoress was born a Jewess.[7]

Indeed, details of the extraordinary autobiography outlined by Brendlah in her 'Introduction' bear close resemblance to the life-history of her heroine Judith. The author of the *de Lissau* novels is more coy. Following the heroine's failure to convert in *Sophia de Lissau*, the sequel introduces her sister Emma's story with a renewed stress on its veracity:

> In consequence of various letters and remarks, respecting 'Sophia,' from persons of the first respectability in England and Scotland, addressed to the Author, or communicated to her by her friends, which, though they conveyed a very flattering approbation of that work, yet expressed doubts of its *authenticity*, she thinks it necessary to offer a few brief remarks.
>
> When she first designed to offer to the public, a sketch of the domestic and religious peculiarities of a people, ever interesting to a reflective mind, and more especially so, to Christians, she found that the *mere* detail, would necessarily be dry and heavy reading. She therefore adopted, (as a vehicle to convey the necessary information,) events with which she was intimately connected, and could therefore detail, with fidelity and accuracy. Many persons have questioned the *truth* of these details. The Author *knows* them to be affecting realities.[8]

The writer argues here that the story was merely a vehicle for presenting information about Judaism, which was the primary purpose of the book. However, almost immediately she goes on to titillate the reader about the origin of the story and the real source of its authenticity:

> In the narrative of 'Emma', (as previously in that of 'Sophia',) dates and

names are changed, and anachronisms purposely committed, for substantial reasons. Many events are wholly omitted, to have given *all* the Author *could* have detailed, would have extended the work to twice its present size. The Author has documents in her possession, to which no reference is made in the work, though connected with subjects not uninteresting.[9]

Henry Webb's 'Preface' to the second edition sees further need for reassurance: 'I have known the Author of Emma de Lissau for many years, and have good reasons for believing, that that, which she has written is true'.[10] In *The Orphans of Lissau*, published two years later, which relates the earlier family history of the de Lissaus, the author reveals that 'the following authentic narrative is extracted from the journals of a departed relative'.[11] The 'Recommendatory Preface' to a new edition of the same novel reprinted in the 1850s, however, blurs the distinction between biography and autobiography: 'Her touching and varied narratives are founded on direct information, or the closest personal observation. Some of them, though artificially constructed, describe, with as much precision as prudence dictates, the affecting history of her own conversations and subsequent trials'.[12] Indeed the structure of the author's own preface to *Emma de Lissau* suggests an identification between her sufferings and the sufferings of her heroine:

Respecting the defective style of composition, visible in the Author's productions, she at once acknowledges it. – Her's [sic] are *native* abilities, if she possesses *any*, – Education has done little for her, – Her reading has been very confined, – added to which disadvantages, 'Emma de Lissau' has been written under much indisposition of body, heightened by the painful anxiety, connected with straitened temporal circumstances. She needs, therefore, the generous allowance of her Christian readers, and confidently believes she shall not be disappointed.

The narrative closes at the period when Emma became an outcast for the truth's sake, prudential reasons render this needful. The trials of Emma since that period have been of a nature, the details of which, would injure the sacred cause, in the opinion of the world, and perhaps grieve and deter, weak converts among her nation.[13]

A similar gesture is made by Leila Ada's editor, whose oblique references to the persecutory power of Leila's family explain his reluctance to publish further work concerning her; the eventual publication of the book, under such circumstances, becomes additional evidence of its authenticity.[14] The idea of the book produced under stress is an important authenticating device: the respective introductions to the sequel to *Sophia de Lissau* and the subsequent volumes of

Leila Ada's work argue that their continuing production is justified by public demand; they are not, they claim, novels written for profit, but on the contrary, narratives written in self-sacrifice for the sake of truth.

I will be suggesting several linked reasons why authenticity seems to be such a key concern for these writers. The first is to do with their cultural context. These texts register a puritan distrust of fiction; they must be considered not only as autobiographies, but as Evangelical narratives. In drawing a line between her past self represented in the novel and her present self writing the novel, the author names her text as a confession. By publishing her own confession she hopes to multiply it, by revealing her own errors she hopes to illuminate others'. These texts are written not as a testimony of subjectivity, but as argument and evidence for universal truth, evidence which is strengthened by every addition to the genre. They are not about the search for a narrative of the self, but the submission of the self to an already-written narrative. Thus, I would suggest, these texts effectively write autobiography against itself, the individual voice dissolving easily into the universal story.

Yet, at the same time, the autobiographical form's capacity to privilege the individual voice has a particular significance for the Evangelical writer. As Jane Rendall writes, Evangelical theology stressed 'the possibility of salvation through the conversion and rebirth of the individual'.[15] This emphasis on individual consciousness also needs to be contextualized historically in the rise to dominance of Evangelicalism during the social changes of early-nineteenth-century Britain. Catherine Hall has shown how the Evangelical Revival coincided with the formation of the new industrial bourgeois class, and its ideology came to represent the changing consciousness of this class.[16] The theology of individualism also underlies the conservative political stance of the Evangelical movement, which, despite its campaign for the abolition of slavery at the beginning of the century, was not generally in favour of structural change through the redistribution of political power, but advocated reform from within: self-emancipation.[17] This resulted in a very particular understanding of the role of the individual within the nation: 'It was the religious consciousness of England, they argued, which determined her political condition'.[18]

I want to link this individualistic ideology with the form of the novels I have been discussing. Conversionist novels as a genre were produced by the Evangelical preference for self-emancipation through conversion, as opposed to political emancipation and social reform. If enlightenment is the responsibility of the individual not society, the Evangelical writer uses the novel form to underline this emphasis. Autobiography stresses interiority; revelation comes to the heroine of *Tales of a Jewess* in her locked room, in private, silent communion with the Word. Among her Jewish family she experiences 'an instinctive longing to be alone, again to open *that forbidden book*, which she could not overcome'.[19] Leila Ada's memoir embodies this privacy of faith in the self-communing of a private diary, 'a secret correspondence with her own heart'.[20] Her editor explains that 'writing was ever Leila's stronghold. Often when beset with sorrows she found a precious solace in this – partly because it engaged her thoughts; but especially because in it she found a channel for her earnest feeling'.[21] Yet this exploration of subjectivity seems also to be denied in the search for truth: she resolves 'that I will live only to serve God and for the good of others. Never seek my own pleasure or satisfaction at the expense of that of any one else; but as far as possible I will forget that there is a self to please'.[22] The diary articulates contradictions: both selflessness and extreme introspection, objectivity and subjectivity, and although never intended for publication it somehow made its way into print.

The problem of these paradoxes leads me to what I consider the most important reason for the emphasis on authenticity in these texts – that they are fakes. The gender, religion, culture and life-story of the subjects of these autobiographies are in fact literary strategies. For despite the claims to provide secret insider knowledge, much of the information about Jewish customs in *Tales of a Jewess* and the *Leila Ada* texts is garbled and seems second-hand. There are also more general mistakes, like the claim by Leila's editor Trenery Heighway that her diary and correspondence had to be translated from Hebrew because Jews habitually communicated in that language.[23] Historically, this is wholly unlikely, though it was a commonly held opinion about the Jews. Stylistically, as well, there seems to be little development in 'Leila''s forms of literary self-expression between her early teenagerhood and her adulthood. The *de Lissau* novels, on the other hand, appear to be accurate in the information they offer. However, the anonymous author was in fact Amelia Bristow, later editor of *The Christian Lady's Friend and Family Repository*, one of several conversionist periodicals which devoted considerable attention to documenting and encouraging the conversion of Jews. Like Heighway's and Brendlah's texts, Bristow's narrative is formulaic, showing the awakening of a woman to Christianity through reading the New Testament, her persecution by her family, her inquisition by rabbis and finally her escape or death. Heighway's and Bristow's novels were all reprinted in the late 1850s by the Evangelical publisher Simpkin, Marshall and Co. as part of the 'Run and Read Library, consisting of tales uniting Taste, Humor, and Sound Principles, and written by competent Christian writers with a view to elevate the character of our popular fiction'. The *Jewish Chronicle*, British Jewry's official newspaper, considered the 'Leila Ada' books an obvious conversionist fraud: 'We immediately perceived, from unmistakable evidence, both internal and external, that the book was a fabrication, and as much the invention of the fertile imagination of the author as the innumerable other works of fiction'.[24] The newspaper noted with gleeful irony the successful prosecution of Heighway by his publisher in 1857 for attempting to sell the copyright to another fraudulent memoir, the profits of which were supposed to go to the 'diarist's' poor dependants. The proceedings were reprinted in full, so readers 'may judge of what stuff an author patronised by the conversionists is made, who panders to the morbid taste of a sickly religious public, and in how far credence is to be attached to productions which speculate upon human feelings as the devices of the swindler upon the purse of his neighbour'.[25] Pouring scorn on Heighway's disingenuous profit-making, the *Jewish Chronicle* also recognized that for a reader, Jewish or non-Jewish, without a considerable degree of knowledge and experience of Anglo-Jewish religious and social practice, there are few reasons to question the origins of these texts. This is primarily due to their extremely sophisticated authenticating mechanisms, which use all the apparatus of autobiography, its construction and analysis of subjectivity, and its foregrounding of questions about editorship and authority.

But if Jewish female subjectivity is not what is being explored in these texts, then what is? If we are going to treat these novels as highly self-conscious examples of the *use* of autobiography, how indeed are its features employed, and to what end?

Firstly I want to discuss the reasons why women's autobiography was used as a vehicle for the Evangelical project of the conversion of the Jews. This is a question to some extent of literary precedent. Literary representations of the Jewess had always emphasized her ambiguous, almost intermediate status, her assumed dissatisfaction and therefore less determined adherence to her heredi- tary religion and culture.[26] The Jewess' physical beauty was conventionally the route to her salvation as it could attract a Christian man who would save her. Thus the female Jew tended to be used to represent a belief in the Hebrews' perpetual potential for redemption and conformity, as opposed to their utter irredeemability and otherness, conventionally signified by the male. I would also suggest that it was the enormous popularity of Scott's *Ivanhoe*, showing a Jewish woman who defiantly refuses to convert, which prompted the subsequent proliferation of Evangelical books about zealously converting Jewesses.

However, I think there are more important political functions of using women's autobiography for this project. These writings appeared in the wake of the granting of political emancipation to Protestant Dissenters and Catholics, and during the campaign by British Jews, who were still barred from public office, the professions and the universities, for similar emancipation. The question of the place of Jews within the British polity was a highly public, contentious issue which struck at the heart of the Protestant and liberal identification of the British state.[27] On the other hand, the novels which I have been discussing frame Jewishness in a very different context; they tell of the lives of middle-class women, and their subject matter is correspondingly domestic. The stories centre around family relationships, spiritual contemplation, moral reflection: the typical content of the bourgeois domestic novel. The space outside the domestic environment is random and uninterpretable in *Tales of a Jewess*, non-existent in *Sophia de Lissau*, and represented entirely in terms of religious allegory in the diary of Leila Ada (for example her long account of her travels across Europe to Palestine). For the female characters in these novels, being Jewish does not constitute a political identity in the terms of contemporary public debate: Jewishness is manifested entirely in the home, in domestic practices and domestic relations. Thus the autobiographical form's emphasis on interiority focuses the sphere of the domestic novel even further inward. In the diary of Leila Ada in particular, there appears to be no public self at all; Leila exists only through her communion with herself. Using women's autobiography necessitates a different kind of emphasis, determined by contemporary constructions of femininity and the female sphere, and this conjunction enables Evangelical discourse to produce a different account of Jewishness. This is not to say that such representations deliberately avoid reference to the more conventional narrative of the political and social persecution of the Jews. However, in all these novels it is the Jewish *woman* who suffers persecution, and this persecution never takes place outside the domestic sphere. Centring the Jewess in these texts crucially changes the political resonance of the figure of the Jew. The conversionist heroine is the victim not of the anti-semite but of her own family. Persecution is not an external phenomenon, a question of legal and social status, as it is for Scott's heroine Rebecca; instead it is domesticated. The displacement of the political by the personal through the use of autobiography in these Evangelical novels constitutes a significant silence around the relationship between Jews and anti-semitism in British history.

However, autobiography as a form is crucially modified in all these texts. Despite the elaborate devices of authentication, the autobiographical voice is implicitly admitted to be inadequate as a vehicle for information, which, as I showed earlier, Bristow claimed was her primary concern. The personal voice, its introspection lapsing into private language, creates gaps in comprehension which need to be filled for the reader. Cultural difference needs annotation – these texts are unable to sustain their dependence for authority on the individual female voice, and the 'truth' of testimony ultimately shows its limitations. This suggests that the focus in these texts is not only on the account of conversion. The narrators in fact seem as eager to fix their cultural 'origins' as to document the story of their personal development. For this purpose, paratextual commentary appears in all the novels, purporting to explain the arcane. This editorializing takes different forms; in the *de Lissau* series and *Tales of a Jewess* the story is accompanied by a series of scholarly notes which are set apart from the main narrative. In *Tales of a Jewess* the notes soberly and often lengthily debate details of Jewish thought, language and practice and stand in striking contrast to the rambling and irreverent text. Sometimes, however, the voices cross over each other, combining anthropology with judgment:

> The modern Jews are very religious, or rather superstitious, observers
> of the Sabbath. If a beast by accident fall into a ditch on this day, they
> do not take him out, as they formerly did, but only feed him there. They
> neither carry arms, nor gold, nor silver about them; nor are they

permitted so much as to touch them. The very rubbing the dirt off their shoes, is a breach of the Sabbath; and their scruples go so far, as even to grant a truce to the fleas.[28]

There is a similar ambivalence in the *Leila Ada* books. Leila's words are introduced by an editor, then commented upon by him throughout, thus annotation is incorporated into the body of the narrative. Her own writings are also supplemented with the testimonies of others who knew her, and often, significantly, the voices of Leila and the editor appear to merge.

Cultural difference had been represented by this form before, notably in Maria Edgeworth's novel on Irishness, *Castle Rackrent* (1800), and Sydney Morgan's *The Wild Irish Girl* (1806), examples of the early-nineteenth-century female genre of the national tale which both use a double narrative structure. However, it is in the editorializing that an ambivalence about the functions of these texts always emerges. Ina Ferris sees the notes in *The Wild Irish Girl* as 'more than scholarly references; they are also political acts, at once vindicating and constructing Irish culture', and thus 'the authorial and narrative worlds in the end confound each other'.[29] Gary Kelly, on the other hand, argues that in *Castle Rackrent* the notes satirize the first-person narrative. In Edgeworth's novel the 'editorial apparatus repeatedly draws attention to the irrational, improvident nature of Irish popular culture, and emphasizes the "otherness" of this culture further by notes on Irish peculiarities of pronunciation and phrasing'.[30] This is precisely the effect in the conversionist texts. Kelly suggests that in *Castle Rackrent* 'the "editor" dominates the text as a whole while operating from its margins ... and the mere narrative is continually interrupted, controlled, or supervised by the notes, which represent a literate and learned consciousness very different from that of the "illiterate" narrator'.[31]

I would argue that the notes are crucial in modifying autobiography in these texts, in regulating its meaning. Indeed the 'simple, lovely-spirited writings' of 'Leila Ada', who apparently never intentionally wrote for the public, need to be subjected to ventriloquization by a male, Christian editor.[32] Annotation defamiliarizes what autobiography has made familiar. At the same time, the autobiographical voice defines the function of the notes, drawing their apparently neutral information into a conversionist teleology in which its significance cannot be misinterpreted. And yet, do not the notes also, to some extent, exceed this purpose, *vindicating* as well as constructing Jewishness as in *The Wild Irish Girl*? How useful are the categories of 'fake' and 'authentic'; does it actually matter that these texts are not, like Sydney Morgan's novel, expressions of an ideology of romantic nationalism or cultural preservation, but, on the contrary, written with the purpose of disparaging their subject and relegating it to ancient history?

My concern here is not, in the end, with which register is able to confer authority and regulate meaning. Rather it is with the effects of the difference and interaction between authoritative discourses within these texts. In the narrative of *Tales of a Jewess*, Jewishness is subject to ridicule and inevitable refutation. In the footnotes, which assume a sober, scholarly tone, Jewishness becomes a subject of knowledge. The Western 'Orientalist' production of the Orient through the creation of knowledge about it is replicated here in the codification of knowledge about Jews and Judaism. This was, as Edward Said has argued in his analysis of nineteenth-century Orientalism, an aspect of the power relationship between the Occident and its 'Other'.[33] As the Rev. John Wilson of the Free Church of Scotland's mission, Bombay, wrote in his 'Recommendatory Preface' to Amelia Bristow's novel about Polish Jewry, *The Orphans of Lissau*, 'the more that is known of their present tenets, feelings, observances, and religious and social customs, the more intense will be the interest that is felt in the work of their instruction and enlightenment'.[34]

Robin Gilmour writes of autobiography as paradigmatic for Victorian culture, an introspective version of the age's preoccupations with ancestry, genealogy, links between the present and the past:

> Holding the world together within, finding a coherence in the self which would at the same time impose some meaning and coherence on a rapidly changing world outside: this involved searching for the logic in one's own memories, which is the task of autobiography. The autobiographical pressure which is felt so strongly in Victorian writing of all kinds – fiction, poetry, literary criticism, theology – is an expression of the desire to make sense of an evolutionary universe by discovering evolution in one's own universe of memory.[35]

Describing Jewishness in the texts I have discussed in this paper is in a sense Christian culture searching for its roots, reclaiming its religious origins. Certainly one of the reasons for the new interest in Jews at this time was a return to the puritan tradition of English Protestantism, recognizing 'a kinship which drew inspiration from the Old Testament', regarding Jews not as Christ-killers but as Christ-bearers.[36] However, these texts suggest that for Victorian Evangelicals the production of an evolutionary autobiographical narrative involved identifying, defining and classifying the unfamiliar as well as the familial.

Notes

1 Mel Scult (1978) *Millennial Expectations and Jewish Liberties: A Study of the Efforts to Convert the Jews in Britain, up to the Mid Nineteenth Century*, Leiden: E.J. Brill, Chapters 6 and 7. The conversion of the Jews was of particular importance to millenarian Evangelicals, who believed that it was necessary as a prelude to the Second Coming.

2 Scult 1978, p. 126.
3 For an account of literary representations of the Jew in the novel and the theatre from the seventeenth to the nineteenth century see Edgar Rosenberg (1960) *From Shylock to Svengali: Jewish Stereotypes in English Fiction*, London: Peter Owen.
4 M.C.N. Salbstein (1982) *The Emancipation of the Jews in Britain: The Question of the Admission of the Jews to Parliament, 1828–1860*. Rutherford, Madison, Teaneck: Fairleigh Dickinson University Press; London and Toronto: Associated University Presses, p. 37.
5 Osborn W. Trenery Heighway (1853) *Leila Ada, the Jewish Convert. An Authentic Memoir*, third edition, London: Partridge and Oakey, p. viii.
6 *Ibid.*, p. 207.
7 Madame Brendlah (1838) *Tales of a Jewess, illustrating the domestic manners and customs of the Jews. Interspersed with original anecdotes of Napoleon.* London: Simpkin, Marshall and Co., p. v.
8 [Amelia Bristow] (1828) *Emma de Lissau; a Narrative of striking vicissitudes, and peculiar trials; with explanatory notes, Illustrative of the manners and customs of the Jews*, by the author of 'Sophia de Lissau', 'Elizabeth Allen', etc. etc., London: T. Gardiner and Son, pp. iii–iv.
9 *Ibid.*, p. iv.
10 [Amelia Bristow] (1829) *Emma de Lissau; a Narrative of Striking Vicissitudes, and peculiar trials: with Notes, illustrative of the manners and customs of the Jews*, by the author of 'Sophia de Lissau', 'Elizabeth Allen', etc. etc., second edition, London: T. Gardiner and Son, p. vi.
11 [Amelia Bristow] (1830) *The Orphans of Lissau, and other interesting narratives, immediately concerned with Jewish customs, domestic and religious, with explanatory notes*, by the author of 'Sophia de Lissau', 'Emma de Lissau', etc., London: T. Gardiner and Son, p. 4.
12 [Amelia Bristow] (n.d. [1859]) *The Orphans of Lissau, and other narratives*, by the author of 'Emma de Lissau', 'Sophia de Lissau', etc. etc. etc., new edition, revised, London; Simpkin, Marshall and Co., p. x.
13 [Bristow] 1828, pp. iv–v.
14 Osborn W. Trenery Heighway (1854) *Select Extracts from the Diary, Correspondence, &c., of Leila Ada*, London: Partridge, Oakey and Co., pp. vi–vii.
15 Jane Rendall (1985) *The Origins of Modern Feminism: Women in Britain, France and the United States 1780–1860*, Houndmills: Macmillan, p. 74.
16 Catherine Hall (1979) 'The Early Formation of Victorian Domestic Ideology', in Sandra Burman (Ed.) *Fit Work for Women*, London; Croom Helm; Canberra: Australian National University Press, pp. 19–20.
17 Paradoxically, many of the prominent campaigners in the parliamentary campaign for Jewish emancipation later in the century were Evangelicals. However, they were not advocating social reform for its own sake, but, they hoped, as an aid to eventual conversion. See Scult 1978.
18 Hall 1979, p. 19.
19 Brendlah 1838, p. 82.
20 Heighway 1853, p. 7.
21 Heighway 1854, p. 172.

22 Heighway 1853, pp. 19–20.
23 Heighway 1854, p. viii.
24 'A Pious Fraud', *Jewish Chronicle*, 15 January 1858, p. 35.
25 *Ibid.*
26 This is discussed at greater length in my forthcoming 'Gender and Jewishness in Nineteenth Century British Literature', unpublished PhD thesis, University of London.
27 See David Feldman (1994) *Englishmen and Jews: Social Relations and Political Culture, 1840–1914*, New Haven: Yale University Press. For an account of the continuing resonance of this debate in English literature see Bryan Cheyette (1993) *Construction of the Jew in English Literature and Society: Racial Representations 1875–1945*, Cambridge: Cambridge University Press.
28 Brendlah 1838, p. 213.
29 Ina Ferris (1991) *The Achievement of Literary Authority: Gender, History, and the Waverley Novels*, Ithaca and London: Cornell University Press, p. 126.
30 Gary Kelly (1989) *English Fiction of the Romantic Period 1789–1830*, London and New York: Longman, p. 77.
31 *Ibid.*, p. 78.
32 Heighway 1854, p. v.
33 See Edward Said (1991) *Orientalism: Western Conceptions of the Orient*, Harmondsworth: Penguin, 'Introduction'.
34 [Bristow] n.d. [1859], p. ix.
35 Robin Gilmour (1993) *The Victorian Period: The Intellectual and Cultural Context of English Literature 1830–1890*, London and New York: Longman, p. 27.
36 Salbstein 1982, pp. 29–30.

Chapter 7

Sisterhood and Self-censorship in the Nineteenth Century

PART ONE

Writing herself: The diary of Alice James

Janet Bottoms

Diary writing is sometimes perceived as a private and spontaneous activity; unstructured, uninhibited, it flows on from day to day, a modest little stream of consciousness. In reality it is very far from this, though the writer may not be fully conscious of the process of selection and structuring which is taking place. When Alice James – sister of Henry, the novelist, and William, the author of *Principles of Psychology* – began her journal she was 40 years old, an invalid and alone, apart from her nurse, having moved to England a few years earlier for what had been intended to be a short visit. Like many other diary writers, therefore, her decision that to write a little every day might 'bring relief as an outlet to that geyser of emotions, sensations, speculations, and reflections which ferments perpetually within my poor old carcass for its sins',[1] was motivated by a desperate sense of isolation.

One of the most noticeable things about her diary, however, is that it is *not* a 'geyser of emotions'. If the first instinct of the diarist is towards freedom of expression, the second instinct is to retreat, for no sooner does pen touch paper than the writer becomes also a reader, and a complex of inhibitions and an inculcated self-consciousness come into play. The diary is very much a woman's form because it is secret – it makes no open claim to notice – and yet to record oneself in this manner is, after all, to make an assertion that one is worthy of record. In many diaries we find that combination of defensive self-mockery and self-assertion which is also to be found in Emily Dickinson's equally 'secret', self-reflexive poetry.

I'm Nobody! Who are you?
Are you – Nobody – Too?
Then there's a pair of us?
Don't tell![2]

Alice James referred to this poem in her diary while recording how she had been asked whether she had herself (like her famous brothers) ever written for the press. She repudiated the suggestion vehemently[3] and with scorn, yet her friend and amanuensis Katharine Loring was quite sure that she wanted her diary to be made public eventually.

Secondly, the diarist is a reader *before* she is a writer. Alice James brings together both the writing and reading processes when she speaks of the value of being able to 'get on to my sofa and occupy myself for four hours, at intervals, thro' the day, scribbling my notes and able to read the books that belong to me, in that *they clarify the density and shape the formless mass within*' (*Diary*, 5 May 1890; my emphasis). Apparently it is this need to clarify, to give form, which lies at the root of much diary writing. Some kind of defining shape is constantly being sought and imposed upon contingency – but in this process the diarist is necessarily influenced by the way her or his idea of self has already been constructed, through society and its narratives.

The diarist, then, is both writer and reader, observed and observer, in a way which replicates the life experience of many women. A woman, John Berger has said, learns continually to watch herself because how she appears to others is so important to what is, or at least traditionally has been seen as, her 'success' in life.

> So she comes to consider the *surveyor* and the *surveyed* within her as the two constituent yet always distinct elements of her identity as a woman. . . . Her own sense of being in herself is supplanted by a sense of being appreciated as herself by another.[4]

The diary may be a private form of writing, but it is remarkable how many diarists do, in fact, address themselves to someone or something, to a fantasized reader who is a part of themselves and yet separated in order to give the affirmation, the appreciation which they dare not claim consciously. The way that the reader is conceived of must therefore make a difference to the selecting and shaping process by which experience is translated into written record. Most female diarists imagine a female *alter ego*, but Alice James' 'Dear Inconnu' is male, a fact to which she draws self-mocking attention, and which can surely be understood in the light of the dominant role played in her life by her father and brothers, as well as her 'failure' to acquire the husband who would have given her a social validity. Berger's comment that 'the surveyor of woman in herself is male: the surveyed female' is therefore particularly relevant to Alice James.

It is a male view of herself which the diary shows her both adopting and unconsciously wrestling with, and it is for a male-gendered reader that she seems to be 'writing' herself (though there is an unquantifiable extra dimension in the fact that from the beginning of 1891 every entry was dictated through a woman).

Diaries, and women's diaries in particular, are excellent examples of the autobiographical process at work precisely because they are not spontaneous outpourings but are shaped, however unconsciously, and the *Diary* of Alice James is a fascinating example of the inconsistencies and attempts to create something consistent, the self-projection and self-censoring, the compulsion to truth and the 'bracketing' of it, which underlies diary writing for many women. Her 'reader' is defined as male, as I have noted, and in the James family 'male' meant intelligence, wit, and having a 'moral' being and individual identity in a way which being female did not. Henry James senior, an eccentric but respected writer on the philosophy of religion, had developed a theory of moral evolution seen at work in man, for whom an apprehension and experience of evil was a necessary part of his development. Women, on the other hand, were different – their purpose being to inspire and comfort rather than to have a moral consciousness of their own. In this he was encouraged and confirmed by Mrs James, 'the very incarnation of *banality*', according to one contemporary observer,[5] but whom it was an article of faith with all the James children to see as the epitome of self-effacement and maternal devotion.

Consciously at least, the family ideology was not to be questioned – too much emotional capital was invested in it – and nor could a daughter consciously question the priority given to her obviously brilliant brothers. At 18 she subscribed herself in a letter to William, 'Your loving *idiotoid* sister', and at the end of a life marked by an accelerating series of psychological and physical breakdowns, she wrote to him again:

> But you must believe that you greatly exaggerate the tragic element in my commonplace little journey.... You must also remember that a woman, by nature, needs much less to feed upon than a man, a few emotions & she is satisfied.[6]

'Matrimony', she had early concluded, 'seems the only successful occupation that a woman can undertake', but matrimony was denied to her, and her hope of being able to find a similar role as the comfort and support of her widowed father was thwarted by his apparently willed death within the year.[7] This was the point at which, as she wrote later in her diary, 'my scaffolding began to fall' – the point at which the 'meaning' of her life as it had been written for and by her until that point seemed to disappear.

Alice's diary was begun six years later, and ended with her death from breast cancer at the age of 43. There are two main aspects to it – a day to day record of ideas and incidents, and, increasingly towards the end, a retrospective view of her life. Naturally, a selecting process is at work in both, but the shaping tools are different. On the first level, she makes use of a defensive irony and ambiguity. Much of her diary is a record of her lively interest in political and social issues and her extensive reading. Her brother Henry wrote to William that her 'vigour of mind and decision of character' as well as her 'brilliant and trenchant conversation' were much admired in England,[8] but Alice herself exhibits a compulsion to avoid any appearance of taking herself seriously.

> I wonder whether, if I had had any education I should have been more, or less, of a fool than I am. It would have deprived me surely of those exquisite moments of mental flatulence which every now and then inflate the cerebral vacuum with a delicious sense of latent possibilities – of stretching oneself to cosmic limits. (*Diary*, 12 December 1889)

She can only safely lay claim to the ability partially to follow in the intellectual footsteps of a man, 'one's mind stretching to the limits of his', and 'such a subtle flattery emanating from his perfection in "putting it" as to make an absolutely ignorant creature like me vibrate, as with knowledge, in response to the truth of his exquisitely subtle perceptions' (*Diary*, 12 June 1889). When this happens, she writes, her whole being is 'vivified with the sense of the *Intelligent* revealed!' but whether she means revealed in him or in herself is left ambiguous. Moreover, in case she appears to be taking herself too seriously, there is always that bolt-hole word 'flattery': a woman comparing her mental abilities with a man must be either flattering herself, or being flattered.

She depicts herself as a traditional object of comedy – a 'grotesque'.

> Yesterday Nurse and I had a good laugh but I must allow that decidedly she 'had' me. I was thinking of something that interested me very much and my mind was suddenly flooded by one of those luminous waves that sweep out of consciousness all but the living sense and overpower one with joy in the rich, throbbing complexity of life, when suddenly I looked up at Nurse, who was dressing me, and saw her primitive, rudimentary expression (so common here) as of no inherited quarrel with her destiny of putting petticoats over my head; the poverty and deadness of it contrasted to the tide of speculation that was coursing thro' my brain made me exclaim, 'Oh! Nurse, don't you wish you were inside of *me*!' – her look of dismay and vehement disclaimer – 'Inside of you, Miss, when you have just had a sick head-ache for five days!' – gave a greater blow to my vanity than that much battered article had ever received. (*Diary*, 12 July 1889)

To be reminded so abruptly that, even when within her she felt 'the potency of a Bismarck', to the world her 'glorious role was to stand for *Sick headache* to mankind!' was enough to make her retreat again into defensive irony.

> To sit by and watch these absurdities is amusing in its way and reminds
> me of how I used to *listen* to my 'company manners' in the days when
> I had 'em, and how ridiculous they sounded.

Such comments are a reminder that *irony* – the simultaneous acceptance of and
protest against incongruity or injustice – is the weapon of the relatively
powerless. It may be turned on other people or the context in which the ironist
is unwillingly placed, but if, for reasons of emotional need, she dare not
consciously criticize those who are responsible for her situation, she will tend to
divide and turn upon her own self. Alice seems to have felt, subconsciously, that
if she was to justify herself her critical comments on other people and institutions
– a necessary exercise, for her, of the 'acrid strain to stiffen the sinews' (*Diary*
12 January 1890) but an expression of the 'hardness' which she recalls her father
deploring in her – she must turn her satirist's eye inwards first of all.

Her comments on the journals of other women writers show a scorn – and
a fear – of self-pity. Her physicians having impressed upon her that the way to
health was to ignore all her symptoms and emotional moods, 'be they
temporarily pleasant or unpleasant',[9] she came to regard the voicing of them as
typically female and feeble. The *Journal* of the young Russian artist Marie
Bashkirtseff, begun in passionate eagerness at the age of 15 and broken off in
despair shortly before she died of tuberculosis at the age of 24, had just been
published and was the subject of everyone's conversation. Alice James, however,
consciously reading it, noted:

> I imagine her the perverse of the perverse and what part so dreary to read
> of, or what part so easy to act as we walk across our little stage lighted
> up by our self-conscious foot-lights (*Diary* 16 June 1890)

She was shocked by the 'futile whining' and 'superlative solemnity' about
herself of George Eliot, a writer she had ardently admired. 'What a lifeless,
diseased, *self-conscious* being she must have been!' she exclaims in disgust, 'As
if it weren't degrading eno[ugh] to have head-aches, without jotting them down
in a row to stare at one for all time' (*Diary* 28 May 1889; my emphasis). For
Alice James, dignity went hand-in-hand with a sense of humour, and both of
them were part of the pride of being a James.

Her record of the past was also highly selective. Her childhood; her
enthusiasm for riding; gossipy adolescent friendships; and great tracts of her life
as a young woman growing up during the Civil War, or as a Bostonian lady
involved in some of the social and educational reform movements of the post-
war period are ignored. Instead, what emerges is a gradually evolving narrative
of what had come to seem significant to her subjectively conceived self, and here

her preferred tool was metaphor. She searched, in her own reading, for images through which to write her 'story'. At first this took the form of unexplored jottings. In the opening pages of the diary she refers to a sketch of the Cobb at Lyme Regis, 'off which dear, sweet Louisa Musgrove jumped', adding enigmatically: 'Think of my being so mentally clumsy as not to have seen her ghost of my own motion' (*Diary* 1 June 1889). Three days later she noted, 'What one reads, or rather all that comes to us is surely only of interest and value in proportion as we find ourselves therein, form given to what was vague, what slumbered stirred to life'. What was it that was given form by the image of Louisa Musgrove's disastrous jump in *Persuasion*? On the face of it there is little similarity between the impetuous, wilful Louisa and 'poor Alice', the Bostonian invalid spinster. Does Louisa stand for 'the expectant', which 'palpitated within' her in childhood, and which took the form of such excitement at a promised visit, on one occasion, that her mother decided she must be denied it in order to bring her back to a more level emotional state?[10] Youth, she commented later in the diary, was the most difficult period of life.

> The blank youthful mind, ignorant of catastrophe, stands crushed and bewildered before the perpetual postponement of its hopes, things promised in the dawn that the sunset ne'er fulfils. Owing to muscular circumstances my youth was not of the most ardent, but I had to peg away pretty hard between 12 and 24, 'killing myself,' as some one calls it – absorbing into the bone that the better part is to clothe oneself in neutral tints, walk by still waters, and possess one's soul in silence ... How I recall the low grey Newport sky in that winter of 62–63, as I used to wander about over the cliffs, my young soul struggling out of its swaddling-clothes as the knowledge crystallized within me of what Life meant for me. (*Diary* 21 February 1890)

Nothing she had written at that earlier period suggests any such knowledge.

Gradually, her autobiographical narrative began to take shape as she discovered the metaphors through which to express it, but it was in looking back that she was enabled to impose structure on her experience – negative suffering transposed into positive control. One of the best examples of the process is in one of her longer autobiographical passages, inspired by her brother William's paper on the 'Hidden Self'. In this he had described how 'the nervous victim "abandons" certain portions of his consciousness', an 'excellent expression' in her view, even though she herself had never been able to abandon her own consciousness enough to get even five minutes' rest.

> I have passed thro' an infinite succession of conscious abandonments and in looking back now I see how it began in my childhood, altho' I wasn't conscious of the necessity until '67 or '68 when I broke down

first, acutely, and had violent turns of hysteria. (*Diary* 26 October 1890)

In the complete physical collapse which followed the storm, but with her mind 'luminous and active', she saw, as she says, 'distinctly', that life was to be, for her, one long battle between her body and her will, 'a battle in which the former [the female body rather than the "male" intellect or will] was to be triumphant to the end'.

'Owing to some physical weakness, excess of nervous susceptibility', she continues, 'the moral power *pauses*; as it were for a moment, and refuses to maintain muscular sanity, worn out with the strain of its constabulary functions'. The body, it may be noted, is now apparently also criminal. And against what law does it offend?

> As I used to sit immovable reading in the library with waves of violent inclination suddenly invading my muscles taking some one of their myriad forms such as throwing myself out of the window, or knocking off the head of the benignant pater as he sat with his silver locks, writing at his table, it used to seem to me that the only difference between me and the insane was that I had not only all the horrors and suffering of insanity but the duties of doctor, nurse, and strait-jacket imposed upon me, too. (*Diary* 26 October 1890)

The pater, the head – literally and figuratively – was the object of both her bitter resentment and her need to love, of kisses and of violence. She might well have said, with Othello:

> Excellent wretch, perdition catch my soul
> But I do love thee, and when I love thee not
> Chaos is come again.

It was the pater who insisted, all through her life, on writing her as patient and sweet. In her earliest extant letter, at the age of 12, Alice promised him, 'I will try to be good and sweet till you come back, and merit the daisy curtains, and get a chance at your dear old pate again'.[11] Surely it must be better to kill herself rather than to attack such a head. And yet even suicide, as an expression of a rebellion against 'being good', was denied her because when she asked her father whether he thought suicide was a sin, he had replied that it might be seen as a rational response to intolerable suffering, and therefore she had his full permission to end her life when she pleased.[12]

Paralysis, figured as a self-imposed strait-jacket (self-imposed but also 'imposed upon me') was all that was left to her at that period. Later, in her diary, she found the tool which enabled her to face and construct her narrative. In this context, also, she could also appeal for understanding. The language shifts from narrative mode to apostrophe – an appeal to that reader who is both herself and the male 'Inconnu'.

> Conceive of never being without the sense that if you let yourself go for a moment your mechanism will fall into pie and that at some given moment you must abandon it all, let the dykes break and the flood sweep in, acknowledging yourself abjectly impotent before the immutable laws. (*Diary* 26 October 1890)

The force of that word 'abject' suggests a powerful self-disgust, and yet the abject victim is also source of the destructive flood – both Maggie and the Floss in spate. This is now no longer an account of that period in the past, her first breakdown, but of the story of her life – the key she has discovered to her own autobiography. 'When all one's moral and natural stock in trade is a temperament forbidding the abandonment of an inch or the relaxation of a muscle, 'tis a never-ending fight.' Anything which might start up those expectant or ambitious feelings again must be guarded against, 'until life becomes one long flight from remote suggestion and complicated eluding of the multi-fold traps set for your undoing'.

Alice's ability to construct her life as a pattern of 'flight' *from* the unfaceable had finally been brought about by her ability to see the goal she is moving *to*. The process of selection involved in diary writing depends very much upon a sense of direction or purpose, and the long autobiographical passage quoted above was written when it had finally become clear to everyone involved that her death was inevitable. This seems to have given her the sense of closure, of a complete narrative structure, within which to place what could now be seen as significant in the past. From wondering what she could possibly 'stand for' – 'a collection simply of fantastic *un*productive emotions enclosed within tissue paper ... all safety valves shut down in the way of "the busy ineffectiveness of women"' (*Diary* 7 November 1890) – she begins to lay claim to 'a clearer perception of the significance of experience' (*Diary* 23 March 1891).

> One becomes suddenly picturesque to oneself, and one's wavering little individuality stands out with a cameo effect and one has the tenderest indulgence for all the abortive little *stretchings out* which crowd in upon the memory. (*Diary* 1 June 1891)

The significance of a life, like the structure now given to her diary, was to be discovered in its ending. The deaths of acquaintances and relatives now seemed to clarify their lives and make clear what, essentially, they 'stood for', while her own death was seen to rank as her life's work, to rival, finally, her brothers'. In June of 1891 she sums up their achievements in the last year – Henry's novels and plays, William's *Principles of Psychology* – as 'not a bad show for one family! especially if I get myself dead, the hardest job of all' (*Diary* 16 June 1891). Six months later she commented, with exasperation, 'The difficulty about all this dying is that you can't tell a fellow anything about it, so where does the fun come in?' (*Diary* 11 December 1891), but the irony at her own expense and that of others, the cool observation and the 'hard core', remained.

> How wearing to the substance and exasperating to the nerves is the perpetual bewailing, wondering at and wishing to alter things happened, as if all personal concern didn't vanish as the 'happened' crystallizes into history. Of what matter can it be whether pain or pleasure has shaped and stamped the pulp within, as one is absorbed in the supreme interest of watching the outline and the tracery as the lines broaden for eternity. (*Diary* 29 February 1892)

This is the penultimate entry in the diary. On the last day of her life, as her friend Katharine Loring noted, 'Alice was making sentences', and one of the last things she said was to correct the wording of the final entry. As she 'crystallized into history' Alice James succeeded finally in writing her own 'story'.

Notes

1   L. Edel (Ed.) (1982) *The Diary of Alice James*, Harmondsworth: Penguin, p. 25. All subsequent references to the *Diary* are to this edition.
2   T.H. Johnson (Ed.) (1975) *The Complete Poems of Emily Dickinson*, London: Faber and Faber, p. 133.
3   *Diary*, p. 227. Alice James quotes the second stanza of Dickinson's poem, 'How dreary to be somebody ...' before recording her vehement rejection of the 'imputation'. After Alice's death, Katharine Loring had copies of the *Diary* privately printed for her brothers, and encouraged its later publication, telling William's daughter, Margaret James Porter, that 'though [Alice] never said so, I understood that she would like to have it published'; R. Yeazell (1981) *The Death and Letters of Alice James*, Berkeley and London: University of California Press, p. 5.
4   J. Berger (1972) *Ways of Seeing*, Harmondsworth: Penguin, pp. 46–7.
5   J. Strouse (1980) *Alice James: A Biography*, Boston: Houghton Mifflin, p. 44.
6   Letter to William James, 6 August 1867; Strouse 1980, pp. 115–16. Letter to William James, 30 July 1891; Yeazell 1981, pp. 186–7.
7   Letter to her friend, Annie Ashburner, about the artistic ambitions of another young woman, 12 April 1876; Yeazell 1981, p. 72. Mrs James died in January 1882. Alice's aunt, Katharine Walsh, commented that 'her mother's death seems to have brought new life to Alice', and her brother Henry wrote that 'as she is a person of great ability it is an extreme good fortune that she is now able to exert herself'. However, Henry James senior was to die in December of the same year: Katharine Loring wrote to

Robertson James, 'He gets over the delay in dying by asserting that he has already died': Strouse 1980, pp. 202, 208.

8   Henry James to William James, 9 May 1886; Strouse 1980, p. 254.

9   Alice spent the winter of 1866/67 under the care of Dr Charles Fayette Taylor whose system for the treatment of neurasthenic young women, outlined in *Theory and Practice of the Movement Cure* (1861), included impressing upon the patient that 'she must not regard her symptoms, ... but should ignore them as much as possible, taking a course to secure ultimate immunity from them': quoted in Strouse 1980, p. 107.

10   Strouse 1980, pp. 67–8.

11   Letter to Henry James senior, 11 March 1860; Yeazell 1981, p. 49. Twenty years on, Alice would write, 'How sick one gets of being "good", how much I should respect myself if I could burst out and make every one wretched for 24 hours ... If it were only voluntary and one made a conscious choice, it might enrich the soul a bit, but when it has become simply automatic thro' a sense of the expedient – of the grotesque futility of the perverse – it's degrading! And then the dolts praise one for being "amiable!"': Edel 1982, p. 64.

12   Strouse 1980, p. 186.

PART TWO

Gender negotiations in nineteenth-century women's autobiographical writing

Pam Hirsch

Joanna Russ' provocative book *How to Suppress Women's Writing* has demonstrated the process of 'false categorizing' which operates in order to distract attention away from the woman writer towards her love affair(s).[1] So, for example, the mythology surrounding Elizabeth Barrett has suggested a pale semi-invalid, a Victorian Sleeping Beauty, dreaming unproductively until awoken by the kiss of Robert Browning into mature poethood. In the case of George Sand, similarly, volumes have been written about her love affairs, representing her as a kind of groupie, attaching herself to men of genius. One of the 'uses of autobiography' for both these women was the articulation of their struggles to construct themselves as writing subjects. Their autobiographical writings represent both 'the process of being gendered, and the project of putting that process into discourse'.[2] I am taking it as axiomatic that gender identification is not a fixed and stable given, but always liable to negotiation and renegotiation. To give an example: Elaine Showalter in *A Literature of Their Own* has pointed out that a common trait among nineteenth-century writers was 'their identification with, and dependence upon, the father; and either loss of, or alienation from, the mother'.[3] This cannot be a surprise: the socially dependent but ambitious daughter desired for herself the privileges of freedom of movement and superior education that her father exemplified. However, this identification with the parent of the other sex often became conflicted as the girl moved from childhood to adolescence; the project of rethinking gender identification was often painful, prolonged and possibly never fully resolved.

Elizabeth Barrett's diary written in 1820, when she was 14, is my first example of an aspiring woman writer struggling with these gender negotiations. Her tiny manuscript diary, only five inches by three inches, cut, folded and sewn together in order to fit into her pocket, ready to be fished out when she wanted to write something, could easily have been lost to us. It was discovered by Robert Browning after her death and subsequently entrusted to their son, Pen. After his death it came into the public domain and its very existence reveals both that poetry was the aim and object of her life from an early age, and also, that female ambition was inextricably linked with a conflict of gender.[4]

Briefly, the family politics were as follows: Elizabeth Barrett was the eldest of eleven children living with her parents at 'Hope End' in Ledbury, Herefordshire. As a small child her precocious talent was recognized and rewarded by her father. In her diary she wrote: 'In my sixth year for some lines on virtue which I had penned with great care I received from Papa a ten shilling note enclosed in a letter which was addressed to the Poet Laureat [sic] of Hope End'.[5] Encouraged by paternal approval she continued to turn out masses of apprentice stuff, generally rehashes of works by male authors, such as her 'Battle of Marathon' in imitation of Pope. Of all her siblings, she was closest to her brother Edward, nicknamed Bro', born in 1807, one year after Elizabeth. They spent all their time together – climbing, fishing, horseriding, organizing plays and picnics. She shared Bro''s tutor, Mr McSwiney, and learned Greek with him. But when Bro' left for Charterhouse Mr McSwiney left too. On the last page of the diary there is a striking sense of an ungendered Paradise Lost: 'My past days now appear as a bright star glimmering far, faraway and I feel almost agony to turn from it for ever!' She plotted that when she was grown-up she would 'wear men's clothes and live on a Greek island, the sea melting into turquoise all around it'.[6]

The day Bro' left for school at the age of 13, Elizabeth realized that there was an inescapable difference between being a clever boy and being a clever girl. She was literally 'left behind' at what now seemed the aptly named 'Hope End'. Figuratively she was afraid of being left behind intellectually and was consumed with envy of the previously beloved brother. He wrote to her all the time complaining that she hardly ever wrote back. She assumed, in the teeth of contrary evidence, that Bro' had become expert in Latin at school, and this caused her anguish:

> Whenever I am employed in any literary undertaking which requires much depth of thought and learned reference I cannot help feeling uneasy and imagining that if I were conversant with such languages I might perhaps come to a descision [sic] at once on a point which now occupies days in conjecture!! This is tormenting and sometimes agitates me to a painful and almost nervous degree.[7]

Elizabeth's life at home meandered through extended visits to relations, a typically middle-class way of keeping girls occupied, because they had no sustained education to interrupt. If boys' departure to school was a masculine middle-class rite of passage, the equivalent rite of passage for girls (at approximately the same age) was the onset of menstruation, which for the middle-class girl was often accompanied by restraints on girls' outdoor romping. It became apparent to Elizabeth at this point that her mother's life, and not her father's, was the model that she was supposed to be studying. It seems hardly surprising that it was not a life she would choose for herself. Her mother, Mary, had been married in 1805, and had, from then on, produced children with almost monotonous regularity (1806, 1807, 1809, 1810, 1812, 1813, 1814, 1816, 1818, 1820, 1822, 1824). After the birth of her twelfth child Mary Barrett never fully regained her health and in 1828 she died. Thinking back about her mother's life much later, when she herself was contemplating marriage, Elizabeth wrote to her fiancé that her mother was 'one of those women who never can resist; but, in submitting and bowing in on themselves, make a mark, a plait, within – a sign of suffering'.[8] This use of the word 'plait' (now commonly superseded by the word 'pleat') is interesting. Literally it means a crease in any natural structure, thus a 'plait between the brows' simply means a frown. However, its figurative meaning is that of a hidden recess, often carrying with it an association of sinuosity of character. I'd like to suggest that to evoke an image of a 'hidden recess' in close conjunction with a woman unable to 'resist' reveals Elizabeth's fears about the reproductive fate of women. I see that in the same letter she referred to her mother's 'sweet gentle nature, which the thunder a little turned from its sweetness – as when it turns milk'. As Elizabeth's father was nicknamed the Thunderer and 'milk' is yet another image associated with the female body and its reproductive history, it seems that the soon-to-be bride was trying to convey to her lover her acute anxiety that her poet-self could be destroyed by maternity.

But, back in 1820, Elizabeth was in the process of changing from a happy child to an unhappy adolescent. The reasons for this, or at least some of them, can be unpicked from her diary. She had read Mary Wollstonecraft's *A Vindication of the Rights of Women* when she was about 12 years old and I think this text resonates in some of the diary's pronouncements:

> My mind, wrote Elizabeth, is naturally independent and spurns that subserviency of opinion which is generally considered necessary to feminine softness. But this is a subject on which I always feel strongly, for I feel within me an almost proud consciousness of independance [sic] which prompts me to defend my opinions and to yield them only to conviction!!! ... Better, oh how much better, to be the ridicule of mankind, the scoff of society than lose the self respect which tho' this heart were bursting would elevate me above misery – above wretchedness and above abasement!!! It is not – I feel it is not vanity that dictates them! it is not – I know it is not an encroachment on Masculine prerogative but it is a proud sentiment which will never, never allow me to be humbled in my own eyes!!![9]

The tone of the assertion is both defiant and anxious: the anxiety, on the one hand, that vanity is a particularly feminine vice and, on the other, that only masculine minds possess intellectual toughness points to the problem of gendering her writing self. This gender anxiety is repeated in her comment that she had 'made a secret vow never to pause at undertaking any literary difficulty if convinced of its final utility, but manfully to wade thro' the waves of learning, stopping my ears against the enchanted voice of the Syren'.[10] Learning is clearly identified by Elizabeth with the masculine, and femininity, signified by the siren, is represented as the undoer of masculine learning.

It is unclear what happened to her immediately following the writing of this diary. From being a healthy outdoor sort of child Elizabeth fell suddenly into a mysterious invalid state. This has been variously attributed by her biographers to the result of a fall from a pony, a wasting disease of the spine, an undiagnosed case of anorexia, or ME, and so on. Certainly no contemporary doctor seemed able to diagnose her condition. Without wishing to dwell on or develop this argument, one can at any rate note that her invalidism meant that she was not required to fulfil the tasks eldest daughters usually undertook in nineteenth-century middle-class homes, even after the death of her mother. She continued to study, to write, and to meditate on the particular conundrum of what it meant to be a woman and a writer. Bro' was to die in a sailing accident in 1840. In 1846 she married another poet, Robert Browning, who first fell in love with her poetry and then with the woman. Aged 43, despite all the years of invalidism, she gave birth to a healthy son. Many critics have seen *Aurora Leigh* (1857) as her finest work. It is an epic poem, whose form bespeaks her 'masculine' studies, but here she triumphantly makes the 'condition of the poem's very existence the fact that its protagonist is a woman and a poet'.[11] It is, among other things, even in its name 'Aurora', a homage to her contemporary female idol, the French writer, Aurore Dudevant, a.k.a. George Sand, and the poem's insistent 'I ... I ... I ... I ... I ... I write' suggests that for Elizabeth Barrett Browning the earlier gendered crisis had been triumphantly resolved.

Elizabeth Barrett's diary was the private meditation of a young girl right at the beginning of her writing career. George Sand's *Histoire de ma Vie*, on the other hand, was the autobiography of a mature writer who had already published thirty novels.[12] She signed a contract in December 1847 to produce, in instalments, a five-volume autobiography. A deal was struck of 130000 francs, money she needed to keep herself, her children and her household at Nohant. This was the most immediate use of *writing* her autobiography. However, *reading* the autobiography, one is ineluctably drawn to psychoanalytic perspectives, because the text 'produces' the reader as analyst. If we accept (like analysts) that the family is the primary locus where the psyche assumes a gender and a history, we feel that what we are being offered by this story is a case study of repetitious family dynamics. Here, I can only sketch in the elements pertinent to my theme very briefly.

On Aurore Dupin's father's side the family were aristocratic, with royal forebears. Her father Maurice was the only son of Claude Dupin de Franceuil and Aurore de Saxe; her mother Sophie Delaborde was the daughter of a Paris birdseller whom Maurice had met when serving as Murat's aide-de-camp during the Napoleonic campaigns. In wedding Sophie, Maurice had defied the wishes of his mother; the older and the younger woman became locked in a deadly sexual rivalry. Maurice's early death in a riding accident made the 4-year-old Aurore the legitimate heir to the family estate of Nohant, in Berry. The two women's rival love for Maurice was now displaced onto the small girl. Aurore de Saxe reasserted old class distinctions and pensioned Sophie off to Paris on an allowance when Aurore was 9, severely restricting Sophie's subsequent visits to Nohant.[13] Aurore persistently and passionately dreamed of the time when she and her mother would be reunited. This mother-want, primarily for a recuperated, ideal mother is a persistent trope in Sand's fictional work.[14]

But the psychic reality for Aurore Dupin at Nohant was an identification with her dead father; he was 'the real author of the story of my life'.[15] In the psychoanalyst R.D. Laing's words: 'the young are introduced to the parts the dead once played'.[16] Aurore was her father's living double: 'My voice, features, manners, taste – everything about me reminded [my grandmother] of her son as a child, to the point where sometimes, while watching me play, she would have a kind of hallucination, call me Maurice and speak of me as her son'.[17]

The identification with the dead father was further reinforced by Deschartes, Maurice's tutor, who took Aurore at the dead of night to kiss her father's skull in the family grave:

> Having taught only boys, I think [Deschartes] was eager to see me as male and convince himself I was one. My skirts disturbed the seriousness of his teaching, and it is true that when I took his advice and donned the masculine smock, cap, and gaiters, he became ten times more pedantic and crushed me under his Latin, presuming that I could understand it much better.[18]

Because the grandmother's only passion had been the maternal one, it redoubled in intensity towards her granddaughter. To protect her self from being overwhelmed, Aurore took refuge in a 'poetic and fantastic world'.[19] At its centre was the imaginary figure of Corambé, a kind of bisexual muse who was simultaneously the hero/heroine of a continuous novel in her head and also a kind of personal god/goddess. 'Corambé ... was as pure and charitable as Jesus, as shining and handsome as Gabriel, but ... it often appeared to me with female features'.[20] Her play and her reveries protected her until Aurore de Saxe, furious because, despite all her efforts, the young girl still wanted to be with her mother, 'settled on the most baleful means of all' to win the struggle.[21] She told Aurore that Sophie had been a garrison wife, an army camp-follower and a prostitute and that if Aurore were to live with her mother, she too would inevitably be prostituted. At the moment of puberty, then, a crucial epoch in the complicated process of gender identification, 14-year-old Aurore was told that her mother was a disgraceful and disgraced woman. The consequences were devastating:

> I no longer knew if I loved or hated anyone, I no longer felt impassioned over anyone or resentful towards anyone. I had what seemed like an enormous burn inside me and a searing emptiness where my heart should have been. I was aware only of a kind of contempt for the whole

universe and a bitter disdain for life as it would henceforth be for me: I no longer loved myself. If my mother was detestable and hateful, then I, the fruit of her womb was too ... I gave up my sweet reveries. No more novel, no more daydreams. Corambé was silent.[22]

Aurore's immediate response was to suffer one of the first of several bouts of anorexia she experienced during her life. She wrote that her 'mute anger' had the effect that her 'stomach rejected all food: my throat tightened, nothing would go down, and I could not repress a secret pleasure in telling myself that death by starvation would occur without my having a hand in it'.[23] She was full of rage against both 'bonne-mamam' (grandmother) and her 'bad mother' (Sophie), but, incapable of stopping loving them, either of them, her rage was turned in on her own body, the female body which she now knew to be deeply unreliable.

In a move which seems strikingly like a punishment for not repudiating her mother, the grandmother sent Aurore to live and be educated in the English Convent in Paris. Although cut off from the outside world she also had two years' respite from the family conflict. Once again Aurore experimented with gender roles. Firstly, she joined the *diables*, that is the group of girls with a reputation for wild escapades, the sort of girls who are often called 'tomboys'. This was succeeded by a sudden perverse reaction, when she became almost pathologically pious, mortifying her flesh. At the end of the two years she decided that she would enter the convent permanently when she reached her majority of 21. Instead, following her grandmother's death in 1821 she finally achieved her desire of being reunited with her mother. Although mother and daughter found it difficult to live with one another after a separation that had effectively established Aurore in a different class to that of her mother, nevertheless, this interregnum appears to have been very important. She wrote: 'If destiny had made me pass immediately from my grandmother's control to that of a husband or a convent, it is possible that ... I would never have become myself'.[24] It was during this period that she was once more able to conjure up Corambé, that 'eternal poem ... where I felt myself true to my emotions'.[25]

It is, I think clear from her account that the self she refers to is her writing self, 'George Sand'. This pen-name is in itself curious, an ungendered sign, in that the French masculine form would be 'Georges'. Arguably, her pen-name signals an identification with her 'dream-muse', Corambé, in that it is not securely masculine *or* feminine. In 1822, Aurore married Casimir Dudevant (later Baron Dudevant) and had two children, a son Maurice (named after her father) in 1823 and a daughter Solange in 1828. The marriage broke down quite quickly and in 1831 Aurore decided to live in Paris and make her living from writing. On her first attempt to get impartial advice in Paris she was told: 'a woman shouldn't write ... don't make books, make babies'.[26] She started to 'pass' as a young man: 'having dressed like a boy during my childhood, then having hunted in smock and gaiters with Deschartes' she had a 'sentry box redingote (the male fashion of the day) made for myself, out of thick grey cloth, with matching trousers and vest. With a grey hat and wide wool tie, I was the perfect little first-year student'.[27] In this outfit she enjoyed the same freedom as young male students; her clothing, she wrote, made her feel 'fearless'. Her cross-dressing and her identification with her soldier-father seem to have been psychologically necessary to safeguard her from a deep-rooted fear of the female.

In her fictional writing, however, she dwelled with great intensity on the problems of growing up female.[28] She used her autobiography to 'prove' that her father had loved her mother. If her father loved her mother, her mother was no longer disgraced. In recuperating the reputation of her mother, she simultaneously attempted to recuperate her own 'daughterliness', which she equated with 'femininity'. Nevertheless, to the reader/analyst, her gender oscillations seem doomed never to be fully resolved. She rarely bonded with other women (except a very few, and those few did not include her daughter). She wrote endlessly, even obsessively, her creative writing operating out of her daydreams, which played and replayed the original family romance. In the case of George Sand, one might say, it was the never-to-be-resolved anxiety and fragility of her gender identification that was one of the most powerful sources of her creative drive.[29]

Notes

1 Joanna Russ (1983) *How to Suppress Women's Writing*, London: The Women's Press.

2 Elspeth Probyn (1993) *Sexing the Self: Gendered Positions in Cultural Studies*, London and New York: Routledge, p. 2.

3 Elaine Showalter (1978) *A Literature of Their Own*, London: Virago, p. 61.

4 Elizabeth Barrett (1914) *Glimpses into My Own Life and Literary Character*, Boston: The Bibliophile Society.

5 *Ibid.*, p. 7.

6 Introduction by H. Buxton Forman to Barrett 1914, p. xxxv.

7 Barrett 1914, p. 25.

8 *The Letters of Robert Browning and Elizabeth Barrett 1845–1846* (1969), 2 vols, ed. Elvan Kintner, Cambridge, Mass.: Harvard University Press, vol. II, p. 1012.

9 Barrett 1914, p. 24.

10 *Ibid.*, p. 25.

11 Cora Kaplan's introduction to Elizabeth Barrett (1982) *Aurora Leigh*, London: The Women's Press.

12 It was written in installments between 1846 and 1854. I will be quoting from: *Story of My Life: the Autobiography of George Sand* (1991), a group translation, edited by Thelma Jurgrau, Albany: State University of New York Press.

13 See Wendy Deutelbaum and Cynthia Huff (1985) 'Class, Gender and Family System: The Case of George Sand', in Shirley Nelson Garner, Claire Kahane and Madelon Sprengnether (Eds) *The (M)other Tongue: Essays in Feminist Psychoana-*

lytic Interpretation, Ithaca and London: Cornell University Press.

14 I have argued this case in my MA 'Scheherezade and her Half-sisters' (University of Essex, 1989) and in Chapter 3 of my PhD thesis 'Barbara Leigh Smith Bodichon and George Eliot: An Examination of Their Work and Friendship' (Anglia Polytechnic University in collaboration with the University of Essex, 1992).

15 Sand 1991, p. 169.

16 R.D. Laing (1972) *The Politics of the Family and Other Essays*, New York: Vintage, p. 29. See Freud's essay, 'Creative Writers and Day-Dreaming', in *The Complete Psychological Works of Sigmund Freud* (1959), tr. from the German under the general editorship of James Strachey in collaboration with Anna Freud, London: Hogarth Press, vol. 9, pp. 143–53, in which he writes: 'You will not forget that the stress [my model] lays on childhood memories in the writer's life ... is ultimately derived from the assumption that a piece of creative writing, like a day-dream, is a continuation of, and a substitute for, what was once the play of childhood' (p. 152). George Sand wrote that the name Corambé was merely a 'fortuitous collection of syllables' (*ibid.*, p. 605). Hélène Deutsch (1946) *Psychology of Women*, London: Research Books, offers this account: 'When Aurore was small and her father was away, her mother tried to teach her the alphabet. The little one showed application and talent. But she had one curious difficulty: the letter "b" did not exist for her ... it seems to me that the "b" repressed in her childhood is identical with the "bé" that later turned up as the suffix to "coram" [Latin for "in the presence of"]. The whole word could then mean, "in the presence of 'b'". If the "b" repressed in childhood referred to the absent father, whom she hardly knew at the time, then its turning up in Corambé would be quite understandable' (p. 246).

17 Sand 1991, p. 467.

18 *Ibid.*, p. 781.

19 *Ibid.*, p. 60.

20 Sand 1991, p. 605.

21 Sand 1991, p. 633.

22 *Ibid.*, pp. 634–5.

23 *Ibid.*, p. 824.

24 *Ibid.*, p. 752.

25 *Ibid.*, p. 804.

26 *Ibid.*, p. 915.

27 *Ibid.*, p. 893.

28 See Michael Danahy (1982) 'Growing Up Female: George Sand's View in La Petite Fadette', in Natalie Datlof (Ed.) *The George Sand Papers: Conference Proceedings 1978*, New York: AMS Press.

29 'Only in artistic dreaming did George Sand realize her aborted femininity', Deutsch 1946, p. 241.

Chapter 8

The Educative 'I' in Nineteenth-century Women's Autobiographies

PART ONE

Catharine Cappe of York (1822)

Ruth A. Symes

In 1812, a Unitarian woman, Catharine Cappe of York, wrote the *Memoir* of her life.[1] The book, edited after her death, in 1822, by her stepdaughter, Mary, and published by a local firm, is a rare instance of a full-length, fully-finished and public autobiographical narrative by a woman in this period.

Cappe's *Memoir* might disappoint critics who attempt to read it as characteristic of the romantic age in which it was written. Asking to be read simultaneously as a self-history and as an educational textbook for middle-class parents, the text looks grey and uninspiring, the educative 'I' stiff and matronly, when compared with the colourful and soulful effusion of the romantic poets in the same period. Criticism of autobiography, as it stands, cannot deal with Cappe because her *Memoir* distorts accepted versions of literary history and begs us to treat self-history as a philosophical as much as a literary artefact.

I want to suggest a method of reading the context and contours of Cappe's *Memoir* in ways which highlight its pedagogy as a well-thought-out poetics of autobiography – a poetics which specifically allows for the writing of female self-history in this period. In doing this, I hope to establish Cappe as an autobiographical subject worthy of serious critical attention and by extension to show how the writing of self-history in this period was distinctively conditioned by factors of gender.

Cappe's *Memoir* is educative in design and purpose: she constantly and unapologetically refers to the 'uses' of autobiography – the 'usefulness' of her own life. In the Preface to the *Memoir*, Cappe expounds these uses at length. It is, she declares, not 'through any vain expectation of an imaginary life in the fleeting breath of those who succeed her' that she has written this *Memoir*: rather it is her intention to guide ordinary people through the pitfalls of life on their journey towards God: to teach parents the best method of educating their children by recounting her own childhood experiences; and to outline the histories and education of various people with whom she has been connected.[2]

Though contemporary feminist criticism[3] might suggest that such disclaimers are disguises under which Cappe felt free to pursue her real aim – that of telling the true story of her life, the succeeding *Memoir* bears her statements out as integral to, and not divorced from, her notion of self-history. Cappe senses no contradiction between telling the story of her own life and shaping that life into educational anecdotes for the consumption of middle-class parents. Evidently, there are very different ideas about selfhood, autobiographical writing and education at work in this *Memoir* from those which characterize Wordsworth's *Prelude* (1801), for example. The key to bridging the historical gap between Cappe's life and our own, lies in the realization that for her autobiography and pedagogy necessarily walk hand-in-hand.

A realization that this partnership lies at the heart of Cappe's life and writing necessitates particular kinds of methodological investigation. First, Cappe's Unitarian belief and her practical activity as an educationalist and philanthropist might be seen as a context for the production of her text. Second, the partnership reveals itself on the level of the text. The language and structure of the *Memoir* show how one educational theory in particular – the theory of association – was instrumental in shaping Cappe's ideas about how self-history might be written; textual analysis also reveals how those ideas occasionally come into conflict with more romantic notions of experience and the self. In all these respects Cappe's *Memoir* owes much to the rationalist thinking of the Enlightenment which is channelled through her Unitarianism and inflected by considerations of gender.

In contrast to the often fragmentary narratives penned by Quaker and Methodist women in the early eighteenth century, Cappe's *Memoir* is a well-structured and carefully planned full-length account of a life that is both spiritual and practical – a life-history that in content and form reflects the specific preoccupations of her Unitarian religion.[4]

The Unitarians were a relatively small dissenting sect led by Joseph Priestley who preached to his first congregation in 1764 at Millhill, Leeds, in a chapel later to be attended by Cappe herself.[5] In theological terms, the Unitarians rejected many of the creeds and articles of faith of the Anglican Church and subscribed instead to a belief in the humanity of Christ, the non-existence of the Trinity and the perfectibility of mankind through education. Cappe was spiritually, intellectually and personally involved with the Unitarian movement almost from its inception; many of its leading Ministers were her friends and, in some senses, her *Memoir* is a history of Unitarianism told from a domestic rather than a theological perspective.[6]

The Unitarians seem to have been preoccupied with the educational potential of life-writing. Several of them, including Cappe herself, wrote lives of Christ;[7] obituary writing for the two main Unitarian magazines, *The Monthly Magazine* and the *Monthly Repository*, became something of an art form; and a number wrote Memoirs.[8] These Memoir writers commonly mention in their opening pages that as ordinary men rather than 'great statesmen', 'politicians' or 'warriors', they were particularly well-suited to the task of writing exemplary lives that might be emulated by the common man.

Cappe shared this Unitarian belief in the educational purpose of life-writing but her view of education and consequently her view of life-writing was one which played on her 'middle-class' femininity as much as her ordinariness. Though in the preface to her *Memoir* she makes the conventional differentiation between Unitarians and 'eminent statesmen, profound politicians or successful warriors', her book on charity schools (published in the same year that the *Memoir* was written, and dedicated to the 'ladies of Britain'), gives this statement a gendered inflection. It is Cappe's contention that women's distance from the 'ceaseless anxieties of the conscientious legislator; the great fatigues and multiplied dangers of the military commander; the temptations, inquietudes, and degrading compliancies of the ambitious statesman'[9] gives them the edge over their male counterparts in matters such as education.

Little research has been done on the role of women in Unitarianism.[10] As a doctrine for life, it did offer some autonomy to those women who became involved in it. The practical bias of the religion and the emphasis on education and philanthropy provided an active if secondary role for females. Cappe's life-history reveals her long involvement in pedagogical and philanthropic projects of many kinds. She was, for example, one of the earliest founders of the Sunday School: she supervised the activities of the Grey Coat School in York and set up a spinning school there; she also helped to extend what had become something of a national network of Female Benefit Societies to towns in the North of England.[11] As much of her other writing testifies, Cappe was acutely aware of the need for 'promoters, patronesses and conductors' to visit schools, hospitals, prisons and lunatic asylums for example.[12] For Cappe, whose own education had been characterized by the misogyny of her father and a showy training in accomplishments at a boarding school in York, educational and philanthropic concerns were best carried out under the surveillance of 'eminently respectable' and 'useful' middle-class females. In the *Memoir* it is apparent that this surveillance extends to the management of self-history itself.

In general, Cappe's *Memoir* is clear and candid. The tempo is controlled and slow and the detail predominantly domestic. Cappe details the small losses and gains of middle-class families such as her own. She dwells on matters of health and the fortitude with which she has overcome the obstacles that life has thrown in her path. In all this exposition, a rigorous method is imposed. There is a tight interweaving of event and interpretation. Incidents yield to generalization. Abstract remarks are always tied back to the material. The life-story is chopped up and rearranged in order to maximize its educational potential. The passage below is typical of Cappe's ability simultaneously to render the autobiographical import of her writing and the pedagogical one; to move from the personal and particular to the general and public:

> It being one of my objects, as already mentioned, to throw some light for the benefit of others, on what passes in the infant mind, as far as I can do it, by instances adduced from my own recollection, I will here put down as faithfully as it lies in my power, the effects which I remember to have been produced, whether by something original in my own disposition, or by *very early associations arising from particular situations, from accidental occurrences, or from incidental conversations.*[13]

The language used here by Cappe is exactly that of contemporary educational texts written by women for the instruction of girls and young children. The statement, like the *Memoir* as a whole, depends on a recognition of the importance of early associations originating in the incidents occurring in youth. These associations are responsible for the development of adult morals and it is the memory of them which facilitates the writing of self-history.

Association might be considered to be the poetics of Cappe's *Memoir*. It is a poetics which derives from the doctrine of association, a philosophy common to many branches of rational inquiry in the eighteenth century but one which by the last decades of the century had become specifically connected with the pedagogical activities of middle-class women.

In order to explain exactly how association had come to be a gendered concept in this period, it is worth tracing its history a little way. The principle of association originated in the writings of John Locke at the end of the seventeenth century but was later developed by David Hartley in his *Observations of Man* (1749).[14] Hartley suggested that the brain actively combined different sensory perceptions by association to produce more complex ideas. Out of these complex ideas, the moral sense developed. So, for example, a child learnt to associate the sight of a flame with heat and the notion of fire with danger. He would then learn that starting a fire was morally wrong.

In the light of Hartley's writing, the minds of children were seen as particularly vulnerable to new sensations and impressions. By extension, it became obvious that those in charge of children might have an enormous influence on the way in which they came to associate various elements of the world around them. It followed that through their superior associative powers, educators played a hitherto unforeseen importance in guiding a child's moral sense.

The theory of association had paradoxical connotations of gender. It was frequently assumed that women, especially lower-class women, were less able to associate events than men.[15] Nursery maids and servant girls were considered to make imaginative rather than rational associations between events and were therefore considered a dangerous influence on middle-class children. In educational literature, however, middle-class women educators, mothers or governesses, were seen as the answer to this problem. Their powers of teaching accurate association to their children were constantly emphasized. Increasingly in the debates on education at the end of the eighteenth century, the class distinction between women was seen in terms of their associative abilities.[16]

Cappe's use of associative techniques within her *Memoir* may be attributed partly to the fact that Hartleyanism was central to Unitarianism. Her husband had been involved in the on-going project of republishing and reinterpreting Hartley's works and Cappe refers to Hartley's theory of association by name in the *Memoir*.[17] At the same time, however, Cappe's use of association draws on the growing tradition of educational writing by women in the last decades of the eighteenth and early decades of the nineteenth century. The educational writings of Hester Chapone and Maria and Richard Lovell Edgeworth are mentioned in Cappe's works.[18] These writers and others with whom Cappe would have been familiar, including other women writers in the Unitarian circle, advertised the special talent of middle-class women for association and would have ensured that Cappe's female readers were conversant with the kinds of language she was employing to tell the story of her life.[19]

In her work on charity schools, Cappe acknowledges the associative abilities of middle-class women:

> Upon whom, if not upon us, do the important duties devolve of forming the infant mind of both sexes; of guarding it from *wrong impressions and erroneous associations*; from delusions so confirmed, 'ere reason can assert her sway', that the utmost efforts of her feeble influence, through the whole of after-life, may be quite incapable of emancipating this happy victim? *Thoughts on Charity and Various Other Important Institutions.*[20]

In Cappe's *Memoir*, association serves two main purposes: first, it helps to explain the way identity is developed; second, it provides a methodology for Cappe as autobiographer. It is fundamental to an engagement with Cappe's autobiographical poetics that the reader understands that the associations produced in childhood determine the way that one perceives oneself in adulthood.

Cappe reminds the reader of the impressionability and vulnerability of the infant mind. She describes herself as a child as being 'extremely timid, possessing little courage or fortitude and liable to be long and distressingly affected by too vivid impressions on the imagination'.[21] In this dangerous world of childhood, adult interference is of great importance. As Cappe points out, 'I would again remark how much depends in forming the future character of children on the sentiment and conduct of those who are about them'.[22] Cappe reveals how her middle-class parents provided good examples and associations whilst the maids terrified her with idle stories of 'enchantments, giants, ghosts and robbers' – stories which meant that it was some time before she could bear to be left alone in the dark. The rich too come in for censure. Cappe remarks that her parents should not have allowed her brother to mix with wealthy families in his youth: 'Alas, little did they imagine how very pernicious this early association of respectability and happiness with great riches, would eventually prove to his future character'.[23]

Cappe's associative technique allows her as narrator/mentor to organize her material in the ways she feels are most conducive to educate her readership. Anecdotes chosen for their pedagogical potential define the very business of writing life-history.

> What a striking proof is this little anecdote to the lasting and salutary effects which are sometimes produced on the whole character, by reflections immediately deduced from the circumstances of real life; and what an encouragement to proceed in the employment to the writer of her own Memoirs.[24]

Cappe's associative prowess as a middle-class woman and sometime educator allows her to combine incidents with a common educational thread from various sources within her own life and the lives of her acquaintances. By constantly judging the experiences and associations of her young life through the observations of her later years, she overcomes one of the chief difficulties encountered by autobiographers: the ability simultaneously to render past and present. She recounts anecdotes from her schooldays 'in the hope of their supplying some useful hints to parents, who send their children to such seminaries, and also to the persons themselves to whose care the children are committed'.[25] Cappe's educational recommendations have the effect of reducing the time that has elapsed between her unhappy childhood at a boarding school in York and her mature adulthood as a school supervisor and autobiographer; by extension pedagogical themes may be considered to provide the *Memoir* with continuity and unity.

Though the conviction with which Cappe follows her pedagogical model is impressive, it is not watertight. At a number of moments in the text, Cappe veers away from rationality and towards the imaginative style of contemporary novelists.

In an unhappy love affair with a bewitching Irishman in her youth, Cappe's experience contradicts her rationalist philosophy. The *Memoir* describes the pain of love at first sight and its consequences and Cappe struggles to adduce a lesson from her experience. Significantly she chooses to cast her debate as an argument between the parent or guardian figure with whom she has identified for most of the *Memoir* and the novelist whom she has decried:

> I am aware that all this will be regarded by many readers as extremely romantic and visionary; it was a vision, however, which proved a severe trial to both parties; and perhaps the detail of it may help to correct two errors of a very opposite nature indeed, but both of which frequently prevail, on the subject of sudden attachments. 'Love at first sight,' says the parent or guardian, 'the notion is ridiculous and the thing impossible.' 'So far otherwise,' says the novel writer 'that it forms the criterion by which persons of refinement and genuine sensibility, are most strikingly characterised, and it is quite essential to a happy marriage.' Neither of these assumptions are true.[26]

There is, it would appear, a deadlock here between the rational view of life and the romantic one. Cappe's *Memoir* goes on, however, to come down on the side of the pedagogue. With the danger of romanticism averted, the text remains finally under the control of its 'calm, collected and composed' narrator who, to use Cappe's own words, continues to look 'steadily forward both for herself and for her beloved offspring'.

Ignoring these rare moments of disruption, Cappe's *Memoir* suggests an early-nineteenth-century poetics of self-history that is heavily dependent on a rationalist pedagogical discourse carried over from the late eighteenth century. In Cappe's case, educational ideas are strengthened by Unitarian conviction and inflected by considerations of gender.

Cappe's rationalist view of self-history challenges the notion, sometimes suggested in critical texts on autobiography, that a straightforward transition took place in the early nineteenth century from spiritual to romantic themes. This view is supported by the existence of many other educational texts by women that stop short of describing themselves as Memoirs though they have strong autobiographical undercurrents. Educational discourse and the writing of female lives were, it would seem, of reciprocal importance in this period.

A close analysis of the context and contours of such a Memoir as Catharine Cappe's suggests, therefore, that a number of new questions ought to be asked of autobiographical writing. If there is indeed a distinct connection between usefulness and self-history, between the aims and methods of pedagogy and the aims and methods of autobiography, what kinds of texts might now be considered autobiographical in this period? How might this new emphasis alter perceptions of women's silence as autobiographers? In what other ways were popular philosophical ideas appropriated by autobiographers in the eighteenth and nineteenth centuries? What part do gender and class play in all this? On the other hand, how might our readings of romantic autobiographical writing be changed by an acknowledgment of the importance of 'usefulness' and pedagogy in writing of the early nineteenth century?

Such questions might open up the way for new gender-inflected methods of inquiry into self-history and would certainly rewrite the endeavour of the rational female pedagogue into the history of autobiography.

Notes

1 Catharine Cappe (1822) *Memoir of the Life of the Late Mrs Catharine Cappe*, York: Thomas Wilson and Son.
2 Cappe 1822, pp. 3–4.
3 This approach has been adopted by a number of recent critics of women's autobiography including: Patricia Meyer Spacks (1976) *Imagining A Self: Autobiography and Novel in Eighteenth-Century England*, Cambridge, Mass.: Harvard University Press; Patricia Meyer Spacks (1980) 'Selves in Hiding', in Estelle Jelinek (Ed.) *Women's Autobiography: Essays in Theory and Criticism*, London: Indiana University Press. The view is summed up by Valerie Sanders (1989) in *The Private Lives of Victorian Women*, Brighton: Harvester Wheatsheaf, p. 7: 'those Victorian Women who did [write autobiography] were driven into a variety of rhetorical strategies which fulfilled their need to speak out whilst preserving their aura of reserve and selflessness'.
4 For more on these see Felicity Nussbaum (1989) *The Autobiographical Subject: Gender and Ideology in Eighteenth-Century England*, Baltimore: The Johns Hopkins University Press.
5 For more on the history of the Unitarian Movement see: John Seed (1986) 'Theologies of Power: Unitarianism and The Social Relations of Religious Discourse 1800–1850', in R.J. Morris (Ed.) *Class, Power and Social Structure in British Nineteenth-Century Towns*, Leicester: Leicester University Press, pp. 108–56; Raymond V. Holt (1931) *The Story of Unitarianism*, London: The Lindsay Press; Raymond V. Holt (1938) *The Unitarian Contribution to Social Progress in England*, London; George Allen and Unwin; J. Estlin Carpenter (1922) *Unitarianism: An Historic Survey*, London: The Lindsey Press; David B. Parke (1957) *The Epic of Unitarianism: Original Writings From the History of Liberal Religion*, Boston: Star King Press; and Michael R. Watts (1978) *The Dissenters: From the Reformation to the French Revolution*, Oxford: Clarendon Press.
6 Cappe knew the Reverend Theophilus Lindsey and his wife, Hannah, and was involved in helping them to leave Catterick for London where they established the first Unitarian Chapel in Essex Street in 1773.
7 Catharine Cappe (Ed.) (1809) *A Connected History of the Public Life and Divine Mission of Jesus Christ, as Recorded in the Four Evangelists, with Notes Selected from the Short-Hand Papers of the Late Reverend Newcombe Cappe. To Which are Added, Reflections Arising from the Several Subjects of Each Section*, York: T. Wilson and Sons.
8 See for example, Thomas Belsham, *Memoirs of the late Reverend Theophilus*

Lindsey, M.A. including a brief analysis of his works together with anecdotes and letters of eminent persons, his friends and correspondents, London: J. Johnson; John Williams (1833) *Memoirs of the Late Reverend Thomas Belsham Including a Brief Notice of his Public Works and Copious Extracts From his Diary Together With Letters to and from his Correspondents*, London; Gilbert Wakefield (1804) *Memoirs of the Life of Gilbert Wakefield*, London: J. Johnson.

9 Catharine Cappe (1812) *Thoughts on Various Charitable and Other Important Institutions and on the Best Mode of Conducting Them to Which is Subjoined an Address to the Females of the Rising Generation*. York: Thomas Wilson and Son, p. 99.

10 I know only of the work on a later Victorian autobiographer, Harriet Martineau. See particularly R.K. Webb (1960) *Harriet Martineau: A Radical Victorian*, London: Heinemann.

11 This is mentioned in Hold 1938, p. 247. For more on these philanthropic activities see Cappe's other works: (1800) *An Account of Two Charity Schools for the Education of Girls: And of a Female Friendly Society in York; interspersed with reflections on Charity Schools and Friendly Societies in General*, York: William Blanchard.

12 Cappe 1812, p. 69.

13 Cappe 1822, p. 22; emphasis added.

14 John Locke (1965) *Essay on Human Understanding (1690) ed. John Yolton*, London: J.M. Dent and Sons Ltd; David Hartley (1967) *Observations on Man, His Frame, His Duty and His Expectations (1749)*, Hildesheim: Georg Olms Verlagsbuchhandlung.

15 For more on this see Linda Peterson (1986) *Victorian Autobiography: The Tradition of Self-Interpretation*, New Haven and London: Yale University Press.

16 By 1801, the principle of association had so moved from highbrow philosophical discourse into common educational parlance that Elizabeth Hamilton, a well-known educationalist and a correspondent of Cappe's, remarked: 'the ideas expressed by the term "association" are as easily comprehended by every person of plain sense, as by the scholar and metaphysician'. She went on to explain that mothers were often 'mistresses of the subject of association' without realizing what it was: Elizabeth Hamilton (1801) *Letters on the Elementary Principles of Education*, second edition, Bath: R. Cruthwell, p. 4.

17 This is mentioned by Cappe in her biographical introduction to the Reverend Newcombe Cappe (1805) *Discourses Chiefly on Devotional Subjects*, York: T. Wilson, R. Spence, p. lxxiv. See also Cappe 1822, p. 201.

18 Hester Chapone (1815) *Letters on The Improvement of the Mind (1773)*, London: Scatcherd and Sons; Maria and Richard Lovell (1974) *Practical Education (1798)*, London: Garland Publishing.

19 Examples are the works for children by Anna Laetitia Barbauld and her niece Lucy Aikin.

20 Cappe 1812, p. 100; emphasis added.

21 *Ibid.*, p. 42.

22 *Ibid.*, p. 40.

23 *Ibid.*, p. 68.

24 Cappe 1822, p. 353.
25 *Ibid.*, p. 45.
26 *Ibid.*, pp. 132–3.

PART TWO

'What I earnestly longed for ...': Elizabeth Missing Sewell, writing, autobiography and Victorian womanhood

Brian Ridgers

One of the defining aspects of Victorian culture is its insistent concern with representing itself, with retelling its own history. Nineteenth-century texts display a commitment to revealing the triumphs of the personal against the pressures of public life, from Samuel Smiles' autobiographical manual *Self Help* (1859) to Isabella Beeton's concern for domestic detail within the middle-class home in her *Book of Household Management* (1861), from Charles Dickens' manipulations of self-history and the heroic search for selfhood in *David Copperfield* (1850) to Charlotte Brontë's quest for independence within matrimony in *Jane Eyre* (1847). Vastly different kinds of narrative in the nineteenth century involve elements of biographical and autobiographical discourse as an important central influence for writers of both sexes in interrogating the Victorian self.

Recent studies of nineteenth-century autobiography have emphasized the links between a questioning of the identity of the individual and the development of autobiography as a form of writing distinct from biography:

> The perceived instability and hybridity of 'autobiography' are inextrica-
> bly linked to the problematics of selfhood and identity, with the
> boundaries between 'inner' and 'outer', 'private' and 'public' becoming
> the sites of the greatest concern. Autobiographical discourse in the
> nineteenth century, following on from eighteenth-century accounts of
> 'self-examination', reveals the extent to which the 'inner' of the self is
> constituted as both a sacred place and a site of danger. Introspection,
> moreover, divides the self.[1]

Elizabeth Helsinger develops the idea of autobiography as a kind of writing marked by introspection. Her discussion of Ruskin's autobiography *Praeterita* (1885) and Tennyson's poem *In Memoriam* (1850) identifies in both texts an attempt to resist this labelling of the self. It is Ruskin particularly who resists the self-absorption and isolation of the introspective autobiography by turning attention away from himself to the landscapes he travels through (the mountains at Schaffhausen and the Col de la Faucille) or the art he views in Italy. Autobiography becomes, then, 'a way of describing the self while at the same time extending the self'.[2] In this sense Ruskin is developing the influential autobiographical model of Wordsworth's poem *The Prelude* (first published 1850). Written at the end of his life, it is here that Wordsworth establishes a confidence that he can represent his life as a movement in a single direction, partly revealed by moments of private vision, of self-revelation. It is this model that writers such as Ruskin and Tennyson attempt to follow and finally reject.

The establishment of a textual tradition of autobiography that relies upon male authors has been countered by modern feminist criticism which seeks to meet the male lineage with a female one. Well established works on nineteenth-century women's writing (such as Showalter 1978 and Gilbert and Gubar 1979) re-examine nineteenth-century literature within the terms of the double lives of women writers, their public conformity to men and their representation of the privacy of the imagination and its potential for rebellion.[3] Christina Crosby, acknowledging their strategy, places this female tradition within a process of historicization which seeks to locate women and women's writing within 'a fundamental experience which unites all women, the experience of being "the other"'.[4] Divisions of gender within Victorian culture are met at each turn by equal divisions of class, a confrontation that Julia Swindells links specifically to female identity, emphasizing working women's use of the concept of the 'literary' against the writing of their masculine counterparts, able to write within the specific identification of employment:

> While working-class men may frequently organise their autobiographies around particular notions of advance in waged labour – through acquiring skill or various modes of organisation – working women are more likely to turn to 'the literary', to genres for terms in which to express and construct the experiences central to their lives.[5]

Literary models, then, appear as relevant to the high profile autobiographies of men such as John Ruskin as to the less well-known autobiographies of women such as Elizabeth Missing Sewell (1815–1906) whose autobiography, published posthumously by her niece in 1907, covers the divisions between the public image of the respectable churchwoman and teacher and the private image of the creative young woman, struggling to find her identity within the space of the Victorian middle-class family.

Sewell's work as a popular authoress, alongside such contemporaries as Mrs Emma Marshall and Charlotte Yonge, promoted the model of the pure young girl, apprentice Angel in the House. As a writer Sewell produced a wide range of works, including thirteen novels and three volumes of short stories, religious and educational treatises, history and language textbooks and travel books. Aiming her writing primarily at the young, she described herself in the 1840s as 'a successful popular authoress whose chosen audience would be girls and women of the educated class'.[6]

Sewell's background reveals an orthodox Victorian history: born in Newport, on the Isle of Wight, in 1815, the second daughter of a prosperous middle-class household, she never married, she dedicated herself to domestic duty and to promoting the moral and social attitudes necessary for a life built upon Christian principles. Her father was a respectable solicitor and land agent in Newport and a figure of local importance who held the office of Mayor twice and was for a time the Deputy Governor of the island. Her brothers, all older than she, were outwardly successful figures of social and professional respectability. Her eldest brother William, Elizabeth's closest influence, was a prominent figure in the Oxford Movement, a fellow of Exeter College, Oxford and Professor of Moral Philosophy, as well as the founder of two public schools.[7] After attending a boarding school in Bath she came home when she was 15 to teach her two younger sisters. In 1852 Sewell established, with her elder sister Ellen, a girls' school in the family house, using her brothers' daughters as a nucleus alongside some outside pupils. A keen supporter of female education and of Church schooling, she went on to found a larger school for girls in 1866, St Boniface at Ventnor on the Isle of Wight. It was the insolvency and subsequent death of her father and the severe debts incurred by her brother William that forced Sewell to provide for the family herself. To do this she turned to writing, and, with her sister Ellen, to teaching.

Sewell was not the kind of high-profile authoress that attracted great social attention, like those women interviewed by Mrs Helen Black in 1893 as 'Notable Women Authors of the Day'.[8] Her early work was heavily influenced by William. Despite the success of *Amy Herbert* (1844), her first novels appeared under his name as editor, subtitled 'written by a lady'. Her name first appeared in 1852 on the title page of her novel *The Experience of Life*, the first work published after the Sewell family turned to Elizabeth for financial support. Despite her low personal profile, the success of her work can be seen as we catch a contemporary glimpse of the broader appeal in marketable terms of Sewell's work. In Frank Smedley's novel *Lewis Arundel* (1852),[9] a shrewd London publisher discusses the financial potential of the model of a character like Miss Morton, the governess in *Amy Herbert*, with a potential authoress:

> Clever book, *Amy Herbert*, very. So much tenderness in it, ma'am nothing pays better than judicious tenderness; the mothers of England like it to read about – the daughters of England like it – the little girls of England like it – and so the husbands of England are forced to pay for it. If you recollect ma'am there's a pathetic governess in *Amy Herbert* who calls the children 'dearest;' well imagined character, that. She's sold many copies, that governess.[10]

Clearly Sewell had been financially successful as a writer as well as morally acceptable by 1844 but she remained ambivalent about her own position, revealing a complex mixture of repression and insurrection. It was during the early years of her writing, when the success of novels like *Amy Herbert* was bringing her financial reward, that she expressed her frustrations at her brother's controlling hand, writing in her journal: 'What I earnestly longed for was to get my money into my own hands, and draw it when and how I liked'.[11]

*

Sewell's autobiography begins with a decision about literary origins and the pressures of subjective representation. Asked by her mother on her deathbed to 'finish an account she had begun of her early life, and other family circumstances', Sewell responds:

> Of course I gave the promise, though I felt at the time that it would be very difficult to keep it. The history of a family, told by one of its members, must, in a certain degree, resolve itself into the history of the person who writes. This must especially be the case now, because, as nearly the youngest of twelve children, my recollections cannot go back very far to the childhood of the others. *I can only state what I have heard, and relate my own impressions*; and a great part of the circumstances, which would have been important in my dear mother's eyes, passed before I could understand them.[12]

Any attempt at a narrative of the family immediately refers back to herself, and the limitations she feels she would encounter. She can only write about herself: 'I can only state what I have heard, and relate my own impressions'. Yet after this she appears to contradict herself, relying upon family duty, her responsibility to her mother, to overcome this by an act of will. The language seems impersonal against the subjective force of her last statement:

> Still I would try to do my best, because I felt that many things in one's life were worth recording. We have all as a family been singularly cared for, and, on looking back, I can trace the most clear working of God's Providence for our good, both as regards myself and others. It seems as if I could see the meaning of almost every joy and every sorrow.[13]

The troubled emphasis of duty to represent her family forces Sewell to react against her instinct to write introspectively. The division that this kind of language suggests is not present in such a direct way in other autobiographies of the period. Male writers appear less anxious about the act of writing on the self: for example, Trollope's autobiography begins 'It will not be so much my intention to speak of the little details of my private life, as of what I, and perhaps others round me, have done in literature'.[14] This is the kind of autobiography that Leslie Stephen was describing in the *Cornhill Magazine* in 1881, drawing on exclusively male examples: 'The true autobiography is written by one who feels an irresistible longing for confidential expansion'.[15]

If anything Sewell works hard to deny this move to 'confidential expansion'.

Her brother William played a central and acknowledged role in forming his younger sister's sense of self-worth. Elizabeth, with the benefit of hindsight, describes her feelings for him with a measure of distance:

> I really idolised my brother William, whose great abilities, fervent piety and warm affection I was beginning to understand and appreciate; and who captivated me with his sermons and poetry and conversation. I never loved any one else in the same intense way ... But the feeling, like everything else of its kind, brought suffering with it, very acute at times.[16]

The suffering that Sewell refers to could be cruelly direct at times:

> My mind had become much quieted and strengthened by the reading of Butler's *Analogy* ... I took it up for curiosity and read it through nearly, but not quite to the end; feeling very much afraid all the time that some one would inquire into my studies, and being greatly humiliated by an observation made by William, who one day found me with it in my hand. His surprised tone, as he exclaimed, 'You can't understand that,' made me shrink into my shell of reserve, and for years I never owned to anyone that Butler's *Analogy* had been to me ... the stay of a troubled intellect and a weak faith.[17]

The status of her intellectual inquiry and the promise of her creativity are denied by William's bullying manner which firmly puts her in what he considers to be her place as a young girl. The impression is that Butler's text is beyond her grasp because of her gender, an idea belied by the effect Sewell describes from reading the book. William's words are hardly commented upon except to measure their harmful repressive effects, the division he causes between her affection and her unspoken judgment.

The irony is that economic circumstances led her to write for money. The failure of two local banks in 1840 and her father's death forced her to take on the role of breadwinner for the family.[18]

> My writings had now become a pecuniary necessity for the whole family. My mother fully recognised it, for she said to me one day that she would rather be dependent upon me than upon any one else. Not that my brothers failed in assisting me to the utmost of their power, but the business claims were still a perpetual anxiety, and the pressure upon us all was so great that any one who made or could make money was called upon, as a matter of course, to give it to the general fund.[19]

Her brother showed less business sense than his sister. Resembling a character from a Wilkie Collins novel, the respectable clergyman mismanaged the affairs of Radley, the school he had founded at Abingdon in 1847. This led to the closure of the school and the sequestration of his fellowship at Exeter College, and in 1862 he fled abroad to avoid his creditors.[20] Despite her public repudiation of her brother's actions in her autobiography ('He was not a man of business habits, and his delight in seeing beauty around him after showed itself in a way which caused him to be misjudged and thought careless of expense'[21] her private comments reveal a more critical approach. After one of William's financial crises she wrote in her journal 'as usual [he] thought Bonchurch [the family home] a kind of pit in which money was buried'.[22]

*

Sewell's fiction re-enacts the narrative of her autobiography, the division between self-conscious introspection and public female duty to the family. Many of the novels are acknowledged by Sewell as autobiographical and set out to celebrate the apparently uneventful existence of the domestic life. In the most autobiographical of her novels, *The Experience of Life* (1853), the first-person narrator is the firm-minded, unmarried heroine Sally:

> I am not going to write a tale, not at least what is usually so called ... this is not a real representation of human experience. For one person whose life has been marked by some very striking event, there are hundreds who pass to their graves with nothing to distinguish the different periods of their probation ... They hope and enjoy, they are disappointed and sad but no one points to the history of their lives as containing warning or example.[23]

The domestic sphere of home is at the centre of her narrative, 'the Paradise of my brightest joys and holiest affections'. Sally who appears at first as a shy and retiring child dedicates herself to the service of others, her model being a spinster aunt from whom she learns the discipline of self-mastery:

> Trials in some shape or other have followed me from my youth, but there has been no 'must be miserable'. The must, if I believed it to exist, was of my own creation – a phantom which had only to be rightly confronted and it vanished.[24]

Almost by an act of will the phantom that 'only had to be rightly confronted' easily disappears by drawing upon the strengthening restraints of a Christian, moral personality. Any dangerous subjectivity, any introspective emotion is swept away by the act of confrontation, a willed act of self-control. Sewell seems to be rehearsing the moments in her autobiography where she has to face the problems of an emotional introspection. The figure of the morally upright spinster aunt is a recurring character in Sewell's fiction, mirroring her own position as a schoolteacher, but offering the image of the strong woman as a model to the characters in the book and to the reader.[25]

A similar model of characterization is repeated in another novel, *Amy Herbert* (1844), 'a little tale [that] was written by a lady for the use of a young member of her own family'. Here the young eponymous heroine Amy finds her model in a meek governess, Miss Morton 'whose daily life was one of wearying mortification and self-denial; and yet Emily Morton had never been heard to utter a single murmur ... her heart was a perpetual well spring of quiet gratitude, which made the heaviest trials of her life sources of improvement to herself, and of blessing to those around her'.[26] The model reiterates the formula of repressed subjectivity and strength through silent trial. Miss Morton's example serves to teach the tempted Amy the correct path towards a form of womanhood that privileges self-restraint above the dangers of confession or an emotional response to the trials of life. The character of the governess, outwardly spiritual and impervious to the threat of self-doubt and 'wearying mortification', suggests another rewriting of autobiography, the perfect figure able to offer herself as an example by virtue of her silence.

Sewell's own struggle in the *Autobiography* with the force of her personality and the corresponding contest with representation itself offer an interesting counterpart to this fictional model of female behaviour. Here the record is of an intense, strongly religious childhood that struggles more defiantly with confinement and restraint. The submissive exterior of Sewell the child conceals an inner life of imagination and forthrightness, 'a morbid and overstrained conscience' which is revealed in her confessional passion for self-recrimination. The heightened emotional narrative of an overly rigorous evangelical teaching is in her fictional counterpart of Amy Herbert easily resolved. Amy learns to look upon what are often considered trifling faults in a child – ill temper, indolence, vanity and greed – as grievous sins in the eyes of God, which must be checked at the very beginning by 'all who wish to continue what they were made at their baptism – His children'.[27] In the narrative of Sewell's 'real' life, similar concerns with childhood piety reveal a sense of conflict: 'I had a very violent temper, and was extremely self willed'.[28] What is also revealed is the child's difficulty in separating the pressures of a dominating religious faith from imaginative fancy, that expression of a vicarious self-will:

> I was always given to strange, scrupulous fancies, and not long before
> had made myself miserable, after reading about Jepthath's vow, because
> I imagined that every time the thought of making a vow came into my
> head I had actually made it, and was bound to keep it. I even went so
> far as to worry myself with the question whether or not I was bound to
> kill my mother, because I thought I had made a vow that I would.[29]

The death of her mother figures as a battle with authority in the rebellious imagination of Sewell's childhood. Despite the figure of her brother, her mother was a strong influence in the Sewell family, insisting on the girls' education, even at a young age, an experience that was at first hard on the young Elizabeth. The authority present to make claims against was, at this stage, female: her harsh teacher (the appropriately named Miss Crooke) and her mother, of whom she exhibits feelings of defiance expressed by the incantation of her vows, deviating from their religious root but still potent in their linguistic force. These are the very opposite to the words that Sally's aunt in *The Experience of Life* teaches her young charge to say in moments of self-doubt, recalling the defiant silence of Miss Morton in *Amy Herbert*. What remains is the faith that Sewell places in the power of her vows; once they are spoken their force means that they remain, even if they utter the unmentionable and the unthinkable, the death of a parent or the destruction of the family.

The child in the autobiography develops a compulsive urge for confession. Her school, a grim counterpart to Jane Eyre's Lowood, is a place that offers 'the great worm-eaten four-poster bedsteads, without an atom of curtain or drapery; the uncarpeted floor, and the two blocked-up windows, with a third which we were forbidden ever to look out of, on pain of paying half a crown'.[30] The blocked windows reveal the extent of the physical repression of her early education but could be read as symbols of an urge for introspection: prevented from looking out, the children are forced to develop a life of imagination.

It is language itself which makes any sign of individuality or deviance from the codes of behaviour a form of punishment. At Miss Crooke's establishment a child is punished for lying by being made to stand for hours in a long black gown wearing a piece of red cloth resembling a tongue with the word 'Liar' spelled out in large red letters. The physical image of the language of public humiliation presents a violent alternative to self-expression.

In these wretched surroundings Sewell's rebellious spirit comes out further, when she inscribes an exercise book with the initials 'O.W.', referring to Miss Crooke as an 'Old Witch' and then conceals the book from her teacher. As a result she suffers the agonies of conscience that lead to the necessity of a very public confession:

> My conscience, however, went on working; having once begun to confess, the practice became a necessity, and I begged that I might be allowed to tell every day the things I had done wrong, because I felt so wicked. Miss Crooke at first treated me as a converted penitent, but by degrees she must have become alarmed. My confessions verged on the ludicrous, and the climax must have been reached when having received an order in common with my companions to mention if we saw any black beetles in the school room, I made it a subject of confession that I had seen a large black beetle crawl out from under a large bureau, and had not told it.[31]

The narrative of confession if allowed full flow leads to the door of both fancy and fictional representation rather than the strictness of religious contemplation. Sewell feels she goes too far when, in confessing, she breaches the boundaries of fact and fiction, boundaries which she has stated at the very beginning of her autobiography are confused or ignored at the peril of a dangerously non-representative, subjective account.

Ultimately Sewell shies away from the display of authorship. In the autobiography we find that it is Sewell herself who wants, at first, to publish anonymously:

> I had no delight in being an authoress. My objection to the name existed in full force, and when the little book – *Stories on the Lord's Prayer* – appeared, I flattered myself that it would not be in good taste for any one to speak to me about it.[32]

The shying away from praise is met by another example of her brother's insensitivity towards her, presented in the text as a telling memory. On the occasion of a visit from the writer Charles Trevelyan Sewell, she thinks that he has come 'simply to look at me and see what I was like' and refuses to 'meet him on literary ground'. This leads her to recount, 'as my brother once said of me to a lady who made some inquiries about me, "My sister Elizabeth isn't remarkable in any way;" and I heartily endorsed the opinion'.[33] Her ready assent is, perhaps, as much a test of her self-control as the chance to hide beneath the identity of the woman almost invisible beneath the figures of the men in her family. This is a vastly different image to Helen Black's interview with the sensational novelist Rhoda Broughton in 1893 which emphasizes her readiness to discuss her talents: 'It is a surprise to hear her great gifts, her originality of style, her wondrous description of scenery, subtle humour are not hereditary. Keenly interested you ask her how then, the idea of writing occurred to her.'[34]

It is the spectacle of the author that so troubles Sewell when she visits the poet William Wordsworth in September 1849, with the future poet Algernon Swinburne (then aged 12), a friend of the Sewell family:[35]

> I never felt anything like the uncomfortableness of expectation I had then, except when I have been going to a dentist. We all hated the intrusion, though Algernon was greatly interested at the thought of seeing the great poet; it was so intensely awkward, and so odious, going to see a person merely to say you have seen him.[36]

The visit doesn't go well, the mundane nature of the encounter being met by Sewell's feelings of the inappropriateness of the meeting:

> I could almost say I am sorry I went, though I dare say by-and-by I shall

be glad. We were all stiff and restrained, and talked at intervals – with fearful pauses – a little about the Lakes and the scenery, and Mrs Smith's family . . . and we said how many people there were in the world with the name of Smith, and how they tried to vary the spelling . . . Somehow (I am afraid I am overfastidious), but I wished the writings and the privilege had been kept in the background; and I wished too that it had not been so evidently a favour conferred upon us to be admitted to him, and that there had been some apology, as in ordinary cases there must have been, for the length of time we had waited.[37]

It is fitting that Sewell is the person initiating the meeting of two 'famous' male poets of different generations. The representation of the masculine tradition of writing is undercut somewhat by her distaste for the conversation and for the display of the celebrity of the great author. What is even more significant is that, given Sewell's rejection of the introspective model of autobiography initiated by Wordsworth himself in *The Prelude*, she should meet the poet and re-enact her rejection of this form of representation within his own drawing room:

I feel rather vexed with myself for not having looked about more, but I dislike feeling curious, even by myself. The room was dark – one of the windows blocked up by a sofa. We waited an immense time. Mrs Wordsworth came at last . . . Wordsworth himself came a few minutes after. He was much older and more feeble than I had expected, and I had a painful feeling of having intruded upon him.[38]

Resisting the impulse of curiosity Sewell denies herself the chance to explore. Her vexation is tempered immediately by her sense of propriety: offered the opportunity to investigate the Wordsworths' house, she resists, obeying the decorum of a genteel Victorian lady. The allusion to the blocked window, obliquely recalling the blocked windows of her bedroom at Miss Crooke's school, allows a sense of the fictional to enter the narrative. There is a suggestion that Sewell's representation deliberately empties the event of any sense of drama. The account of the meeting signally fails to record her response to Wordsworth as Elizabeth Sewell the authoress, except to censure herself for the sin of curiosity. The episode provides a fitting example for Sewell the autobiographer, seeking to control the representation of the private by emphasizing her public identity as a Victorian woman, a testimony perhaps to a kind of writer honoured by George Eliot at the end of *Middlemarch* as one of 'the growing good [in a] world partly dependent on unhistoric acts, [one of] the number who lived faithfully in a hidden life and rest in unvisited tombs'.[39]

Notes

1 L. Marcus (1994) *Auto/biographical Discourses: Theory, Criticism, Practice*, Manchester, Manchester University Press, p. 15.

2 E.K. Helsinger (1979) 'Ulysses to Penelope: Victorian Experiments in Auto-biography', in G.P. Landow (Ed.) *Approaches to Victorian Autobiography*, Ohio: Ohio University Press, pp. 3–35, p. 14.

3 See, for example, E. Showalter (1978) *A Literature of Their Own: British Women Novelists from Brontë to Lessing*, London: Virago; S. Gilbert and S. Gubar (1979) *The Madwoman in the Attic: The Woman Writer and the Nineteenth Century Literary Imagination*, New Haven: Yale University Press.

4 C. Crosby (1991) *The Ends of History; Victorians and 'The Woman Question'*, London: Routledge, p. 153.

5 J. Swindells (1985) *Victorian Writing and Working Women*, Cambridge: Polity, p. 140.

6 Sewell's novels were pointedly directed at an adolescent market, following the development of a young girl within a severely religious family. Sewell's most urgent religious novel however, was meant for an adult audience. *Margaret Percival*, published in 1847, was written at the urging of her brother William and intended to put down the Catholic tendencies in the Church after Newman's defection. Her other works include *Laneton Parsonage* (1846), *Katherine Ashton* (1858) and the influential textbook *Principles of Education* (1865). She wrote regularly for Charlotte Yonge's *Monthly Packet*. Her *Autobiography*, published in 1907, the year after her death, is edited by her niece Eleanor Sewell: E.L. Sewell (Ed.) (1907) *The Autobiography of Elizabeth M. Sewell*, London: Longman. For discussions of Sewell's life and work see V. Colby (1974) *Yesterday's Woman: Domestic Realism in the English Novel*, Princeton: Princeton University Press; S. Foster (1985) 'Elizabeth Sewell: The Triumph of Singleness', in *Victorian Women's Fiction: Marriage, Freedom and the Individual*, New Jersey: Barnes and Noble, pp. 110–35; S.C. Frerichs (1979) 'Elizabeth Missing Sewell: Concealment and Revelation in a Victorian Everywoman', in G.P. Landow (Ed.) *Approaches to Victorian Autobiography*, Ohio: Ohio University Press, pp. 3–25; J. Rowbotham (1989) *Good Girls Make Good Wives: Guidance for Girls in Victorian Fiction*, Oxford: Basil Blackwell, especially Chapters 1 and 2.

7 William Sewell was involved in the early stages of the Oxford Movement, a group interested in ecclesiastical reform, but withdrew after it strayed into Catholicism. He was famous for his strong opinions: 'On the appearance of J.A. Froude's *Nemesis of Faith* in 1849, Sewell after reading it, declared to his class the next morning (27 Feb) on the wickedness of the book; and when one of the pupils, Arthur Bolfield admitted ... that he possessed a copy, Sewell seized it, tore it to pieces and threw it on the hall fire (*Daily News*, 2 May 1892). This incident gave rise to a commonly received report that Froude's [work] was publically burnt by the authorities of the university': S. Lee (Ed.) (1897) The Dictionary of National Biography, London: Smith and Elder, vol. 51, p. 291.

8 H. Black (1893) *Notable Women Authors of the Day*, Glasgow: David Bryce and Son.

9 Smedley was a minor novelist, whose work resembled elements of Dickens, was illustrated by Phiz and carried itself a strong autobiographical content.

10 A. Cruse (1935) *The Victorians and Their Books*, London: Allen and Unwin, p. 60.

11 E.M. Sewell (1891) *Extracts from a Journal Kept from 1846 to 1891*, Edinburgh: St Giles, p. 75.

12 Sewell 1907, p. 1; emphasis added.

13 *Ibid.*, p. 2. The autobiography was first printed for private circulation in Edinburgh in 1893; the first published edition, published in 1907 after Sewell's death, is edited by her niece, Eleanor Sewell. She presents a brief preface and introduces the various appendices written mainly by eminent women either influenced or taught by Sewell. In a sense the text is mediated by another (literary) female family member. Eleanor's preface opens with something resonant of Elizabeth's link to her mother: 'I have been entrusted by my aunt ... with her autobiography and feel that I am carrying out her wishes in having it published, so that many to whom the record of her life will be of interest may have it in her own words': Sewell 1907, p. v.

14 A. Trollope (1883) *An Autobiography*, London: Williams and Norgate, p. 1.

15 L. Stephen (1881) 'Rambles among Books No. II: Autobiography', *The Cornhill Magazine*, vol. 43, April, pp. 410–29, p. 410.

16 Sewell 1907, p. 42.

17 *Ibid.*, pp. 53–4.

18 For details of the perils of bankruptcy for the family see: L. Davidoff and C. Hall (1987) *Family Fortunes: Men and Women of the English Middle Class 1780–1850*, London: Routledge, pp. 245–7.

19 Sewell 1907, pp. 101–2.

20 Lee 1897, p. 187.

21 Sewell 1907, p. 165.

22 Sewell 1891, p. 75.

23 E.M. Sewell (1853) *The Experience of Life*, London: Longman, Book I, Chapter 1. The plot of *The Experience of Life* is minimal: what there is revolves more around the revelation of fortitude of character than any development of a story. An envious cousin appears who causes the narrator brief unhappiness and the proposal of marriage from a clergyman which she refuses, quite sorrowfully, because she is (like Sewell herself) the main financial support for her mother and her younger sisters.

24 Sewell 1853, Book I, Chapter 6.

25 Her early schoolteaching was organized around an extended family situation. Her first pupils were her nieces, and those pupils who were brought in from outside were obliged to address her as 'aunt' as well. This was a tradition which Sewell carried on throughout most of her professional career.

26 E.M. Sewell (1844) *Amy Herbert*, London: Longman, Book I, Chapter 5.

27 Sewell 1844, Book I, Chapter 7.

28 Sewell 1907, p. 18.

29 *Ibid.*, p. 20.

30 *Ibid.*, p. 24.

31 *Ibid.*, pp. 26–7.

32 *Ibid.*, pp. 75–6.

33 *Ibid.*, p. 96.

34 H. Black (1893) *Notable Women Authors of the Day*, Glasgow: David Bryce and Son, p. 41.
35 For references to the visit to Wordsworth by Sewell and the young Swinburne see also P. Henderson (1974) *Swinburne: Portrait of a Poet*, London: Macmillan, pp. 16–17; E. Gosse (1917) *The Life of Algernon Swinburne*, London; Macmillan and Co., p. 337. There is a reference to Sewell's death in a letter from Swinburne to his younger sister dated 'Aug. 22, '6.': 'I was glad after what you had told me of her sad state, to see that our dear old friend of very early days, Miss. Eliz. Sewell, had – to use the best and most beautiful phrase ever found for our common passage out of life – "entered into rest"': D. Leith (1917) *The Boyhood of ACS: Personal Recollections by his Cousin Mrs Disney Leith (with extracts from some of his private letters)*, London: Chatto and Windus, p. 207.
36 Sewell 1907, p. 106.
37 *Ibid.*, p. 108.
38 *Ibid.*, p. 107.
39 G. Eliot (1871) *Middlemarch*, 1965 edition, Harmondsworth: Penguin, p. 896.

Chapter 9

Autobiography and Educational Change

'I wanted to nurse. Father wanted teachers.'

Bobbie Wells and Peter Cunningham

Our particular 'use of autobiography' arises from a funded research project on teacher training and professional identity in the early twentieth century.[1] This chapter incorporates a digest of our seminar presentation at the Homerton 'Uses of Autobiography' conference, together with some points of reflection which arose from the discussion.

The principal focus for our research is the development of a particular form of teacher training, neglected in the traditional historical record, but of considerable significance for the present day. Teachers, a large occupational group, are worth considering by the social historian because of their role as transmitters of culture and their potential influence over a younger generation, as agents in the distribution of life changes or in the policing of youth. In the first half of the century, teachers were an upwardly mobile workforce, gaining recognition and status with the expansion and extension of formal schooling. Personal accounts of their experiences have much to tell us.

An episode in the history of teacher training

The Student Teacher Scheme is an almost forgotten episode in the history of teacher training, in operation from 1907 until 1939. During its lifetime it attracted both enthusiastic support and a great deal of criticism. Perhaps because it is an example of how quickly and easily educational innovation and change can be forgotten it deserves our attention for its own sake. It does, however, have another and more compelling attraction in that it provides us with the opportunity to re-examine the question, of concern in current educational debate, as to what impact school-based teacher-training has on the individual teacher-practitioner as well as on the profession's corporate sense of its identity.

Before 1907 many elementary schoolteachers made their first steps into the profession through the Pupil-Teacher route. This will be better known to most readers. The scheme ran from 1846, and was recognized to have shortcomings by the turn of the century. By 1899 the compulsory school-leaving age for most pupils was 13 and only a tiny minority of elementary school children proceeded to secondary school. Nevertheless, young people of very limited means aspiring to be elementary teachers could begin their 'apprenticeship' from the age of 14 by means of the Pupil-Teacher Scheme. At the same time some minimal extension of their personal education would continue either under the tuition of the headteacher or in a pupil-teacher centre, in the hope of later admission, on grant aid, to teacher training college. However, there was an increasing sense that the intending teacher needed education in a secondary school to acquire the cultural capital expected of members of an emergent profession.

The Student Teacher Scheme was distinctive in that, as teacher education began to edge its way towards an increasingly college-based training, the scheme itself continued to emphasize a school-based element, providing a year's paid work in an elementary school, but only after completing a *secondary* school education on a bursary, and preceding two years at a teacher training college. Amongst other things, it provided a means of getting a free Sixth Form education. Our informant, Miss P, at secondary school until 1915, records of her scholarship examination at age 11:

> my parents didn't pay any fees. And they didn't pay fees because at the end of the three years [*aged 15*] I was allowed a bursary because I said then that I wanted to be a teacher. So that gave me another two years at the secondary school and then ready to go to college.

However, before college the intending teacher could spend a year, not unusually in the elementary school from which she or he had progressed to secondary education, absorbing some of the practical skills of the profession. At its best the Student Teacher Scheme promised to be highly organized with regular Local Authority inspection, careful supervision by school teaching staff, student record books, and a well-planned day each week back in the student's own secondary school for the purposes of maintaining intellectual development.

In the 1920s many students entered teaching by this route. Indeed, in 1924–5 over 42 per cent of all admissions to teacher training colleges were student teachers.[2] However, by this time there were those who questioned the value of the scheme[3] – it required for instance, as Miss P indicated, a very early commitment to the profession. There were also doubts about the nature of the practical experience gained as compared with that of the pupil-teacher. Too many student teachers were said to be spending their time on menial tasks and under inadequate supervision. Furthermore, training colleges were also critical, complaining that the teaching experience gained was old-fashioned or that it inculcated 'bad habits' of practice. In addition, it was claimed that the student's intellectual development, stimulated by advanced work in the secondary school, was interrupted and impaired by the scheme.

Increasingly, teacher training college was regarded as the most appropriate and immediate destination of the intending elementary schoolteacher on leaving school and by 1934 the scheme was considerably reduced. Nevertheless, in its lifetime, over 70,000 teachers began their classroom careers in this way. How did they evaluate this early experience? How did they, as students, reconcile their school-based training with the college education which followed? What impact did the scheme have on their developing sense of professional identity? With all these questions in mind we turned to the teachers themselves to give us some picture of this important stage, believing that their autobiographies or personal histories would provide not only an account of commonalities and diversity in their careers but also a unique record of a significant event in the history of the profession itself.

Autobiographical sources for educational history

Our methodological concern is to explore how teachers' accounts of their personal experience contribute to our understanding of educational history. Whilst principally an oral history project, we also draw on aspects of life-history studies; between oral history and life-history there is a complementariness but also a creative tension for our project. Scarce, but enlightening too, are published autobiographical accounts already available.

Teachers' autobiographies

There are a number of classic autobiographical writings by teachers, a few of which bear more or less directly on the areas which we set out to investigate.[4] Those who have spent a lifetime in the profession may find it difficult to stop teaching, and it would therefore not be surprising to find that their autobiographies have some kind of point to make. Spencer's objectives were explicit, simple and humble:

> Of course it is an account of the life, chiefly of the external life, of the writer. Were it no more than a personal record, it would not have been worth writing, nor, in such a case, would it have been worth reading. It is offered as a 'document': for I belong to a rapidly dying class. Never again will anybody become a Pupil Teacher. No one with my history,

which, in its essentials, is that of thousands of others, will ever fill the posts I filled. Our type of our generation is probably worth a record.[5]

Spencer recalls that no-one asked him whether or not he wished to teach, but if they had he should probably have answered 'no', the natural answer for a boy of 14. His father, a skilled artisan, had intellectual aspirations for his son which would have overruled such a reaction.[6]

Leah Manning's intentions may be inferred from the last chapter of her autobiography. Despite an account of progress through educational and social reform, she felt frustrated by inadequacies which persisted, but saw her own work as a foundation on which more could be built.[7] Of the career decisions that interest us in our research, little is explicit in Manning's account of her childhood. Several factors can be inferred, however, as can the process by which she came to spend a year teaching in elementary school before following a teacher's certificate course at Homerton College.[8]

There are limitations to the usefulness of teachers' published autobiographies as a source. In the small sample available, there is often relatively little, and certainly no consistent treatment, of occupational choice or of the experience of professional training. They certainly do not provide consistent answers for a structured investigation of training. But autobiography of this kind does offer some useful pointers for aspects of professional image and self-image. The hopes and the despair, the crowded yet lonely life of elementary and primary teaching echo across a century between Runciman and Steedman.[9]

Life-histories

One tantalizing aspect of reading autobiography of those long dead is that it lacks the possibility of interrogation, especially crucial when exploring professional identity. On the other hand, the possibilities of making such inquiries are more than evident in life-histories. Many of the classic life-histories are open-ended and all-embracing – data gathered over time with only the gentlest guidance from the social science researcher.[10] However, Swindells, amongst others, warns us to be sceptical of the authenticity of voices which are conditioned by power relationships inherent in the circumstances of their collection .[11]

With regard to teachers, a classic recent life-history research project was that of Sikes, Measor and Woods.[12] Taking a small sample, and adopting interactionist techniques, they engaged in a sequence of interviews with secondary teachers to explore their entire career and biography. For us, a more salient example is the work of Nias, which comes close to life-history in its methodology.[13] She conducted long, semi-structured interviews to explore the development of personal and professional identity in the early years of their career of specifically *primary* teachers. Three conclusions graphically emerging from the powerful evidence which she collated were:

(1) A critical role for the primary teacher is the 'sense of self'; teaching as work requires practitioners to place high value on self-investment and on a personal relationship with pupils.
(2) The teaching task is central to teachers' lives; there are potentially high rewards but also great demands – the variety of organizational and inter-personal skills that are brought into play, the sheer hard work and the loneliness encountered.
(3) In apparent contradiction with the last feature is the powerful sense of collective responsibility with one's colleagues within the school. The crucial issue for us was how to elicit, within a relatively short interview directed towards a personal but nevertheless 'factual' account of the teacher training experience, this quality of reflection on professional identity.[14]

Oral history

The main concern of our project is the recovery of oral history accounts of teachers' live and careers. But at the same time we ask respondents to reflect on what is essentially a sociological construct – professional identity. Our goal is to establish the actuality of 60 years ago, the workings of the Student Teacher Scheme. This is where the predominant emphasis of our research lies.

The main claims for oral history in relation to our project are three. First, it recognizes the value of individual experience of teachers. This is especially important where histories of this occupational group have often been seen in terms of teacher unions – the profession acting collectively.[15] Second, it amplifies the written record. Much of the documentation about educational systems in general, and the Student Teacher Scheme in particular, tell what was supposed to happen rather than what did actually happen, and these are two often quite distinct things.[16]

Third, oral history gives us the opportunity to collect unique personal testimony which will soon be lost. The interior life of schools is relatively ill documented, and this is just as true for the inter-war years as for the late nineteenth century. Happily, for the more recent period, teachers' personal memories are still available.

'Real teachers'

Our project is concerned with the mechanisms and individual experience of the Student Teacher Scheme. It is also concerned with the Scheme's relationship to college-based training and with the impact both had on the development of professional identity. By integrating the personal testimony of oral history with documentary evidence, our intention is to explore how change in the form and content of professional training was perceived and experienced by students themselves.

The collection of this testimony has raised a number of issues, among them the importance of seeking out and representing both diversity and commonality, those varieties of experience which contribute to the making of professional identity. We have also been profoundly aware of the need to give 'voice' to our respondents. While this may be at the cost of subordinating other methodological and theoretical issues[17] it is also clear that their vivid recollections and reflections have added considerably to our quest to explore the nature and origins of professional identity. There is also the issue, particularly where so many of our respondents are elderly retired women teachers from a profession frequently but not unproblematically represented as 'feminized', of integrating questions of gender into our inquiry without changing its focus. Finally, to add to our quest there has been the desire to rediscover classroom interiors of former times. Just a few examples of findings from the initial stages of our research are presented below.

We identified a number of possible respondents through press appeals and through direct contact with teacher training institutions and their former student associations. So far the search has yielded over 40 former student teachers, including those with memories of an Edwardian schooling, as well as those who entered the profession more directly without school-based training. To all who responded to our appeals we sent an initial questionnaire to give us some kind of background account and, where necessary, as a prompt for further discussion. The questionnaire was essentially an outline of our inquiry, inviting respondents to give us some of their reasons for wanting to teach, the means by which they entered the profession and a brief reflection on what it has meant to them. We have been surprised and moved by the promptness of response as well as by the nature of that response in that our questions were more than amply answered.

Our next concern was with the character of the interview which we would conduct as a consequence of the replies to our questionnaire, whether it was to be carefully structured with a more or less rigid interview schedule or whether it should be conducted in a less formal and more conversational manner. Bearing in mind the important methodological point that a rigid interview agenda discourages respondents from pursuing their own recollections and reflections[18] we sought to devise a minimal semi-structured schedule for use more as an aide-mémoire[19] than as a route map. To do this we constructed a detailed interview schedule which we then reduced after much discussion to a prompt sheet in order to enable respondents to offer personal response, evaluation and judgment rather than a recital of facts and events and to provide the opportunity to reflect as fully as possible on matters of particular meaning to them.

Such reflection is rarely neatly packaged. The business of sifting through the past in this way involves both reconstruction and re-evaluation and may require the interviewer to put aside prepared agendas. It also requires concentrated listening on the part of the interviewer. Our respondent, Mrs D, for instance, reflected at length on her own secondary education, providing a wealth of detail to add to what is still a patchy history of the schooling of middle-class girls[20] and the tensions between private and state educational provision, and, more importantly, of their contribution to the preparation of intending teachers. As she remembered,

> Well it was a government ... ordinary state school. It wasn't the high school. There again, mother didn't approve of the headmistress of the high school ... so I went to the secondary school ... I was taught at home first for a bit and then when I went there it was in the middle of a term which wasn't really a wise thing to do ... Mother had taught me French ... but when I got into this form they'd been doing phonetics and I knew nothing about phonetics and I was at sea.

Such reflections are personal and intimate. In conducting our interviews our concern has been to value, respect and protect the individual voice. This has meant that our respondents have retained control over the material generated by the interviews. A copy of each transcript has been sent for review, annotation and comment, and a final version has been retained by the respondent as their own record. We have tried to follow faithfully the instructions they have given us as to the nature and dissemination of that record, for example, where requested, we have expunged names or details which might identify individuals or institutions.[21] Indeed, the reputation of long dead colleagues or mentors remains a matter of great concern to our respondents for whom the past is far from being a foreign country.

*

For the rest of this chapter we shall focus on interviews with two of our respondents, Miss P (aged 96) and Mrs D (aged 90), in order to develop some of the issues arising from our oral history of aspects of teacher training as discussed above. As we have already noted, we are uncovering varieties of experience as well as commonality. Although admission to teacher training required prescribed academic standards, individuals made differing assessments of their own abilities. Mrs D, for instance, was highly critical of her own academic performance at her girls' secondary school:

> much to my annoyance the headmistress decided I *could* work. My results were not comparable with what I could do. I hadn't worked hard enough ... I was always more interested in games ... I had to stay down and take that wretched exam [Lower School Certificate] again.

On the other hand, Miss P, the daughter of less prosperous parents, was well aware of the ambiguous status of the 'scholarship girl' whatever her academic success.

> The first year I was in the secondary school with my scholarship ... lots of girls in the form whose parents paid ... rather looked down upon us ... We were called 'the scholars'. Now we thought that was nasty but since then I've thought, I'm jolly proud that I was called a scholar.

In terms of commonality and in spite of class difference, both our respondents came from families of teachers and made very early career decisions. Miss P, whose mother had been a pupil-teacher and whose father and sister both taught, communicated an almost dynastic sense of what it meant to be a teacher which she described as having been born in her. Her recollections of her childhood on tape (and elsewhere on video for a Training College archive) underline the importance, emphasized in life-history method and in our own approach, of giving 'voice' to respondents. The construction and reconstruction of childhood stories over a lifetime means that such accounts may become enhanced and embellished.[22] They are nonetheless vivid in their recall. As Miss P remembered,

> Even before I went to school I was only – what – three, four. I had a lot of rag dolls ... I had them all lined up. I can see it now, along the back of the kitchen table ... And do you know, my father made me a little easel and a blackboard ... And I used to keep a register.

Similarly, when asked about the idea of teaching as a career, Mrs D told us,

> Well I never thought about doing anything else ... When I told them at home that I'd said I wanted to be an infant teacher they were all amazed ... nobody else in the family had thought of teaching little children ... Whether in those days they didn't think that was being a proper teacher ... that you were just playing about with young children I don't know.

In this account Mrs D was making her own exploration into the nature of professional identity, in other words what it meant to be a 'proper teacher', here a question relating to the educational sector rather than to professional expertise, qualification or competence.

As we have already indicated, since elementary schoolteaching was dominated in numbers by women in the period of our project,[23] questions of gender are of central importance to our understanding of the construction of gender and the experience of preparation for the role of teacher. In exploring recruitment to the profession it is clear that, as Mrs D reminded us, career limitations were much in evidence for young women: 'In those days there wasn't a lot of choice for girls: nursing, office work, or I suppose, teaching.'

Next, we can almost visualize some of the classroom interiors in which our respondents worked as student teachers, on school teaching practice from college or as newly qualified teachers, bearing in mind the comment made earlier that primary teaching has often been a physically isolating, rewarding but highly demanding experience. Miss P's description of the London County Council school in which she spent her Student Teacher year in 1915 indicates the extent to which any historical investigation into schooling is inevitably seated in the broader context of social history.

> It was a terrifically big one – you know, five hundred on each floor. And each floor had the most marvellous headmistress – or headmaster, of course, up the top and he wore a frock coat to school. And it was really rough ... I mean we did have children – there were no shoes or stockings. It was a poor school ... There were very few classes with less than sixty.

Mrs D began her teaching career some years later in 1924, recalling that at her school there were a number of children who were unable to read. Her comments tell us much about unconventional but imaginative ways of dealing with over-subscribed school accommodation, as well as about standards of literacy.

> Well, you didn't have that in those days ... [the headmistress] decided I should take them and there was nowhere in the school ... I'd take them to Peckham Rye – I don't know if you know Peckham Rye – well, there's a bandstand in the middle and she thought, well, I could take these children ... and I could teach them more or less individually to read ... Little tots sitting on bandsmen chairs. ...

We have been able to compare the experience of the Student Teacher year of our two respondents. For instance, the claim that Student Teachers were given trivial tasks and ill-organized supervision seems to have been borne out in the case of Mrs D's first day's induction at an elementary school in Norwich, where guidance was limited, 'making tea and putting water on the plants. Well, you know, just sort of watching round'. On the other hand, Miss P, whose Student Teacher year had been in London and some six years earlier (indicative of variability in Local Authority interpretation of the scheme) had a more systematic introduction, after first being interviewed by a divisional inspector before being admitted as a Student Teacher. On arrival at her school she was interviewed by the headmistress, who

> would explain what her line was ... We were allotted – there were two of us – we had a week in each class so we started at the bottom and we

worked up the school from the little ones straight up to leaving age.

Thus in expectation of experience of the whole spectrum of elementary education in one London school, she was given a 'bound book ... the official one' (which she had kept for nearly eighty years!). Into this book the authority required to be entered both her lesson plan and the headteacher's comments, all of which had to be made available when she subsequently applied for teaching posts. Each week Miss P spent a day back in her own secondary school with other Student Teachers:

> about six or seven of us used to gather in a classroom and there was a timetable arranged for us ... I don't think they knew what to do with us ... somebody would come in and talk to us about music or about something else. We liked it because we had a good old gossip about our work. I suppose that was good too because we were exchanging goods and bads in the teaching line.

Reminding us that the administration of the scheme was subject to a variety of interpretations, Mrs D, on the other hand, recalled no such experience some six years later. Rather, her recollections speak of isolation within one school, within a limited range of practical experience, and one which detached her from her peers.

> I went straight from school to one elementary school in Norwich and was put there as a Student Teacher full stop. And I was put with one teacher and I worked with her ... I wasn't with other teachers ... I was just a Student Teacher in a classroom with another teacher.

Conclusion

Thus personal accounts provide us with a vivid picture of diversity and commonality, not only in details of the training routes undertaken, which were apparently subject to variation according to place and time, but also in the more intimate aspects of career decision and development, and professional identity. The Student Teacher Scheme, a significant aspect of educational change generally overlooked by textbook accounts, is vividly described by those who underwent it, as is the experience of elementary teaching under different conditions and the professional self-image that emerged from this experience.

Notes

1 'Professional Identity and School Based Teacher Training in the Early Twentieth Century', a research project based at the University of Cambridge Department of Education, and funded by the Leverhulme Trust, no. F.462E.
2 Board of Education *Annual Report 1924–5*: 1826 Cmd. 2695,pp. 118–9.
3 Lance Jones (1923) *The Training of Teachers in England and Wales*, Oxford: Oxford University Press.
4 J. Runciman (1887) *Schools and Scholars*, London, Chatto and Windus; Philip Ballard (1937) *Things I Cannot Forget*, London: University of London Press; F.H. Spencer (1938) *An Inspector's Testament*, London: English Universities Press; Leah Manning (1970) *A Life for Education*; London: Victor Gollancz; Carolyn Steedman (1985) 'Prisonhouses', *Feminist Review*, no. 20, Summer.
5 Spencer 1938, p. v.
6 *Ibid.*
7 Manning 1970.
8 *Ibid.*, pp. 29–32. The Rev. Stewart Headlam, who had taken an interest in her intellectual and cultural development, suggested this route as a practical compromise between her own ambitions for university and the reservations of her family.
9 Steedman 1985; Runciman 1887, p. 9.
10 Ken Plummer (1983) *Documents of Life: An Introduction to the Problems and Literature of a Humanistic Method*, London: Allen and Unwin.
11 Julia Swindells (1985) *Victorian Writing and Working Women*, Cambridge: Polity, Chapter 8.
12 Pat Sikes, Lynda Measor and Peter Woods (1985) *Teacher Careers: Crises and Continuities*, Lewes: Falmer Press.
13 Jennifer Nias (1989) *Primary Teachers Talking: A Study of Teaching as Work*, London: Routledge, pp. 202–6.
14 Questions placed towards the end of our interview schedule are designed to provoke this kind of reflection, but are of course heavily suggestive. It often happens that salient reflections emerge in other sections of the interview.
15 Asher Tropp (1957) *The School Teachers*, London: Heinemann; Peter Gosden (1972) *The Evolution of A Profession*, Oxford: Basil Blackwell; Jenny Ozga and Martin Lawn (1981) *Teachers, Professionalism and Class: A Study of Organised Teachers*, Lewes: Falmer Press; Hilda Kean (1990) *Challenging the State? The Socialist and Feminist Educational Experience 1900–1930*, London: Falmer Press.
16 Phil Gardner has made use of a combination of oral and documentary evidence to help illuminate another obscure area of our educational past – the Victorian private elementary school: Phil Gardner (1984) *The Lost Elementary Schools of Victorian England*, London: Croom Helm, pp. 211–42.
17 Plummer 1983.
18 Sharna Berger Gluck and Daphne Patai (Eds) (1991) *Women's Words: The Feminist Practice of Oral History*, London: Routledge.
19 David Henige (1982) *Oral Historiography*, London: Longmans.
20 Sara Delamont, 'The beach covered hillside: self-presentation in the histories of the

girls' school', in Geoffrey Walford (Ed.) (1993) *The Private Schooling of Girls*, London: Woburn Press.

21 Respecting the wishes of the two respondents quoted in this chapter, their own anonymity is preserved.

22 Plummer 1983.

23 Frances Widdowson, 'Educating Teacher: women and elementary teaching in London, 1900–1914', in Leonore Davidoff and Belinda Westover (1986) *Our Work, Our Lives, Our Words*, Basingstoke: Macmillan Education.

Chapter 10

Life Histories, Adult Learning and Identity

PART ONE

Writing about learning: Using Mass-Observation educational life-histories to explore learning through life

Alistair Thomson

I shall outline here the early stages of a project researching adult learning and life-histories. A data set of 453 educational life-histories which are available at the Mass-Observation Archive in the University of Sussex provide a superb resource for educational research. Here I shall discuss the background to the project and some relevant debates in the life-history literature. Drawing upon two case studies, I shall then outline a range of ways in which these life-histories might be used by researchers, and some of the issues arising from such research.

From oral history to adult education

A further, implicit concern here is the way in which the life-history of the researcher shapes the research agenda and research approaches. This research is an attempt to connect my own background in oral history with a new role as an adult education researcher, and to bring theoretical issues and approaches from life-history work into adult education research.

My academic training is in the field of history, and for much of my working life I have been employed as an oral historian in community, institutional and academic oral history projects. Like many oral historians an initial and on-going impetus for seeking oral testimony has been to recover voices from below, the stories of individuals and communities whose lives have been hidden from history. Yet in the 1970s these democratic aspirations and methods of the resurgent oral history movement were subjected to savage criticisms by traditional, documentary historians.

The main thrust of the criticisms was that memory was unreliable as a historical source because it was distorted by the deterioration of age, by personal bias and nostalgia, and by the influence of other, subsequent versions of the past. Underlying these criticisms was concern about the democratization of the historians' craft being facilitated by oral history groups, and disparagement of oral history's apparent 'discrimination' in favour of women, workers and migrant groups. Goaded by the taunts of documentary historians, the early handbooks of oral history developed a canon to assess the reliability of oral memory (while shrewdly reminding the traditionalists that documentary sources were no less selective and biased). From social psychology and anthropology they showed how to determine the bias and fabulation of memory, the significance of retrospection and the effects of the interviewer upon remembering. From sociology they adopted methods of representative sampling, and from documentary history they brought basic rules for checking the reliability and internal consistency of their source. The new canon provided useful signposts for reading memories, and for combining them with other historical sources to find out what happened in the past.[1]

However, the tendency to defend and use oral history as just another historical source to find out 'how it really was' led to neglect of other values of oral testimony. In their efforts to correct bias and fabulation some practitioners lost sight of the reasons why individuals compose their memories in particular ways, and did not see how the process of remembering could be a key to understanding the way in which certain individual and collective versions of the past are active in the present. By seeking to discover one single, fixed and recoverable history, some oral historians tended to neglect the multivalence of individual memory and the plurality of versions of the past provided by different speakers (as well as different documentary sources). They did not see that the 'distortions' of memory could be a resource as much as a problem.

In recent years oral historians have become more interested in exploring the relationships between memory and subjectivity, and between collective memory and remembering. We are now more self-conscious about the distinctive character of oral testimony, and assert the theoretical and methodological values of the qualitative approach in oral history research.[2] As Paul Thompson commented in the editorial of *Oral History* in Autumn 1989:

> Our early somewhat naive methodological debates and enthusiasm for testimonies of 'how it really was' have matured into a shared understanding of the basic technical and human issues of our craft, and equally important, a much more subtle appreciation of how every life story inextricably intertwines both objective and subjective evidence – of different, but equal value.[3]

For example, in my own oral history research about Australian war veterans, I moved from exploring the hidden histories of working-class soldiers to assessing the impact of the Australian national war legend (the Anzac legend) upon veterans' memories and identities.[4] More recently, now that I have moved into adult education work (in one sense a natural progression from community oral history projects which often served as a site for informal adult education and learning) I am trying to bring the new theoretical and methodological approaches in oral history to bear upon adult education teaching and research. For example, inspired by Swiss approaches to training adult educators, Mary Stuart and myself have created a Postgraduate Diploma in Adult Learning and Life Histories at the University of Sussex. Participants in this course – most of whom teach in community, further or higher education – will focus on their own educational life-histories, and those of other adult learners, in order to explore issues about learning through life. One of the teaching and research resources we are using for this course is the extensive collection of the Mass-Observation Archive, which is based at the University of Sussex.

Autobiographical writing and the Mass-Observation archive

The criticisms suffered by oral historians and oral testimony have also been directed at research using autobiographical writing, and indeed at qualitative research data and methods in general. The example with which I am most familiar is the debate about the Mass-Observation project and archive. Mass-Observation (M-O) was a British social research organization influenced by earlier Polish and Chicago sociological traditions of using life documents for research. It operated between 1937 and 1950 and recruited volunteers to join a 'panel' of writers recording aspects of their everyday life. In 1981, the Tom Harrisson Mass-Observation Archive at the University of Sussex, which houses the diaries and detailed questionnaire responses produced by the original project, initiated a revival of the panel of volunteer writers.

The new M-O was closely related to the development of oral history in the 1970s and 1980s and its aims of validating the lived experiences of 'ordinary people'. Yet the new project differs from oral history by specializing in written material and accumulating sets of autobiographical writing about contemporary rather than past experience. Three or four times a year panel members are invited to respond to open-ended and discursive questionnaires (Directives) about subjects ranging from international and domestic political issues to everyday personal practices. Occasionally panellists are asked to provide detailed one-day diaries, or to record their experiences during the course of a particular event (such as the Falkland and Gulf Wars, and the 1992 General Election). Over 400,000 pages of typed and hand-written material have been amassed, representing the contributions of over 2,500 volunteer writers from all over the United Kingdom.

In the years between the two M-O projects, quantitative sociologists denounced the research validity of M-O material and targeted the inaccuracy of recall, the likelihood of fictionalization, and the unrepresentativeness of a small sample of self-selected respondents. Researchers using either set of M-O material need to meet those criticisms. In response to the latter criticism of the 'unrepresentative sample', it is perfectly possible to produce a profile of M-O writers (including details such as occupational status, gender, age and regional location), and to compare the profile of respondents to a particular directive with the national profile. Indeed, the Archive is currently facilitating such approaches by producing a computerized database of respondents.

However, as Dorothy Sheridan argues '"representativeness" itself is ideo-logically constructed; its dominant meaning focusses on the individual, a single voice, and on the assumption that people can only be seen to represent themselves, and that the quality of representativeness lies *not in what they say*, but in *who they are* (as defined by selected socio-economic characters)'. Sheridan, who is both Archivist and researcher at M-O, asks us to consider who and what the Mass-Observers are writing for and representing. She argues that they often write for 'the experience of others sharing the same or similar historical experiences'. Their writing 'is at the same time singular and collective'. Furthermore, Mass-Observers also write for an audience of inscribed or imagined readers ('people like them', descendants, the archivist, future readers, posterity), so that their writing is negotiated and shaped in relation to that perceived audience.[5]

Sheridan's analysis of M-O writing takes researchers beyond the narrow criticisms of quantitative positivists and opens up exciting issues about the forms, meanings and significance of different types of life-history documents. Sheridan reasserts 'the privileged access which autobiography can provide into a dimension of human reality which would be difficult to come to from other means':

> Through autobiography we may come to learn about people's hopes and fears, their individual choices in relation to wider social and political change, their rational and unconscious motives for acting, and, above all, the meaning and significance which they give their lives.[6]

More than that, I would argue that the search for a representative sample by some M-O users and critics has missed much of the research value of this type of autobiographical writing: that it can be illuminating about how and why people write and represent their lives in particular ways, and about the personal meanings and functional values of such writing. The individual case studies can help us to understand not only how people live their lives in society, but also how they articulate, comprehend and shape their lives in relation to public narratives.

Mass-Observation and educational research

Paul Armstrong has produced an invaluable essay and guide book which outlines practical and theoretical issues for using life-history methods in educational research.[7] He notes that in the past educational research has also been dominated by the quantitative paradigm, but that in recent years there has been a resurgence of research using qualitative strategies. Armstrong lists the following multi-faceted contributions which the life-history method makes to educational research: it facilitates exploratory studies and complements other source material; it enables exploration of individual subjectivity and of the process and change in life-history; it helps researchers to locate particular experiences within individuals' overall life-histories, as well as in the broad socio-historical background; and it encourages critical analysis of educational assumptions and generalizations. Qualitative approaches also facilitate praxis (making links between theory and practice) and participatory research, both of which have been significant features of much adult education research, and arguably adult education's major contributions to research methodology.

Armstrong lists a number of adult education research projects which have used life-history methods. To his list might be added current British projects such as the research into the motivations of Access students being conducted by Mary Lea and Linden West, Mary Stuart's investigations into the educational life-histories of women who have been socially defined as having learning difficulties, and the projects presented at the Life Histories and Learning conference at the University of Sussex in September 1994.[8]

As far as I am aware, M-O has not yet been used for substantial educational research, though it has rich research possibilities in this field, which postgraduate students at Sussex are beginning to explore. (Margaretta Jolly, a contributor to this volume, draws on the resource for her work.) The first part of the Spring Directive of 1991 focused on education (subsequent sections posed questions about the uses of reading and writing, and about taking risks). It asked Mass-Observers to outline their educational life-histories and to reflect upon their experiences of education. 'Education' was defined to include lifelong (formal) learning: 'don't forget to start right at the beginning (nurseries? playgroups?) and bring it right up to date with evening classes and adult education if it applies to you'. Panellists were also asked to record their own thoughts about the value of education, and about the present situation of education in Britain.

Responses to the Education Directive from 453 Mass-Observers now fill four archive boxes, and range from hand-written single sheets to book-length educational life-histories. Becky Garrett, a volunteer in the Archive, has performed an invaluable service for subsequent researchers by profiling Education Directive respondents. She has established that the Directive had a comparatively low response rate (41 per cent of panellists). The gender balance of the 453 respondents – 345 were women and 108 were men – roughly matches that of the panel as a whole. A higher proportion of male respondents were in the older age brackets (two thirds in their 60s or 70s), while the women were more evenly spread out in the 30 to 80 age span, with the highest proportion in their 60s. The south-east of England had the highest geographical representation (28.1 per cent of women and 37.12 per cent of men), but most other regions were reasonably well represented. It is very difficult to ascertain the ethnic background of Mass-Observers, as to date such information has not been gathered or collated. Nor is there an occupational or class breakdown of the Education respondents, though Garrett has established, for example, that about a quarter of the male respondents were graduates.[9] Using the computer database of Mass-Observers which is currently in preparation (for the moment it only includes female observers), it will be possible to contrast the profile of Education Directive respondents with that of Mass-Observers in general, and with the British population as a whole.

Becky Garrett has also produced a document which summarizes the educational life history of each respondent under the categories of pre-school, infant and junior school, secondary school, further and higher education, and adult education. She notes that there is 'a good deal of overlap and there remains considerable work in classifying "grey areas", for example, extra-curricular activities during school years ... and the variety of different forms of education subsumed under "further/higher" and "adult". These last two categories need to be more precisely broken down in future analysis'. Despite such reservations, the summary sheets are an invaluable short cut into the life-histories, and suggest the range and richness of the life-history material as a source for research about adult education and learning.

Using the Education Directive

The Mass-Observation educational life-histories might be used in the following ways for adult education research (other fields of education will have additional issues and concerns):

(1) To pose underlying theoretical and methodological questions, such as:
 • How do people remember and articulate their educational life-histories, and what are the factors influencing that articulation (writing for M-O, the nature of the Directive, the age, educational background, occupation and gender of respondents)?
 • Who responded to this directive and why (influential factors as above), and how does the profile of respondents compare with that of Mass-Observers in general, and of the British population as a whole?
 • What if anything is special or distinctive about the educational experiences and attitudes of respondents (compared with the results of national

quantitative or questionnaire surveys), and to what extent can any differences be attributed to the selective nature of the sample, or to the contribution of qualitative life-history evidence?

(2) To explore specific issues about the nature of adult education and learning:
- How are the nature and values of different educational stages perceived?
- What are people's memories of particular educational institutions and practices, and of the impact of individual teachers and significant others?
- What are the relationships between school experiences and post-compulsory education (or non-participation in post-compulsory education)?
- What are the motivations for participation or non-participation?
- What has been the take-up and significance of different forms of post-school education (higher education, vocational training and continuing professional education, liberal adult education, so-called 'leisure classes', distance learning, informal learning . . .)?
- What is perceived or defined as 'education' or 'educational', and how might the wording of the Directive have shaped those definitions?
- What has been positive or negative about adult education experience?
- What factors facilitated or hindered participation in education at different life stages?
- What have been the varieties of educational pathways and learning routes?
- What have been the outcomes of adult education?
- How have particular educational experiences shaped attitudes to contemporary issues, including contemporary education policy?

(3) We might also consider responses to those questions by specific groupings of respondents: men compared to women; different occupational groups or social classes; graduates compared with people without formal educational qualifications; regional distinctions; age cohorts – younger as opposed to adult respondents.

(4) We could chart changes in educational experiences, over time and for different age cohorts: for example, how was the education of the generation which grew up in the 1940s affected by the war, and how has that experience influenced their subsequent attitudes to, and experiences of, education?

(5) or we could focus on the processes and changes in individual educational life-histories, charting the changing interconnections between social and educational contexts, motivations, needs and experiences (we might even go beyond the Directive responses to produce an additional Directive, or to interview a number of respondents in more detail).

A workshop case study

Some of these possibilities can be illustrated through a case study. At the Homerton conference which generated this chapter, participants read and discussed two of the Education Directive responses. The two respondents are identified by their M-O number; for reasons of confidentiality names are not supplied to researchers. The background information which is readily available (but which might be supplemented by reading other Directive replies by the same panellists, including the autobiographical piece which they supplied upon joining M-O), is as follows:

- A1223: female, 66 years, retired clerk (for whom I'll use the pseudonym 'Joan').
- B1520, male, 71 years, retired printer (for whom I'll use the pseudonym 'George').

One of the exciting features of life-history research is that different readers (or listeners) often find new and unexpected meanings in autobiographical texts. The following reflections on Joan's and George's Education Directive responses have been shaped by feedback at the conference and from colleagues and postgraduate students at the University of Sussex. Researchers who consider the M-O replies in more depth and with different perspectives and questions will almost certainly find other meanings and issues.

The two case study examples were selected on the pragmatic grounds of what could be easily used for workshop discussion – they are both relatively short (about one and a half pages long) and they are typed – and not because I was looking for particular types of response to the Education Directive. I did, however, select one male and one female respondent because I wanted to compare men's and women's experiences, and for the same comparative purpose I selected two people who had been schooled in the inter-war years. Joan attended infant school in Northampton and was a scholarship girl at the local girls' grammar school, where she achieved nine subjects in the School Certificate, including five credits, by the time she left school in 1941 at the age of 16. George attended council infants and elementary schools up to 1934, when he left school without qualifications at the age of 14 to take up an apprenticeship.

The material opportunities and social aspirations structured by class significantly shaped these learning life-histories. Joan's scholarship got her to the grammar school, but George was less fortunate:

> Yet, deep down, I regretted my lack of opportunity to progress to my local grammar school, a private fee-paying school. Although they offered a few scholarship places it was a drop in the bucket with regard to the size of the town and its catchment area and competition was great. I did pass the first examination but got no further. My parents considered paying for me but as I had a younger brother who, of course, would need to be treated alike, it was beyond their means.

George's story, in particular, highlights the limitations and possibilities for agency in learning life-histories. The following extract shows how interventions such as the war and unemployment had dramatic impacts upon educational opportunities, and on George's ability to make or take the learning he wanted. When compared with Joan's account, the extract also illustrates the gendered differences between the experiences and stories of men and women. The forms of autobiographical writing are often as revealing of its meanings as are its content and subject matter, and these two texts suggest that men and women often adopt different *ways* of writing their lives. George's account is mainly structured through short, staccato paragraphs, arranged in strict chronological order, each of which outlines a particular stage in his education and training.

Apprenticed in January 1935 to a local printer on a seven-year term. Attended day release at a local school of art on hand compositor's work.

Broke apprenticeship after three years because family moved to another part of the country, but continued to work without benefit of proper apprenticeship in a small print shop. It was cheap labour for my employer, but I was still learning my trade. Was sacked on my 18th birthday in 1938 because of lack of work.

As war threatened joined Army in September 1938 and attended refresher lessons as part of my army training. Sustained an eye injury which led to being discharged from the army as medically unfit in February 1939.

Resumed employment in another printing office as a junior compositor (again cheap labour, but again I was still learning). This term of unofficial apprenticeship continued for over a year until May 1940 when again the source of work dried up.

This time I took on war work in an aircraft factory which was preceded by five months training as a fitter at a Government Training Centre. So my apprenticeship went on ice for the duration of the war. I was now 19.

Although now in a reserved occupation I was replaced by the entry of women workers, now more and more taking up war work. In May 1941 I was recruited into the Royal Air Force, because of my aircraft experience and who were not so particular about physical standards now that the nation was at war. Then followed another six months of training to turn me into an airframe fitter.

By now I was 21 and wondering when all this training for various occupations was going to end! During the following years of war service I kept the air force flying in various parts of the world. . . .

By contrast, Joan's account is more reflective and thematic. The writing is structured through stories rather than chronology, and whereas George's account very much focuses on his own pathways through education and training, Joan's stories are often as much about significant others, and her relationships with them, as about her own life:

> Considering the fact that my parents were only educated to the age of 13 (Mother) and 14 (Father) I suppose I didn't do too badly, I would dearly have loved to go on to further education, but a girl's education wasn't considered very important in those days, however I did obtain a post with a Building Society in Northampton, which I didn't enjoy very much. I think I would have liked to take a course in Shorthand and Typing and become a secretary, but I couldn't get my parents to agree, you had to pay for private tuition in those days. However my brother, who was a really brilliant student was after passing his Matriculation in everything with distinction, was sent with foresight by my father to be articled to a firm of chartered accountants, and became after the war ended a fully qualified chartered accountant, and went all over the world to work, finally settling down in the U.K. After a few years working for commercial firms and passing exams, as a Lecturer in Accountancy and then took a Masters Degree in Accountancy and Business in German (a competent linguist) and worked at a polytechnic until his retirement. Oh how I wish I could have had such opportunities. With them you can not only do what you enjoy, but also teach where you want to, do the best for yourself and your students. Money is not everything, status and job satisfaction are better. At least my parents found the money to buy my school uniform and send me to the Grammar, not all parents bothered to do that. I found in later years that, that part of my education was invaluable, it helped me to be articulate, and to think much more deeply, and I still find it a help, I was also able to help my two daughters when asked to in their early years, but of course they were both bright and got more advanced than me, however, my husband and I knew the value of a good education, and as they were good enough we let them both go to University, and take degrees, which they both obtained and Judy is now a quite senior civil servant and the young one a Solicitor, which I think is pretty good going, we are very proud of them. . . .

As well as suggesting the different ways in which men and women write their lives, these two extracts highlight the gendered nature of learning life-histories. For working-class men of George's generation education was primarily concerned with training for employment and career development; indeed employment offered and even required significant and continuing courses of vocational training. More generally, education and training was intended to fit men for particular vocational and family roles. George remembers his education in those terms:

Looking back at my days as a schoolboy my education then, let's face it, covered very little more than the three R's. Strangely enough, though, I do not feel as if I have been deprived of much for it has proved adequate enough to see me through my sort of life, to earn a good living, to raise a family, and to be relatively successful.

By contrast, Joan's story is common to many girls and young women of her generation, for whom education beyond a certain point was often deemed to be of less importance than the education of male siblings. Educational opportunities were often mediated through parental expectations and demands. Though Joan was and still is frustrated by that discrimination – 'Oh how I wish I could have had such opportunities' – to a certain extent both she and George internalized gendered social expectations about the extent and types of learning which were appropriate for men and women. Joan describes various 'improvement' courses she took at evening institutes, some for 'my own satisfaction' such as typing, bridge and discussion groups, and others linked to her domestic role, such as 'a cookery course, which has helped me to look after my family reasonably'. George's education in later life continued to be connected to his work interests, and even as he 'was looking forward to retirement', he 'undertook a six-week course to enable me to fuller understand the new composing room technology that now encompassed typesetting'.

The Directive replies are also revealing about the role and perception of learning in later life. Joan claims that she is 'now past the age when I feel the need to improve my education, and don't really have the time and motivation', yet within a few lines she is detailing her participation in bridge courses and discussion groups at 'the local tech', and 'oh yes I also brushed up my French in the last couple of years'. While she assumes a definition of education as training for one's allotted role in life – and thus primarily aimed at younger people – her own experiences highlight the richness and importance of informal, lifelong learning for personal and social development. Participation in Mass-Observation is itself a valued resource for learning and social affirmation: 'I also consider that writing these articles to you are very interesting, and hope that you are able to continue your directives to us all'. Writing for M-O is not simply a process of reflective representation of lived experience for the uses of researchers; it is a process through which participants articulate new meanings for their lives and achieve a sense of collective purpose and identity.

Indeed, Joan's and George's autobiographical writing reveals the complex dialectic between past experience and present sense. For example, their personal experiences of education shape their attitudes about young people and schooling today, just as the stories of their own schooling are refracted through subsequent experiences and public ideologies about education and society. Joan responds to the Directive question about education today:

I don't know very much about current education, but I do find it almost

> impossible to believe that children can leave school without being able to read, write, speak properly, do easy sums in their heads. What a lot they are missing. Is this due to bad teaching methods or bad behaviour [? ...] We had classes of 50 in my day, and we could all read and write etc. by the time we went into junior school by the age of 7 (or else) our fellow pupils took the micky if we couldn't. [...] As for allowing children to do as they like, well we all know what that leads to, anarchy in the classroom ...

Perhaps mindful of his own missed opportunities, George takes a different stance in the education debate:

> Because the whole of humankind deserves a good education its provision must be regarded as a natural right. It therefore follows that education should be taken out of the hands of fee-paying individuals and provided freely and equally to all. [...] the fruits will be a prosperous nation enjoying a high standard of living.

Autobiographical writings by Mass-Observers show how the popular purchase of particular educational ideologies and policies can often be explained in terms of their resonance with individual lived experiences of education. They also show how experience can be contradictory, and that the contradictions may be apparent in the writing though not necessarily recognized or resolved by the writer. For example, the pain of educational frustration is redolent in Joan's account. She is unable to blame her 'brilliant' brother but the detailed telling of his story suggests an unresolved sense of unfairness and even jealousy. 'Those days' are to blame, but not her parents, who 'at least' found the money to buy the school uniform and send Joan to grammar school. Yet Joan's proud account of the role she and her husband played in their daughters' educational and professional success suggests an unspoken – perhaps even unrecognized – comparison with her own parents' failure to adequately support her. Life-histories of learning – such as the collection in the Mass-Observation Archive – can thus be used to explore not only personal and collective experience of education, but also the impact and meanings of educational experience for individuals and their identities.

Notes

1 For a summary of conservative criticisms, see Paul Thompson (1988) *The Voice of the Past: Oral History*, Oxford: Oxford University Press, pp. 68–71, and his editorial in *Oral History*, vol. 18, no. 1, 1990, p. 24. For the Australian debate see the 'Oral History: Facts and Fiction' exchange in *Oral History Association of Australia Journal*, no. 5, 1983–84, *passim*.

2   See the 'Popular Memory' issue of *Oral History*, vol. 18, no. 1, 1990; the revised
     discussion of memory and subjectivity in Thompson 1988, pp. 150–65; the debates in
     the *International Journal of Oral History*, vol. 6, 1985; the international anthology
     edited by Raphael Samuel and Paul Thompson (1990) *Myths We Live By*, London:
     Routledge; and Alistair Thomson, Michael Frisch and Paula Hamilton (1994) 'The
     Memory and History Debates: Some International Perspectives', *Oral History*,
     vol. 22, no. 2, pp. 33–43. For similar developments in the United States see David
     Thelen (1989) 'Memory and American History', *Journal of American History*, vol. 75,
     no. 4, pp. 1117–29; and Michael Frisch (1990) *A Shared Authority: Essays on the Craft
     and Meaning of Oral and Public History*, Albany: State University of New York. For
     Australia see John Murphy (1986) 'The Voice of Memory: History, Autobiography and
     Oral Memory', *Historical Studies*, vol. 22, no. 87, pp. 45–54. For ways in which
     psychology has also taken on these ideas, see David Middleton and Derek Edwards
     (1990) *Collective Remembering*, London: Sage.
3   *Oral History* (1989) vol. 17, no. 2, p. 2.
4   Alistair Thomson (1994) *Anzac Memories: Living With the Legend*, Melbourne:
     Oxford University Press.
5   Dorothy Sheridan (1993) 'Writing For ... Questions of Representation/
     Representativeness, Authorship and Audience', in D. Barton *et al. Ordinary People
     Writing: The Lancaster and Sussex Writing Research Projects*, Centre For Language
     in Social Life, Lancaster University, Working Papers Series, No. 51.
6   Dorothy Sheridan (1993) 'Writing to the Archive: Mass-Observation as Auto-
     biography', *Sociology*, vol. 27, no. 1, p. 28. See also Dorothy Sheridan (1993)
     '"Ordinary Hardworking Folk?": Volunteer Writers in Mass-Observation 1937–50
     and 1981–91', *Feminist Praxis*, vol. 36/37; Dorothy Sheridan (1991) *The Tom
     Harrisson Mass-Observation Archive, A Guide For Researchers*, Brighton: Uni-
     versity of Sussex Library; David Bloome, Dorothy Sheridan and Brian Street (1993)
     'Reading Mass-Observation Writing: Theoretical and Methodological Issues in
     Researching the Mass-Observation Archive', *Mass-Observation Occasional Paper*
     No. 1, University of Sussex; also in British Sociological Association Auto/
     Biography Group *Bulletin*, Spring 1994.
7   Paul F. Armstrong (1987) *Qualitative Strategies in Social and Educational
     Research: The Life History Method in Theory and Practice*, Hull: University of Hull
     School of Adult and Continuing Education.
8   Mary Lea and Linden West (in this volume) 'Motives, Mature Students, The Self and
     Narrative (Life Histories, Adult Learning and Identity)'; Mary Stuart (1993) '"How
     was it for you Mary?": Reflecting on Educational Life History Work With Women
     With Learning Difficulties', in David Jones and Nod Miller (Eds) *Research
     Reflecting Practice*, Boston: SCUTREA; Mary Hoar, Mary Lea, Mary Stuart,
     Alistair Thomson and Linden West (Eds) (1994) *Life Histories and Learning:
     Language, the Self and Education*, Brighton: University of Sussex.
9   Becky Garrett (1992) 'Analysis of Panel Replies to the Spring 1991 (Part 1)
     Directive, Personal Experiences and Attitudes towards Education, Report of Work
     in Progress', unpublished paper, Mass-Observation Archive, University of Sussex;
     an extended form is included in Brian Street and Dorothy Sheridan (1994) 'Literacy
     Practices and the Mass-Observation Archive', ESRC Report R000233728.

Alistair Thomson

Acknowledgment

Mass-Observation Archive material copyright The Trustees of the Mass-Observation Archive at the University of Sussex, reproduced by permission of Curtis Brown Group Ltd, London.

PART TWO

Motives, mature students, the self and narrative

Mary Lea and Linden West

Our research has been concerned to establish a better understanding of mature student motivation in higher education. There is general agreement among researchers that the present level of understanding of student motivation is limited. Research into the reasons adults give for participation suggests that, in the case of qualification-bearing and Access courses, highly instrumental/ vocational factors are the most significant but personal factors are also identified if largely unexplored.[1] We wanted to redress this deficiency by exploring all the factors involved, personal as well as vocational, by providing space for students to reflect on their meaning and significance in the context of past and present lives as well as desired futures. The research indicates that embarking upon higher education is to be seen as part of managing change and seeking a new identity in which revising a self-narrative – the story one tells of oneself and one's personal history – is central to the process. In other words, we suggest that a critical element in reconstituting a self and a life is reconstituting an autobiography.

Methodological issues

Most motivational research has been primarily quantitative in method. Such approaches make it difficult to explore, in depth, processes of decision-making, and their meaning within past and present lives. Surveys relying on data collected in questionnaires provide little or no space for participants to reflect upon the reasons which may underlie particular actions: a box is ticked, an answer given and there the process ends. Our research has gone beyond this by giving space to students to reflect on the meanings underlying their actions. What circumstances have led them to take an Access course? Why might these be significant? Are there common threads which run through the stories?

We used an autobiographical, longitudinal, case study approach in a series of lengthy interviews covering a period of two years and more. Each interview was fully transcribed and given to students as a basis for further dialogue and reflection in subsequent interviews. The unstructured, reflexive nature of the process enabled students to consider experiences in their lives which might be significant in their wish to pursue higher education. During the interviews students explored many different areas including previous education and childhood; the influence of significant others at different periods of their life; family relationships and occupational history; and feelings about self and others over time. The sample consisted of 30 adult returners in Access[2] and similar programmes, selected to include both sexes and a range of occupations, social and ethnic groupings, ages and educational backgrounds. A proportion of the students had completed a year or more in higher education and interviews continued during this phase. The method enabled us to observe how narratives change in the light of the present. A more confident person enjoying higher education tells a different story about past and present than a nervous, diffident beginner.

We are aware of the difficulties in the use of autobiographical methods, with regard, for example, to the problematic boundary between educational research and therapy. Care needs to be taken and the researcher needs to be reflexively aware of her effect, and the impact of the process, on students. Exploring a life and motive can unlock painful and repressed material while research, unlike therapy, offers no long-term framework of support. Moreover, there are methodological questions relating to the nature of remembering, what is recalled, what is forgotten or repressed and why; there are epistemological issues surrounding the meaning of texts and their validity. The interview process itself raises questions about the relationship between the researcher and the researched, and the influence that the researcher may have on the stories being told. As Okely illustrates with respect to ethnographic research in anthropology, the autobiography of the researcher is always present[3] (what is less clear is how it can be interpreted and represented within the research text). However, despite some of these problems, there is a potential richness in the process and the material generated which is absent from more conventional approaches.

The case studies and experiences of the Access course

Initial interviews tended to focus on stated reasons for undertaking an Access course. Many students gave highly vocational rationalizations for their desire to enter higher education. Frustration with an existing career and wanting to follow a new career path were often mentioned. This initial focus on vocational aspirations is understandable in the early material: these were people who had made a conscious decision to change and to move beyond the familiarity of home, community and work, to risk the uncertainty of an unknown environment. Some felt opposition from those closest to them with regard to their actions. In such circumstances they probably found it easier to justify their decision in conventional vocational terms, reflecting the respectability of such motives in the wider culture:

> Personally, I'd like to go into teaching and they're crying out for science teachers. There's a very great shortage of science teachers. So I thought 'well that's the way to go'. It wasn't a particular interest in science. It

was knowing at the end of it that there would probably be a job.

However, the reflexive nature of the interview gave this student the opportunity to explore her initial reasoning further and to look more closely at her personal motivation:

> I think what it is really is that I just don't want a job, I never have just wanted a job. I could go . . . I'm very good on a sewing machine. I could go into a factory on a sewing machine if I just wanted a job. I want more of a career in inverted commas, more of a career perhaps.

In fact much quoted distinctions between vocational and personal motives, public and private worlds and justifications, began to unravel as time was spent talking to mature students in this way. Kathy, a working-class woman in her mid 30s, mentioned, in an early interview, her wish to become a solicitor. When asked for her reasons for wanting to enter higher education, she talked, conventionally, about the importance of a career and the fact of having more time now that her children had begun school. Yet when Kathy considered, in later interviews, what being a solicitor meant to her, these career ambitions became entangled in a story of powerlessness and inner vulnerability across her entire life. She talked of her childhood, and of her parents and their fragile marriage. She talked of doing reasonably well at school, despite low expectations, particularly on the part of her mother, who reflected, as Kathy saw it, the limited expectations of her class and gender.

Kathy recalled wanting to be a solicitor at 14, after her parents separated for the second and final time. Kathy was then at a crucial stage in her schooling and adolescence as her fragile world, ambition and academic career crumbled among the debris of a shattered home. Twenty years later, in the middle of coping with a tragic death and difficulties in a current relationship, she described feeling powerless and inadequate as a child, as she often did as an adult, and wondered what had made her feel this way. Wanting to be a solicitor expressed a wish, however ill-judged the ambition, to be a more socially confident, assertive and respected person, which continued into the present, not the least in relation to her husband and his friends. As in her family of origin and early experience, she continued to feel worthless and empty in her relationships with others: patterns repeated across time.[4]

Even a cursory examination of Kathy's story suggests that her vocational and educational motives are rooted in her most intimate experiences and crises of self and relationships as well as more general forms of cultural oppression. Her story poses numerous questions about why older students turn to higher education, about the relationships between a particular career aspiration and personal history; about what the choice of a specific subject, and attending university more generally, might signify at an intimate level.

Many students mentioned the role of significant others as being critical to their decisions. Kathy's husband had recently been promoted to be an officer in the services which raised difficult questions for her about her background and present identity. He had changed in a way that she did not like while her children had started school; she felt increasingly in crisis and her life and existing identity were falling apart. Significant others appear to play a crucial role at such a time. Close friends or relatives may have recently completed an Access course themselves and have encouraged participants to consider higher education as a possibility:

> A friend mentioned the Access course to me. Well, she was a best friend and she was actually on the Access course so obviously I saw what she was doing and thought 'I can do that'.

Most students had experienced recent periods of change, transition, and crises. Divorce and separation were commonplace while changes in economic circumstances, including unemployment were frequent. A number of the students lived in areas which had suffered major economic decline, such as Thanet and the Medway Towns. Life, including employment, felt fragile and uncertain. Periods of depression and personal instability were widespread, while particular individuals had undergone illness and major breakdowns. As Paul described it:

> I'd been very ill, I'd been working 14, 15 hours a day, 7 days a week. I collapsed at work and went to see the doctor, well my wife made me go to the doctor and I had high cholesterol, very high cholesterol which is hereditary and the doctor said to me 'If you don't slow down, you will be dead within 10 years'. I went home and was absolutely shocked because I play rugby, I swim. I do smoke, but not excessively – probably smoke about 10 cigarettes a day. I was absolutely terrified and we thought well, there must be something else to do. . . .

For the women in the group the experience of being at home with small children, older children going to school, growing up and moving away, were contributory factors in deciding to change direction. The Access course was perceived as a route forward, as a way of managing change and rebuilding. In fact, many students hoped that higher education might resolve some of their problems and help in the process of reconstructing their lives:

> Well, once I'd decided it was straight ahead, no problem. Then I found myself in the situation where I was on my own, boyfriend-wise. I was in my own house, so I was my own boss, nobody to worry about. I'd also just found a cure for my migraines which had dogged me for quite a lot of my life. So I turned a complete corner in my life and I thought

'Take some time. What do you want to do and we'll do that'. I had some friends who were at Kent doing some degrees there and were talking about Computing and I said I don't suppose, you know, older people do that, and he said 'Oh, we've got a man of 60 on our course'. So I thought, 'Oh well, if a man of 60 can do a degree, I jolly well can'. So I made some enquiries, found out they did Bio-chemistry. Thought 'Yes' ...

A common theme surfacing throughout the interviews was one of 'doing something for themselves for the first time'. Participants talked of 'being me here on this course', of being taken seriously for the first time in their lives and of feeling, at long last, grown-up – of being an adult, an independent person, a distinct self:

I don't think I took myself seriously, but now I'm just doing this for me, to prove that I'm capable and to prove I'm not as flippant as the world takes me for.

At the same time, they frequently referred to a past state of alienation, of being marginalized at work or estranged from those closest to them. Many recalled some success at school, often disrupted by family crises. Most were marginal people in the educational sense defined by Hopper and Osborn:[5] caught somewhere in the middle of those who had succeeded in the system and the majority who had been socialized out of the system at an early stage without qualifications of any kind. Some of these students had 'O' and 'A' levels, for example.

Many people spoke about how they had always felt different and life being unsatisfactory until embarking upon the Access course. For some, the move away from family and friends, while having begun long before the course, seemed to gain added impetus during the course itself:

And she must've mentioned it to my sister and obviously my brother-in-law, and the best thing that he really did say about it, what little that he did say, was that he read in the *Sun* newspaper about Art students on the piss every day or something or other. That people could believe that sort of crap is – and that's, that's eased the distancing to me you know, because I couldn't believe that type of thing. I have trouble identifying with them now. And that, that problem of identifying with people who believe that sort of rubbish I found that, with the people that I worked with within the electrical trade, it's horrible and I hate saying it, to categorize people, because it's wrong but, ... people who, with those attitudes tend to be within the trades I think. And that was the reason that I couldn't, that I didn't fit into that any more for some reason. I hope that's not too arrogant, it's not meant to be.

The feeling of alienation from those who had been close is one reason why students need so much support from fellow students and tutors. Rita, in the film *Educating Rita*, was no isolated example. The support of others, and positive reflections of a new self and possibilities in their eyes and responses, appear critical to the development of a new identity.

Experiences of change and personal identity

As students talked about issues of personal change, the development of confidence and doing something which at last felt right for them, the experience of study began to take on a new meaning. It gave them new ways of making sense of their own world which they had never previously experienced. The process of 'meaning-making' seemed to act as a bridge between past and present identities. The acquisition of new insights is important to the restructuring of identity. The following quotation captures aspects of this 'meaning-making', bridging process:

We live in the 1990s. I was born in the 1960s. I know my father's born in the 1920s and my grandpa's born in 1890. I don't know a great deal about those other years bar the fact that there was a war somewhere between '14 and '19 and there was another war later on. They didn't have sanitation. They didn't have cars. You know, I knew those sort of factual things but doing social history, it explains why they didn't have cars. They've explained *why* there was a war. What effect the war had. It explains what living standards were like and why living standards were like that in the late nineteenth century. It explains, for example, why my background or my families' backgrounds had servants and why other people didn't. So effectively I have all these facts ... we've all got them haven't we, all over the place? And it's effectively a link between all these facts, such that at some point you go full circle and you can put that subject into a box. For me, areas that ... if I thoroughly know something I enjoy it and then put it away and then I recall it whenever I want to and enjoy and whatever. So subjects, subjects which I don't know a great deal about, I just have the facts, jumbled up facts and it enables me to put the facts in some sort of order, see it as a whole and then I understand it and that what's so good. It's being able to put all these facts into perspective, relating to other things, the linking.
Q: So is it just relating to other ... is this very specific to the academic world now for you, or does it have implications for the wider ... for your wider world, rather than just the university?

A: Um ... it's a difficult question to answer from the top of my head. I would say that it's academic, it's fulfilling. So, whether it's fulfilling academically or whether it's fulfilling personally doesn't actually matter. It makes me feel fulfilled.

I could give you a little example – my father for example, we went to Margate one day and he happened to point out a shop and he said 'When I was a little boy that was a tourist shop' and he said 'I thought it was an enormous department store'. Well, it was basically just a large corner shop and that was a piece of information I picked up and just put it away, but now having done social history I could see that large shop must have been very large for its time, very innovative for its time, very exciting for a child and I can ... I can take the fact that my father said that was a toyshop and now understand and feel how that must have felt as a new toyshop, so it enables me to get more feelings. Another word is understanding. For me if I can feel the ways something feels that makes me feel good.

Students reflecting on their decisions and their experience of the course made more connections with previous experience, good and bad. Some talked of bad experiences at school or the lack of support and empathy on the part of parents towards them and their studies. Others had been severely hampered by economic circumstances which made it an imperative to leave school. For yet others the experience of school was overwhelmingly bad and they were keen to leave at the earliest moment. The process of higher education, as well as the research, was producing more of these connections, and a positive re-evaluation of self across a life. A fundamental feature of meaning-making was the reappraisal of self implicit to the process: in telling new stories, revising a narrative, they were, in a sense, recomposing themselves.

A quest for identity, authenticity and self seems to be the common thread running through the interviews. Many students initially referred to feelings of emptiness: they talked of holes at their core, or their inner selves being like houses on sand. They were looking for something to fill the gap or strengthen the structure. They had often tried other directions and failed in these: a new job, a new relationship, another child. They talked of incompleteness prior to the course. As the interviews progressed, participants elaborated on their under-standing of their own crises of identity, using material from the courses to do so. One woman used literature to reflect on aspects of her own oppression:

It is almost as if the child hasn't grown up in me, in that sense. ... I have been left in these very emotional situations to fend for myself in some odd ways. I don't mean it in a self-pitying way, but I recognize it and perhaps one of the reasons why I recognize it even more now is because of the books we have been studying in Comparative Literature, where we have seen the Victorian heroine ... she has married in the real world but her unreal world is fairly childlike. And I can see a little bit of myself, maybe lots of people can see a little bit of themselves in this, you know. I think, at the end of the day, there are areas where we are all children. I don't think we ever completely grow up. ...

But I was thinking more of the Victorian wife and mother, the role of wife and mother. And I don't mean that I am an arch-feminist. I'm not, but I believe if you have got an interest, it is good to be able to pursue it if you have that ability or the opportunity or the funds or whatever. A very middle-class attitude that.

Q: Who is your favourite heroine?

A: Well, funny enough, it is a prostitute. ... And the reason I feel sorry for her is because she is within the confines of this coach with all these stereotype people who ostracize her, because she is different, because she is a prostitute, because she is a lady of easy virtue. I don't mean I am saying I am a lady of easy virtue but you know, because she is different and they then realize she has this hamper of food and they are on this very long journey. Oh, she is useful to know, let's get to talk to her. So they chat her up, eat her food and they arrive at an inn to stay overnight, I don't know if you know this story, the Prussians, you know, Prussian, Anglo-Prussian, Franco-Prussians. And the Prussian Officer is interested in her sexually so she doesn't want to know, she is trying to retain her dignity and she eventually gets coerced, emotionally black-mailed, forced, oppressed, call it what you like into going to bed with this chap and is terribly upset afterwards and they all climb back into the coach, by which time they have replenished their food supplies, which they fail to share with. ...

And the last three lines of that story are so real and so painful, I just could draw alongside with her in that she is trying to hold back the tears of hurt and frustration and anger at being cheated when she really has been open and honest.

Changing narratives

The reconsideration of past events and themes within the interviews can be regarded as a form of self-narrative. Self-narratives are, in our view, not simply descriptions of life experiences; as narratives they are more than passive representations of experience. Rather the stories told give meaning to events. As the self is re-evaluated, the nature of personal narrative, and the interpretation of self and history within it, change accordingly. A changing story is the prerequisite of a changing self. Kirby,[6] among others, focuses on the crucial importance of language as constitutive of the self, and talks of narratives as a primary embodiment of our understanding of the world and ultimately our selves. Similarly Giddens,[7] from a sociological viewpoint, argues that a person's identity is not found in behaviour *per se* but in the narratives surrounding it. Survival and well-being depend on what he terms the reflexive project of the self which consists in the sustaining of coherent, yet continuously revised, biographical narratives. As these students' stories are developed, the narratives are clearly both contingent on and constitutive of the experiences they describe. Rather than merely representing a social reality, they in part constitute that reality. The opportunities created for reflexivity in the research process, and the longitudinal nature of the project, meant that students could both re-create the past and in addition construct new identities through the development of their own narratives. Experience never really ends.

Conclusion

We have attempted to illustrate the importance of autobiographical approaches in research as a means of connecting public and private worlds, present motives and previous experience. The material drawn from students' life-histories illustrates the central role of narrative in changing identities and reconstituting the self. Conventional quantitative methods miss these subjective experiences and the meanings attached to them. If adults in higher education are looking for ways to create new meanings within their lives, what are the implications for institutions? How far is today's higher education really able to respond to the challenge of mature adult students and the need to connect academic and more personal worlds? We need to look more closely at life-histories if we truly want to find the answers to these questions.

Notes

1   See Alan Woodley *et al.* (1987) *Choosing to Learn: Adults in Higher Education*, Milton Keynes: Open University/SRHE; see also Veronica McGivney (1990) *Education's for Other People: Access to Education for Non-Participant Adults*, London: NIACE.

2   Access courses in the United Kingdom are designed to prepare non-traditional students, who lack the necessary educational qualifications, for entry to higher education.

3   Judith Okely (1992) 'Anthropology and Autobiography: Participatory Experience and Embodied Knowledge', in Judith Okely and Helen Callaway (Eds) *Anthropology and Autobiography*, London: Routledge.

4   For a fuller discussion of this and other case studies, see Linden West (1995) 'Beyond Fragments: Adults, Motivation and Higher Education', in *Studies in the*

Mary Lea and Linden West

Education of Adults, Leicester: NIACE, October.
5   Earl Hopper and Marilyn Osborn (1975) *Adult Students, Education, Selection and Social Control*, London, Frances Pinter.
6   Paul Kirby (1991) *Narrative and the Self*, Bloomington: Indiana University Press.
7   Anthony Giddens (1991) *Modernity and Self Identity: Self and Society in the Late Modern Age*, London: Polity.

Chapter 11

Assumed Identities: Feminism, Autobiography and Performance Art

Claire MacDonald

It is now time to explore the creative potential of interrupted and conflicted lives. (Mary Catherine Bateson)[1]

Imagine this. On a video screen a middle-aged woman dressed in a white overall and high heels comes into a bare room carrying two bulging plastic carrier bags. Addressing the camera she introduces herself as the artist Bobby Baker and says that the space is her husband's studio where she will make this video of her performance *Drawing on a Mother's Experience*. We must forgive her, she says, because while she is a very experienced artist she is a little nervous in front of the camera. Protecting the floor with a layer of clear plastic covered with a double white sheet, bought, as she explains, in the sales, she turns away and begins to prepare for her performance, unpacking her bags and drawing out cans of Guinness, Tupperware boxes, a food mixer, bottles, jars and bowls, all the while addressing the camera and peppering her work with wry comments about life, art and food.

Her performance is a drawing and in making it Bobby Baker draws, both literally and metaphorically, on her experience as a mother and as an artist. Over the course of an hour she makes a work parodying Jackson Pollock's vigorous masculine action paintings of the 1950s, substituting the materials of a mother's experience for paint since, as she reminds us often, she is a very experienced mother. Marking her sheet with pressed beef, Guinness, milk, fish pie and treacle she covers her sheet with colours and textures, connecting each act of mark-making to an episode in the story of her experience as a mother. Then she clears up. She will leave no trace, no mess, no evidence of work. She has already told us that the sheets will be washed and used again in her next drawing. Her bags are packed as she goes along and every smear of food damped away. Standing over her art work she dredges it in white flour and, having erased it completely, lies down and wraps herself in the sheet so that nothing remains, the story literally sticks to her. Then, as her coda, she dances: in her stained sheet she boogies with difficulty to Nina Simone's 'My Baby Just Cares For Me' and as the music fades she picks up her bags and walks off. There is nothing left but the memory of living and telling.

Bobby Baker's career is exemplary in feminist terms. It both frames the women's movement and marks its changes of agenda, moving from early work in food sculpture to later performances and installations which map the equivalences and commonalities between composing art and composing a life. Now in her early 40s, she trained as a painter, began making art in the early 1970s and had an eight-year-long break to have two children, *Drawing on a Mother's Experience* was made immediately on her return to art-making in 1987. Since then she has continued investigating the relationship of art and lived experience in *Cook Dems, Kitchen Show* and most recently *How to Shop*. Her work is often read as touching and witty, comedic in the tradition of Joyce Grenfell, but while she invokes the tradition of the comedienne she does so in order to subvert it: her work is analytical and highly charged. Outside her performances she refers to her anger, to the need to make work which speaks of the splitting of women's domestic and professional lives, of the difficulties women artists face. Her dilemma as an artist who has achieved popularity with audiences and attention from the art world is one which is current in much writing about autobiography – how an artist or writer who works with herself as subject matter manages to confirm her legitimacy and coherence as a speaker while exploring the complexities and fragmentation of her experience. Over the last twenty years performance has offered a space for feminist artists to explore the self as subject; many of the issues raised by performance have analogies in autobiographical writings and much current theoretical writing about feminist autobiographies also illuminates performance art. This chapter explores some common issues.

Performance art entered the art world as a term in the early 1970s when it was used to describe the events which had been cropping up in galleries, theatres and elsewhere since the mid 1960s, works which might combine poetry, visual events, chance happenings, personal monologues and other occasions which the historian of performance art, Rose Lee Goldberg, has called 'live art by artists'.[2] Feminist artists Judy Chicago and Miriam Shapiro are widely credited with introducing performance as within the programme they ran at Cal Arts in Los Angeles around 1970 and thereafter in Europe and America, performance quickly became a significant medium of expression for women artists.

At the time, women in many spheres of public life were struggling to find alternative ways to express themselves. In an art world dominated by male artists, women still felt themselves to be represented as objects to be looked at by men. Women artists had long struggled to negotiate the relationship between woman as the object of artistic representation and the woman artist as agent and author of her own work. Many women artists began to feel that in the emerging medium of performance they were able to challenge and work with this complex relationship through bringing their own live presence into the work. Performance offered a form in which to speak in new voices and act in new and authentically female ways. Since then performance art has become an established form. Drawing from painting, sculpture and photography and incorporating narrative and movement it is perhaps the medium most alive to changing ideas about the nature of art, the process of art-making and the relationship of representation, lived experience and the construction of the self in art.

It has been important for artists to stress the distinctiveness of performance from theatre. This has been particularly true for feminists, who have emphasized its distance from theatre acting, illusion and the loss of agency associated with taking on a prescribed role. While this might imply a distinction between real life personas as authentic and unmediated and theatrical roles as constructed, the situation is of course more complex. When feminist artists in the 1970s began to make performance art they not only broke the frame of visual representation but addressed the history of woman as a speaking, acting subject in public, invoking a wide and complex history of women as public performers: actresses, prostitutes, preachers, litigants, comediennes, dancers. The history of the public behaviour and conduct of women is clearly linked to questions of performance. In the history of theatre, questions around the public appearance of a woman as herself, rather than in a role, are revealing. In nineteenth-century theatre, for instance, the impropriety of a woman appearing on stage outside a character role, as in equestrian spectacle or as a vaudeville dancer, was much discussed. In acting as herself a woman crossed those boundaries of conduct which always cast her in a prescribed role. A woman could take a role, but not of her own making.

What is important to performance art is that a woman artist's roles are of her own making. The relationship between her identity and agency as an artist and her persona as a performer is central to the work. As the artist and critic Catherine Elwes wrote in 1980, 'performance is the real life presence of the artist, she takes no roles but her own. She is author, subject, activator, director and designer. When a woman speaks within the performance tradition, she's understood to be conveying her own perceptions, her own fantasies, her own analyses'.[3]

When a performance artist stands up in front of an audience she is assumed to be performing as herself. By putting her own body and her own experience forward within a live space the artist becomes both object and subject within the work and is able to use the live space to articulate that relationship. This reference to the real life persona of the artist is central to performance art. For women artists it makes clear the political connection between private experience and public disclosure and so sets performance art clearly within the agenda of feminism. Catherine Elwes' succinct and careful definition of the role of the self in performance art emphasizes the artist's agency – she may take on a role, but it is her own, mediated by her own presence and actions. This is clear in the work of many feminist artists who play across the boundary of reality and fantasy, using impersonation and disguise, multi-voiced texts and cross-dressing to examine the construction of the self in performance. However, American critic Jeanie Forte takes the issue further when she says, 'the performance context is markedly different from that of the stage, in that the performers are not acting, or playing a character in any way removed from themselves; the mode provides women the opportunity for direct address to the audience, unmediated by another author's "scripting". Rather than masking the self, women's performance is born from self-revelation as a political move'.[4]

Comparing these two comments draws attention to the complexity of the politics of identity for women artists. Identifying self-revelation as a political move in women's performance art emphasizes the coherence of a speaking, performing subject and in fact leaves little room for more complex readings. It is a view which is strongly linked to the emergence of performance in the women's movement of the 1970s with its emphasis on women's collective identity and the direct relationship between personal experience and wider politics. While this collective strength gave feminist artists a platform from which to work it masked these dilemmas of self and subject. Looking at artists' practice it is clear that performance has allowed artists to bring the self into play and to investigate what the idea of 'self' might mean. What a performer may be doing instead is assuming identities. These, as Catherine Elwes points out, are still her own invention. In a work where the self is the subject, the relationship of the artist to herself as subject of the work can be a complex one, but it is a complexity which is often overlooked. I read Bobby Baker's work as angry and subversive, using fractured notions of self to work across the divide between self as artist and self as mother. The divisions are signalled in her text and implied, of course, in her title *Drawing on a Mother's Experience*. Bobby Baker's work, however, is often read through only one of the aspects of her self she plays with, the experienced mother. Like Charles Spencer of the *Daily Telegraph*, reviewers feel they are in safe hands, hearing only what mother tells them: 'Ms Baker's achievement is to make what sounds like self-indulgent tosh not only hypnotically watchable, but also strangely touching'.[5] For 'self-indulgent tosh' read 'performance art'. In the subtle irony of her mother persona her seriousness as an artist is overlooked, the 'tosh' of art made safe as it is folded back into the domestic. It is as if in her desire to investigate and even ironize her self as mother in her work she has to forgo a strong, coherent and engaging subject position for herself as artist. This is exactly the dilemma her work speaks about.

It is the relation between self as agent and self as subject which performance artists explore; a gap which can allow for the playful assuming of identities whilst still signalling the real life presence of the artist, enabling an artist to invoke many aspects of herself brought into play through her live presence.

Bobby Baker's housewife persona is both part of herself and a strategy in her self-representation. She speaks as 'I' throughout her performance but her 'I' is not a fixed identity, it is subject to change. Its unsettled nature, signalled in the multiple readings of words, objects and materials throughout the piece, allows the self to operate as a site where the meanings of identity can be contested. The idea that, through a self-revelatory act of performance, a feminist artist has the opportunity to unbind the fix of representation and find an authentic voice is a politically attractive one. It has a refreshing and liberating bite to it when seen in relation to theatrical illusion. Looked at more closely it feels too narrow to account for the complexities which artists use in practice. Feminist performance art now operates on ground which is more contested, more diverse and more complex than ever before. In the 1990s questions of identity and self, gender, ethnicity and representation have become both more uncertain and more urgent.

The notion of performance as directly accessing an artist's real self continues the project to bring the everyday directly into art – whether in person, object, word or action – which has been part of the agenda of avant-garde art in the twentieth century. Starting with dada and surrealism and eventually leading to both conceptual and performance art, avant-garde art practice has sought to close the gap between art and life. However, as artists are aware, there is always a frisson between the two, an edge or boundary over which the everyday is transformed, a space which art seeks to articulate. Art and life are both the same and different. They may be different in content but art is no less mediated than life. The space of the everyday is no less constructed than a performance and performance art is no less constructed than the theatre space. It may be in fact an even more complex space in which to strategize.

In a challenging essay on autobiographical strategies in the collection *Autobiography and Questions of Gender*, Sidonie Smith poses the following question to feminist writers, a question which is equally relevant to performance. She asks 'what kind of autobiographical strategies lead to what kinds of empowerments?'[6] Her question arises from the understanding that, as she says, 'all "I"s are not equal'. In using themselves as subjects, women artists negotiate a complex position in the world. The very strategies of shifting and multiple identity which a woman may want to use can lead to the undermining of her position as an artist. Smith looks for ways in which writers and artists can negotiate new positions which speak of hybridity, conflict and shifting identity whilst still maintaining a powerful and resonant voice. Like many feminist theorists she draws attention to Roland Barthes' autobiographical work. She sees the Barthean strategy of self-effacement as double-edged, affirming the legitimacy of his male identity exactly as it unravels it. Women's social position can never allow them recourse to such audacious deconstruction. Their place is too fragile, too contingent. Women's autobiographical strategies have to confirm them as legitimate subjects so as not to leave them in a position where 'autobiographical practice that promotes endless fragmentation and a reified multiplicity might be counterproductive'. Radical practice in art and writing has sought to address the colonization of woman as other, as object, as illegitimate speaker, by affirming an authentic voice as strong, urgent, genuine and coherent. It is this strategy which Jeanie Forte refers to and applauds. For Smith the strategy is an empty one, one which refers back to a now unusable strait-jacketing essentialism. She pinpoints a double bind which does not only apply to the position of women artists and writers but may be a condition of the politics of identity. Kwame Anthony Appiah in his recent book *In My Father's House: Africa in the Philosophy of Culture* pays attention to this dilemma in his thinking about race. He says that all politics call at some point for the notion of an authentic speaking self who can speak to and for a wider community, and yet this notion itself often essentializes categories in ways which mask the play of identities in lived experience: 'Every human identity is constructed, historical; every one has its share of false presuppositions. . . . Invented histories, invented biologies, invented cultural affinities come with every identity; each is a kind of role that has to be scripted, structured by conventions of narrative to which the world never quite conforms.'[7]

Both Kwame Anthony Appiah and Sidonie Smith call artists, writers and critics to attend to the way in which identities are shaped at a time of political and cultural change, change which may mean setting aside old categories and reframing experience in new ways. Sidonie Smith frames her essay itself as a call to action, a manifesto for autobiographical writing. Her call is for strategies which do not assume false collective identities, which understand hybridity, fragmentation and slippage, speak to the multiplicities of self, but are also alive to the political dilemmas of identity. She invokes Gloria Anzaldúa and Donna Haraway as writers who take on the simultaneous need to be in the world legitimately and yet refuse the traditions of legitimation which have excluded women and others. Above all, Smith argues for work which speaks to the future and exists under the sign of hope. Smith's very writing is performative – racy, rhetorical and questioning, moving register between the informality of the spoken word and high theory, including personal anecdote and acute readings of autobiographical writings. It shapes its desires in its own format. Performance art now needs to be re-read and responded to in the light of such current debate in ways which open out insights like Jeanie Forte's and Catherine Elwes' and see them as historically specific and contingent on their own political context.

Throughout the 1980s performance diversified in relation to this question of the use of the self as subject and its diversity exemplifies some of the critical positions about which I have been speaking. One aspect of this diversity is shown in what Philip Auslander calls the 'rapprochement with entertainment'.[8] In a neat inversion of the current public obsession with self-revelation in the media, artists use performance monologue to tell their own counter-stories, invoking oral traditions of rhetoric, story-telling and stand-up comedy in performances which give testimony to the performer's life experience and, more widely, to the experiences of culturally silenced communities. The genre has been of great significance in the performance of the politics of identity, especially in America where self-revelatory narrative performance is associated especially with AIDS and gay and lesbian activist politics. The genre has become known as auto-performance and a highly specific relationship between performer and perform-ance persona is implied, which when transgressed can be politically explosive. American performance artist Holly Hughes, whose monologues constantly cross the line between lies and life, fantasy and truth, engaged in a long-running argument in the pages of performance journal *TDR* (*The Drama Review*) after being accused of not signalling her identity position clearly in her performances and therefore, while she is a lesbian, not being lesbian enough. Auto-performance brings performance art closer to theatrical monologue, but in content its essence is always assumed to be the real life story of the artist. In a society almost obsessed with self-revelation this makes for interesting alliances and strange readings.

Performance art's shift towards entertainment forms is only one aspect of its recent diversity. While auto-performance stresses self as narrative, other artists have moved away from narrative altogether, returning to the critique of visual representation which gave impetus to so much feminist performance art in the early 1970s and using video, film and photography instead of the live space. While many feminist artists continue to perform and to use personal material as catalyst, their vocabulary is almost entirely non-narrative, seeing narrative and auto-performance as having been coopted by entertainment values. While this may seem negative, even pessimistic, it simply exemplifies the fluidity of a form which always constellates around complex questions of the self and the representation of the self in art.

In all performance art the artist is always present as agent but to allow for a range of readings the subjectivity of the artist must always be left open to question, fluid, ambiguous and unsettled. It is this problem which a mature artist like Bobby Baker negotiates. However, it is also true that in its unsettledness the work takes the risk of being read as less powerful in its politics and analysis. *Drawing on a Mother's Experience* was made and presented at a point of crisis, the point at which the artist re-entered the art world as maker of art having left it to become experienced in another art – being a mother. The work enacts the equivalence of acts of composition – transforming raw materials, mixing food and mixing paint. It creates patterns which are traces of domestic events in the same way that an action painting is composed of the traces it leaves as a record of the artist's process. What she asks us to consider is the value structure inherent in the reading of those acts of composition.

In fact Bobby Baker exemplifies Sidonie Smith's manifesto and assumes identities and slipping between them as her work unfolds in time. She positions herself in constant movement through the piece, wiping away marks like an experienced mother, meditating on colour and texture and questioning the nature of mark-making as an artist. At once hesitant and authoritative, she is both scatter-brained and acutely focused; daubing, pressing, flinging and dancing in her excited parody of the techniques and vocabularies of painting. Bobby Baker enacts the improvisatory and process-based nature of art and life and in doing so she brings into being a self in the continual process of making and unmaking. Her self exists through her actions, her strategies and her composing. Art and life cross over and illuminate one another because the strategies of each are similar and equivalent and demand similar skills. Both address, disrupt and restore order and sense in the world. We build identities through improvising in the face of necessity, through actions and narratives. This does not negate our humanity or make our politics less authentic but may in fact allow us a space for negotiation which we have never before recognized.

In her recent book *Composing a Life* the social anthropologist Mary Catherine Bateson calls for cultural change in a way which mirrors Sidonie Smith's autobiographical manifesto. She cites human success as the ability to adapt to change and asks that we begin to recognize the equivalence between the creative process involved in art and science and the creativity involved in what she calls 'interrupted and conflicted lives'. She asks, 'at what point does desperate improvisation become significant achievement?', saying that discontinuity is the coming challenge of our era, an age in which we are all increasingly 'strangers and sojourners'.[9] The ability to adapt, to assume identities in the face of necessities, to improvise along recurrent themes is, in her view, the strategy of the future. It is a strategy entirely consistent with Bobby Baker's negotiated selves, Sidonie Smith's manifesto and the project of creating a culture of 'affinity politics' which recognizes, with Kwame Anthony Appiah, that all identities are constructed and contingent.

These ideas, articulated as they are in contemporary art and critical practices, require that we respond to them not simply with our intellects but with all the capacities we have to hand, voice and body. At the end of her article Sidonie Smith observes that the autobiographical strategies which question, play with and refuse unitary identities 'help us to hope by insisting on the possibilities of self-conscious breakages in the old repetitions'.[10] The expression could apply equally to the performance strategies of artists like Bobby Baker, recognizing in the affinities and discontinuities between art and life, self and self, that 'I', 'we', 'you' and 'she' may be fluid, ambiguous or obscure but in their unsettled nature they offer new ways in which to remake art and life.

Notes

1 Mary Catherine Bateson (1990) *Composing a Life*, New York: Penguin.
2 Rose Lee Goldberg (1988) *Performance Art: From Futurism to the Present*, revised edition, New York: Abrams.

3 Catherine Elwes (1980) 'Floating Femininity', in Catherine Elwes and Rose Garrard (Eds) *About Time*, London: ICA.

4 Jeanie Forte (1990) 'Women's Performance Art: Feminism and Postmodernism', in Sue-Ellen Case (Ed.) *Performing Feminisms: Feminist Critical Theory and Theatre*, Baltimore and London: The Johns Hopkins University Press.

5 Charles Spencer *Daily Telegraph*.

6 Sidonie Smith (1991) 'The Autobiographical Manifesto: Identities, Temporalities, Politics', in Shirley Neuman (Ed.) *Autobiography and Questions of Gender*, New York: Frank Cass.

7 Kwame Anthony Appiah (1992) *In My Father's House: Africa in the Philosophy of Culture*, Oxford: Oxford University Press.

8 Philip Auslander (1989) 'Going with the Flow: Performance Art and Mass Culture', *The Drama Review* (*TDR*), vol. 33, no. 2, pp. 119–36.

9 Bateson 1990.

10 Smith 1991.

Chapter 12

There are stories and Stories: An Autobiography Workshop

Gillie Bolton and Morag Styles

About a dozen of us, I think. We began by briefly introducing ourselves, a process so fascinating because of the variety of people and of motivation in attending, that my head was full of it – of them – when the first workshop task was set immediately after these introductions. 'Write whatever comes into your head. Nobody will read it,' said Gillie.

'Write whatever comes into your head.' The experience of the Japanese participant is in my head. Inescapable, the thought of what he said. One cancerous eye removed, waiting for the other to follow; autobiography for him means constantly returning to the one August day is Hiroshima.[1] The thought of him more inescapable than the presence of Barbara Castle in our group and the tales of her life she told earlier in the morning. More inescapable than the nature of the others in the group. I want to read the thoughts in their heads of whatever it is they write them to be.

Only one of these people is known to me. It's comfortable to have a familiar face, a friendly one, among strangers. Strangers are over-whelming. The Japanese man told us what he's thinking about, more overwhelming than strangers. Nice people here. One talks to and writes about elderly teachers. A Tory (a Tory? amongst us?) who needed to write autobiographically a belated apology to her life-long socialist father. One writes fiction which – did she say? – is a kind of avoidance of autobiographying. If they can be so divided. That's a nice talking point. One woman bewailing the lack of practising-teacher voices, autobiographical testimony from the classroom. Pity I'm not going to show her the books I've written.

Who else? Academics/administrators tired of the strictures of formal registers who never get involved in autobiography and want to know. A poet who wonders about autobiography; she never writes prose, she says. Can that be? One is concerned with the autobiography-ing of a whole range of people – 'doctors, the unemployed, all sorts'. I'd love to know more. The gold inside these people won't have time to emerge. Who's to know who's compatible ... Did he say he has had his fiftieth birthday, the man with almost no eyes? 'Stop writing.'

(Betty Rosen)

Betty Rosen's account is written as the first exercise of our autobiography writing workshop. We [Morag and Gillie] have only met once before, and are now running our first joint venture. It seemed clear to both of us that what an autobiography conference needed was a session in which people wrote about their own lives rather than just talked about it. Our planning was brief, since we were so in tune with each others' attitudes and ways of working.

We both believe strongly in the power of the process of expressive or reflective writing to illuminate, to clarify, to heal, to remind us of what we know but have forgotten, what we feel but haven't faced. Writing is different from talking which is gone on the air; it stays and can be worked on, mined for even more, and need never be shared. The very process of writing, because of its privacy and concreteness, forces understandings. Yet everyone can do it. And it is so gentle, despite the fears, hesitations and uncertainties that often accompany it.

Now, faced with ten participants – high-powered academics, a famous story-teller, creative artists, a distinguished politician, Gillie and Morag exchange glances: 'Can we trust each other to get this right?' No time to worry – the adrenalin keeps us going.

We start immediately: time is short, and anyway we are here to write together and share that writing. Also, this kind of writing is often best taken by surprise: the memory and imagination ambushed. So Gillie suggests we write whatever comes into our heads for six minutes. The pen isn't to stop and no-one is to worry about whether they're writing rubbish, nonsense, or scandal – today they can't write the wrong thing. Grammar and spelling don't matter; they never do in first draft anyway. This scribble is not for sharing; it is to start the pen moving over that frighteningly blank sheet of paper, capture some fleeting ideas, and possibly lay on one side some nagging but inappropriate worries.

(Betty Rosen)

Memory and imagination ambushed! How right and how well put. There is no time for much conscious thought, to worry about inadequacies or drop into those well-known blocks to creativity and openness. The group leader says 'write' and that's what we do – struggling, doubtful, uncertain, no doubt, but scribbling away together. Betty Rosen's piece was part of the exercise. And so was this:

> This exercise is no good for me.... Writing for me is the desire to record
> an experience I feel is important – even if it's about a quite small or
> humble incident. Or I get the desire to analyse events and ideas and it
> helps if I write them down.
>
> I am too old, too spoiled to write to order when there is nothing I
> want to write about. The best writing discipline I know is to keep a diary.
> At the end of a long day when all you want to do is to go to bed you
> have to sit down and get on paper the main events of the day. It
> concentrates the style wonderfully.
>
> (Barbara Castle)

So was this:

> 6 minutes of enforced writing to get through. And with nothing to say
> about this. What are the others writing about? About this exercise?
> About their breakfast? About last night's episode of 'Beavis and
> Butthead'? About the fifth dimension? More likely about their mother
> or some much-missed face from their youth. But not Barbara Castle
> over there in the corner. There's no honey in her pen. More like brown
> ale spiked with Pimms....
>
> How much time is left? As a student taking exams I struggled
> against the clock. Now I am still struggling, but in the opposite
> direction.
>
> (Edward Fullbrook)

Some grapple combatively with the task, but write vigorously in the very act of
resisting the demands that have been made. For others, it is as if they had been
waiting all their lives for someone to give them permission to write their own
stories.

> Vera and Eva were sisters and sometimes I think their name was
> Hopkins, and they lived a life out in the fens where there is always the
> smell of the sea mixed with the earth, where you can lie down and look
> at the sky and imagine yourself under a green sea. Maybe you drowned,
> maybe this is paradise, maybe you are an angel now. Dogs bark, geese
> fly. Is it the end of summer or the beginning? I see themselves dipping
> and rising over a water butt, laughing. They are washing their hair in
> rain water, dark girls, Jewish perhaps. Their father was a seaman from
> a family of silk weavers.
>
> This picture comforts me. It brings strands together. It accounts for
> loss, terrible irredeemable loss and the loss is counted in the memory of

cool rain water in a butt, of its dark green look when Vera put her face down to it. She is so near to me I can imagine her skin, smell her neck, feel her hair, touch her as I touched her when I was a child. She is my beautiful mother and this picture is a way of bringing together images and ideas from the past and present, my experience, my imagination of her and Eva, two lost girls, lost beneath the sea of time, drowned girls, forever lost to me, their hair trailing under cool green seas.

(Claire MacDonald)

Writing is a staged process. Bits, caught on the wing like this, might either become a beginning which grows and accretes like a snowball, or they can offer vital extra material for an on-going project. Experimenting with ideas and form in writing can give all sorts of insights and leads; but any writer has to be willing to make good use of the waste paper basket! Finished form, such as the sonnet or completed academic article for a referred journal, is usually the final stage. Form is useful for communicating: containing the writer and enticing the reader.

Morag plans to start the autobiographical call rolling by telling a story from her teenage years of a time when she behaved badly. Superficially, it is quite funny and lighthearted, but it carries a charge. Barbara Castle's opening lecture has moved her in another direction. It reminds her of her grandmother, a gutsy Labour Party activist (who always called Barbara 'that fine young lassie') who lived a hard life in working-class Dundee. She wonders whether to tell a story about her. This would deviate from our agreed schedule. Morag suspects Gillie would not mind, but sticks with her original idea anyway. She invites the group to tell each other about a time when they told a lie, behaved shabbily or got into some kind of trouble.

Then Morag told her story about the little man she ditched. Now we have to tell something in similar vein to each other, in pairs. Wait a bit. Someone's questioning the topic – she wants to know why we can't write about something positive, something jolly. Morag looks somewhat pink and a bit startled. . . .

What was significant (as Morag knows full well!) about such an exercise is that what begins as a little spoken anecdote can become a story about what deeply matters when it is explored in autobiographical authorship. Thanks to the exercise, for the first time I felt a real desire to write autobiographically about my own mother. . . .

(Betty Rosen)

Now we are going to write these anecdotes or some aspect of them. Gillie suggests we still write loosely, allowing the story to flow for its own sake. But this time we will be asking if people would like to share all, or part, of the writing afterwards. No-one needs encouragement; pens are poised. Silence for twenty minutes or so, except for a slight scratching, in-drawn breath, shuffle of paper.

Daddy, you'd hardly know me – or I was a teenage Tory
It was that local election when you canvassed one side of the street and
I did the other. Opposite sides. Sides opposite. Or do I imagine that's
what happened?

How did you live alongside that smug little Conservative? Why
were we so different? Will you have me back, daddy, and I can explain,
tell you I'm sorry?
   – And I went to Greenham
   – joined the Labour Party
. . .

And you never asked me what wrought the change, what saved me
from the blue rinse brigade and Tory tea parties. Well, you did. The boy
in the over-sized trousers, the ardent young anti-fascist, the serious
young teacher, the terrifying father at the gate – the man who kept his
socialist faith, never doubting, I hope, that one day his 'pelican
daughter' would be canvassing on the same side of the road. I'm with
you daddy.

(Bobby Wells)

I have been writing letters to my mother for these two weeks, on account
of her ill condition. I am talking and relate my own true feelings but
sometimes I feel it is difficult to write frankly since my end of writing
is to encourage my mother. Anyway writing is very treacherous. Don't
you think so?

Still we read novels, biographies and letters to sniff and find the
truth, though it might be just what we think true, in them. And yet we
want to tell our own stories to others. I know I am now following a circle
and only going round and round, but there is no other way for me now
except this.

Perhaps to throw away these things the best way is to start to write
something about me.

(Kensuke Ueki)

We rest aching wrists and Gillie asks us to read silently through everything we've
written. Sometimes writing created at this speed does seem to flow directly from
the guts to the page, and the re-reading can take the writer by surprise.
Sometimes there are unexpected connections between different parts, particularly the six-minute scribble and the main body of text. (Claire's was a
continuation of her earlier piece about her mother.) We all read through with
attention, marking bits, perhaps adding notes in the margin, selecting that which
is shareable.

The reading out is now about to begin. This is a crucial part of the session. Morag invites those who wish to read their own work to do so, but suggests that some might like to put their writing in the middle of the table. Those who are willing to read someone else's writing aloud should select a script whose handwriting they can manage. Ideally everyone needs time to digest this new piece of writing before reading it aloud, but time is running on apace. The workshop is supposed to last just over an hour and we have already requested an extra fifteen minutes, to which the group has agreed. It is clear to us both that we have to give everyone a chance to read and that we will go over time. A dilemma. We've been a bit ambitious, but we are also surprised to have so many willing and prolific writers.

How to respect and allow time for each participant's contribution, while keeping an eye on the clock. The quality of the writing is almost overwhelming in its variety, authenticity and flair. People are visibly moved; readers take infinite pains to present the writer's work as well as they can; the stories of these lives are compelling and told with such eloquence.

'What I take for granted might be of interest to others', was the comment of one participant. Our lives may seem dull and ordinary to ourselves, but fascinating in the telling, to others.

It's a Sunday morning and the parlour is filled with my dad's cronies, who come round every Sunday morning for a haircut, and the endless political battles rage. In the adjacent scullery, my mother, who works long hours all week, is catching up with the weekly wash, a large boiler on the gas-stove, and at the same time, trying to start the preparations for the Sunday lunch. We live in an old North London three storied house, filled with relatives, grandparents on the first floor and a great-aunt and her two sons on the top.

There is no bathroom, there is a bath with an old geyser in my grandmother's kitchen on the first floor, covered with a piece of wood so that it doubles up as a working space. When I get up, I have to come down by the parlour, through the men's discussion to make my way to the scullery to wash, bombarded by rude comments.

On one particular morning I was washing myself in the scullery. My father was shaving Mr Belkoff, a rabid Zionist, with an open razor and my dad, violently anti-Zionist, was telling him not to be so bloody mad, when my mother took some boiling clothing out of the boiler and accidentally splashed my bare shoulder with the scalding water. I remember the searing pain to this day and the panic that ensued whilst the burn was treated. I remember the anger I felt about the lack of privacy, the lack of a bathroom, the leaking roof, the bitterly cold front room where I had to practise the piano, and the large number of people all living in the house. All these things welled up inside me as I felt the scalding water rip across my shoulders.

(Sheila Miles)

Like Pat, I passed the Scholarship, that dread divider of eleven-plus society. I felt very proud of myself. I liked my new gym slip, the shiny striped tie, my moigashell sax-blue blouse and the matching sash (ah, the clean cloth smell and crisp weave of it, the strokable fresh fringes!) round my middle. A cut above. Without a doubt.

Something occurred at the tea-table one day. Perhaps it had to do with my having to shed my precious uniform before dipping into the cut-glass dishlet for the home-made plum jam. I can't remember precisely what my mother jokingly said but it goaded me into a riposte that silenced everyone, even my father, and lives with me still. I remember only that silence, and my own preceding words: 'What would you know about it? You never even went to a grammar school'.

No. Her father was a lamplighter. Her mother was an Irish immigrant servant girl when they met. My mother had seven brothers and two sisters. They were all merry and musical. My mother could play anything on the piano by ear, with a hundred harmonies, flourishes, arpeggios – anything, as long as she knew the tune or someone could sing it once so she picked it up. . . .

She was more loving than anyone I have ever known.

(Betty Rosen)

Gillie and Morag confide afterwards that good writing always comes from our workshops and we agree that we use no special tricks or techniques to facilitate it. Although our methods are very similar, and extremely simple, we found one difference. Morag likes to start the writing with a period of talking. She feels it is important to gentle people in. Gillie, conversely, has always felt that talking detracts the energy from the writing, that people should be thrown straight into doing it. Opposite attitudes – seemingly. Before this collaborative venture, the group leaders believed that the success they both enjoyed with writing workshops was to do with their particular approaches to groups and writing. But here they were combining two apparently opposing strategies and getting some of the best writing either had ever encountered.

Hitherto, Gillie had been concerned that Morag's spoken story would influence the group's expectations as to the form and content of their own pieces. In the event, it was enabling for some writers. Morag saw that Gillie's six-minute blast technique was extremely effective. The Autobiography Conference gave Gillie and Morag a chance to try out their first experience of co-facilitation, to be open and learn from each other. It was daunting to be faced with such a high-powered group, trying out new approaches and working together. A lot of trust and intuition was involved. But we shared a lot in common. Both of us felt that an opportunity for autobiographical writing was an essential part of such a conference. And we agreed that what matters most is the confidence of the facilitator(s), their belief in people and their belief in writing. So why does this process work, and why was the writing particularly strong that day?

(1) We both profoundly believe that writing is important, and that it is not difficult to do. We recognize fear of writing; we have to deal with defensiveness in every workshop. And, of course, we know that even for the most experienced writers, blocks are common and writing can be painful. Creating a few minutes of autobiographical writing is nevertheless reasonably easy for most people in a supportive environment. A past is one thing we all have in common.

(2) We also believe everyone has a valuable story to tell about their own lives, and that if they can find their own voices, they can write it in a way that will interest others.

(3) We know from experience that the group's shared endeavours will help most people to write and that most will be generous and positive about each other's work. The group will generally silence the odd carping voice.

(4) If the group leaders join in as equal participants, sharing the same deadlines and difficulties, a constructive and purposeful community of writers can be quickly bonded together.

(5) Telling everyone they can't write the wrong thing is wonderfully releasing.

(6) Promising that those who do not wish to read out their writing will not be asked to do so is essential. Donald Graves once said that to be a writer you must be prepared to strip nude in public and we know what he meant. The privacy of writers must be respected and the terrors that can be associated with sharing writing publicly must be acknowledged. The businesslike atmosphere of a writing workshop and the fact that 'everybody is doing it' can, on the other hand, be liberating.

Strange to think how this got underway. How stories beget each other. And there's the dilemma of where precisely to start when in personal experience there are no starts, only a continuity of layering. This is such a little thing; not funny, not outrageous. Certainly not a cancerous cloud, mushrooming for fifty years ... there are stories and Stories. . . .

(Betty Rosen)

Notes

We are deeply indebted to all the participants of the workshop and particularly to those who felt able to contribute their writing. We know it wasn't easy for most of them to do so and we are grateful for their generosity. We would like to offer special thanks to Betty

Rosen for her gift of a personal narrative about the workshop which she wrote and sent to us shortly after the conference.

1   This is a factual error. Kensuke Ueki lost the sight of his left eye in a blast of broken glass at the time of the Hiroshima bomb and his right eye suffers from problems unrelated to cancer or the bomb. We wanted to put the record straight and also to express our gratitude to Professor Ueki whose contribution to the workshop moved us all.

Chapter 13

Conclusion: Autobiography and the Politics of 'The Personal'

Julia Swindells

Autobiography, as many of the accounts in this book have shown, invariably has a political dimension to it. Even the Western European literary tradition has been constructed out of a sense that the autobiographer's voice is often one which is oppositional, heretical or radical in some way.[1] Certainly, discussions of class history have drawn on autobiography for its capacity to yield particularly resonant discussions of class-consciousness and debates about the representation of the experience of oppression.[2] Commentators have drawn attention to what amounts to a tradition of working-class men's autobiographical writing in Britain, emerging from the 1840s.[3] There has also been some attempt, though not over much, to build working-class women into the account of autobiography and class history.[4]

Much of this work has succeeded in redressing the balance in terms of introducing readers to previously unknown or unrecognized autobiographers. Simone de Beauvoir is one example of a woman who has only recently received the critical acclaim handed out to sundry men, in the name of the Western European literary tradition. It is possible to see her *Memoirs of a Dutiful Daughter* and her other autobiographical volumes as the works of a writer and thinker who constitutes, belatedly recognized, a key individual of that tradition, though somewhat more radical than most.[5] (I shall return to questions relating to the influence of that first volume of her memoirs.)

The more important political move, though, is one which moves beyond the life-story of the key individual, and focuses the use of autobiography as part of a political strategy to produce change. Notable in Britain from the earlier part of the century is the publication of *Life as We Have Known It*, by Co-operative working women, one of the earliest texts to draw attention, explicitly, to the relationship between autobiographical statement, political movement and the process of collection of testimonies.[6] That volume could be said to be pioneering in relation to a process which subsequently developed into a widespread commitment within the women's movement, commonly understood in terms of the retrieval of absent or silent women's 'voices'.

This chapter will focus largely on the British women's movement, giving attention to some recent examples of volumes which set out to solicit autobiographical testimony and to present a collection which makes a political statement. I take as my starting point the publication, in the 1970s, of *Dutiful Daughters*, edited by Jean McCrindle and Sheila Rowbotham.[7] *Dutiful Daughters* took up the challenge of Simone de Beauvoir's title, transforming it into a statement about collective as well as individual experience. *Memoirs of a Dutiful Daughter* had charted the process of rebellion in one life, that of the middle-class daughter who resists the familial and social definitions attached to those labels in order to pursue an education, career and relationships on her own terms. *Dutiful Daughters* implies that the constraints against which de Beauvoir rebelled are by no means unique to one woman, and that the type of account she had produced – of the familial and social pressures exerted in the context of the one life, and that a relatively privileged one – could be applied even more graphically to working-class women's lives. Jean McCrindle and Sheila Rowbotham, as editors of the collection, put simply the relationship between their own project and that signalled by de Beauvoir's 'dutiful daughter' title:

> The Women's Movement has shown that shared individual experience is an important part of the social discovery of a common condition. . . . Once we can perceive what is common to women, change and transformation become possible and the cycle of guilt and personal recrimination can be broken.[8]

For McCrindle and Rowbotham, in soliciting and documenting the oral testimonies of working-class women, the 'dutiful daughter' idea is a way of registering a shared experience and common condition of family duty and social constraint. This then provides them with the basis for a political strategy, in which the writing and reading of autobiography becomes part of the process of consciousness-raising, whereby the *perception* of what constitutes a common condition begins to form a precondition for social and political change. The role of editors as scribes and interpreters inevitably raises questions (how far have accounts been shaped to fit the model, and so on?), but it is possible to see the force of this basic idea in individual testimonies, such as that of Linda Peffer:

> I've had the kids . . . and when I had them it was like a nightmare, really. I suddenly realized what it was like to be married and have two kids, you know. Somebody said: 'Motherhood is the best-kept secret in the world'. They're right, because no one really owns up to what it's like. All this rubbish that's written about it. . . . You see, you're not really all keyed up with all these instincts. You don't automatically know what to

do when the baby cries. It's all got to be found out, and I thought, oh Christ, what's wrong with me? ... The housework was hopeless. I suddenly realized – it really dawned on me then – that I really hate housework. Instead of normally sorting it out and thinking, well, there's nothing wrong with me, but there's something wrong with the situation I'm in, I turned it round the other way, which was the only way I could do. I mean all the women I met at the clinics and that were saying, ooh, how lovely and how fulfilled they felt, and I just pretended. I'm much braver, I'm sure, since, because I've met people, you know, who are different. I started voicing opinions. It's surprising after you've said it a couple of times how many women say, ooh yes, you know, really – and they start opening up, and you find that a hell of a lot of women have felt exactly the same as you, only they've just been so scared to say it, you know.[9]

It is Linda Peffer's perception that she can 'turn it round', that there was something wrong with the situation rather than herself, which allows her to break away from guilt and personal recrimination, to begin to voice her opinions, and discover a shared experience and common condition of motherhood and marriage, in which, 'a hell of a lot of women' feel exactly the same as each other. It was this type of context that gave birth to the maxim, 'the personal is political'. The energy behind that maxim lay in the discovery that issues and experiences which *felt* uniquely personal, and therefore felt like matters of personal responsibility and therefore of personal adequacy or inadequacy, were indeed very common experiences, around which there were ideological investments in maintaining certain fictions and mythologies (mostly sustaining a notion of personal liability). Daughterhood was an example, and motherhood, the source of so much representation and idealization in fiction and poetry, even more obviously so. As soon as the recognition of shared experience was made, the possibility of freedom from guilt, and, most importantly, of liberation through social and political change, became available. As Linda Peffer puts it, the discovery was that the *situation* might be wrong rather than the person.

McCrindle and Rowbotham register, in a slightly disturbing apologia, that one of the ironies surrounding women being the subjects of so many powerful fictions and mythologies of motherhood and family duty, was that women's own record of their own lives was likely to see their experiences dismissed as trivial. Literary and cultural modes and forces had succeeded in constituting women's own testimonies, first-person accounts of experience, as inherently less valuable than the fictional or poetic version.

We wanted to show through the interviews that if the experience of most women is regarded as unworthy of recording it is not because it is in itself uninteresting, meaningless or trivial, but because of the criteria which are normally brought to bear when the decision to record is taken.[10]

A number of the autobiographical collections published since *Dutiful Daughters* have tended to make use of these key ideas about women arriving at a sense of shared experience and common condition, from out of a position of isolation, difference and alienation. The risk though, was always that the definition of 'the personal' would slip away from the experience of oppression, and back in the direction of the individualized account of relative privilege. In other words, as critics of mainstream white, middle-class feminism were about to point out, the registering of a supposedly common condition could be exclusive in its turn, if the basis for that common condition was a shared experience of anything approaching privilege rather than oppression.[11] *Truth, Dare or Promise*, published in the mid-1980s, was, in principle, as committed as *Dutiful Daughters* had been, to a feminist politics.[12] The contributors are described as 'twelve women who grew into feminism in the 1970s', whose political credentials extend beyond feminism to other commitments, 'to socialism, anti-racism, or to other recognitions of ways in which the world needs to be changed'.[13] But the cracks had begun to show, for, whatever their considerable credentials as activists, what the contributors do not apparently share is an experience of the condition of oppression. Beguiling though these accounts of 'girls growing up in the fifties' are, the book cannot really live up to its claim to be 'as much about the future as it is about the past', for the simple reason that, however impoverished and deprived the childhoods of the contributors to the collection may have been, their experience in the present is characterized more by relative fame in the public sphere, albeit as feminist activists, than by powerlessness and exploitation in the private sphere.

There is also a sense in which radicalism itself is taken as a given in the project. These people are children of the post-war decade and of the 1960s, of 'the year 1945 and its immediate aftermath, [which] ignited that fever of optimism which was to accompany a large portion of our generation all through childhood' and of 'the high point in the "sixties", the time universally regarded as our true historical moment'.[14] These historical moments, whatever their limitations, 'form the momentum of our generation', and it is as if to say that this is a radical generation by virtue of its historical placing. Part of the project of 'being as much about the future' as the past entails observations about the 1980s and the book's contemporary political culture. The Welfare State is described as 'increasingly impoverished', but in what appears as something of a surprising contradiction of that bleak and all too prophetic comment on the reduction of state services, women today supposedly 'have the possibility of being more fulfilled as mothers'.[15] It is hard to imagine quite how this can be the case on 1980s levels of Child Benefit, low pay and women's poverty.

The tension is around the relationship between political radicalism in the past and in the present. The accounts of 1950s and 1960s childhoods largely avoid nostalgia, and perhaps do constitute a unity, or collective experience, out of radical perspectives on childhood, but the attempt to bring that radicalism to bear on the 1980s and the future proves more elusive. (And is there perhaps just a slight suggestion that these individuals, the contributors, have liberated themselves and solved the problem, and so it no longer exists?)

Three years after the publication of *Truth, Dare or Promise*, Virago published *Very Heaven: Looking Back at the 1960s*, edited by Sara Maitland.[16] This collection runs some of the same risks as *Truth, Dare or Promise*, in that it is set up in terms of nostalgia for a golden age of political action and liberation. The editor, Sara Maitland, shows her consciousness of the danger from the beginning:

> As the times get harder and it seems increasingly difficult even to manage decent strategies of resistance, let alone any truly creative political intervention against Thatcherism and the social injustices which are daily escalating, it seems to me more and more that I, at least, have to understand the sixties better, explore that terrain more carefully for signs both of hope and of self-criticism. That is why I wanted to edit this book ... I wanted to edit it, rather than write it, because one of the most important things of the time was the liberating of individual voices into defining collective experience.[17]

Sara Maitland holds out for collective experience as distinct from the individual voice (against publishers wanting her testimony as that of a key individual in the Western European literary tradition?), in a move reminiscent of Jean McCrindle's and Sheila Rowbotham's commitment in *Dutiful Daughters*. Sara Maitland acknowledges the difficulties of sustaining that move 'as the times get harder'. Also, as with *Truth, Dare or Promise*, the momentum is behind the significance of history, and nostalgia for the political activism of the past. At the same time, Sara Maitland finds herself keeping a certain scepticism in play. She goes on to describe in her introduction to the collection that most of the contributors tend to believe that the 'real' 1960s were happening somewhere else. Also, she observes that they suffer from amnesia in attempting to recall precise events, in a way that is not characteristic of a response to other decades, and which may or may not be related to an apparent embarrassment experienced by many women in recalling their own 'moral seriousness' in the 1960s. Another problem, and a salutary defence against any nostalgic idea of women's power and visibility in the 1960s, is what she now sees as the 'amazing' absence of women from so many public events of that time.

Perhaps what is most significant about *Very Heaven* for this account is a phenomenon about which Sara Maitland makes a passing observation. Many of the contributors had difficulty in believing that they had significance as individuals in the history she is attempting to persuade them to recall. She attributes this to their having 'absorbed the message of collectivity' and 'learned that there was no such thing as individual leadership, or authority'. It is hoped that Sara Maitland is right in this analysis. An alternative, bleaker interpretation is that, like some of the 'diffident' women whose accounts McCrindle and Rowbotham solicited for *Dutiful Daughters*, many women still have difficulty crediting their own experience as significant, rather than as 'uninteresting, meaningless or trivial'. One of the reasons why it is difficult to decide between the two interpretations is that, as Sara Maitland notes, the experiences that are being recalled and described are in some senses 'pre-feminist', and therefore did not necessarily carry with them, at the time, an explicit feminist commitment to collectivity. Sara Maitland inflects the argument in relation to the future as well as the past:

> Many, although not all, of the contributors here would identify themselves now as feminists; practically none of them do so remembering their younger selves. But since there are now women around claiming to be 'post feminist' I have no qualms whatever in identifying these writers' lives as 'pre-feminist' in an important way.[18]

The challenge to post-feminism is welcome, but the comment also highlights a problem shared with *Truth, Dare or Promise*, that contributors have been selected *for their identification as feminists*, which is not necessarily coterminous with having experienced a common condition of oppression. Also, this is a particular version of feminism, centring upon an identity constructed, as Sara Maitland acknowledges, out of a particular relationship of the present to the past. That this identity, in the sense of a personal history which 'progresses' from pre-feminist to feminist alongside a visible political movement (that is, 'second wave' feminism), is not available in the same form to the younger generation, to the daughters of the 1980s, is treated with humour and tolerance (and some measure of guilt?) by Maitland.

> My daughter and her friends, all born in the early seventies, laugh at the sixties: their laughter was the starting point of this book. I responded to it by an earnest and intense desire to explain. But in fairness I felt that I had to give them a space to express that ridicule.[19]

The daughter and her friend, Gaynor Griffiths and Mildred Lee, do indeed make use of this opportunity to express ridicule: 'The sixties were a mess. . . . Mocking one's parents about their past – teenagers' favourite pastime. Well, if you were an upwardly mobile trendy would you like to admit the hippies we described above were your parents . . .?' All good fun, but in another recent autobiographical collection, *Surviving the Blues*, the editor, Joan Scanlon, makes a more serious point out of the relationship between the 'daughters' of the 1980s and the political past.[20] Sara Maitland had cast some doubt over the 'very heaven' of the 1960s. Joan Scanlon challenges that idea directly:

> It is understandable that for some of those who have lived through the Britain of the sixties and seventies there is a return to that history for models of political activism. And it is no wonder that, at a superficial level, the Women's Liberation Movement of the post-'68 decade looks to those women who were involved in it as if it offered possibilities for dramatic and rapid change which no longer seems available. Much of the nostalgia, however, is for a fiction which misrepresents the historical and international complexity of that movement as much as it denies possibilities for political activism in the present.[21]

Surviving the Blues concentrates on the contemporary political culture of the 1980s, without seeking to ratify collective experience in terms of any kind of spurious unity provided by history, nostalgia or the notoriety of contributors. The women contributing to the book have grown up in the 1980s, and they look at the women's movement in terms of 'the present reality of Thatcher's Britain', coming to feminism 'with a particular commitment to change, one unclouded by false hopefulness and unrealistic expectations'. Problems with feminism are not smoothed away, as is trenchantly articulated in Noral Al-Ani's description of working as a cleaner in a women's resource centre.[22] Feminism does not provide the raison d'être of the collection, either in terms of success stories – from pre-feminist to feminist – or as an unproblematic source of common identity characterizing all contributors. Rather, it is a terrain of engagement, which is also an engagement with the types of account included in *Truth, Dare or Promise* and *Very Heaven*. Many of the autobiographers capture the tensions in their testimonies. Louise Donald writes:

> I was exposed for the first time in my life to the word 'feminist', and had the chance to meet a few of them. Describing those women as 'them' makes them sound as though they were completely unlike myself. I did feel we had nothing in common, that their histories somehow made it possible for them to be feminists, but that mine couldn't accommodate the theory or the practice. Feminism seemed a student preoccupation, and could never be adapted to life in Wishaw.[23]

It is the personal histories of the feminists she meets, perhaps lived through the 'fever of optimism' of the post-war decade or 'the high point of the sixties' rather than Thatcher's Britain and its contempt for women, which appear to give them their political credentials. Mary Smeeth, in 'Can You Hear Me at the Front?', also articulates this tension over history, reaching a telling conclusion:

> Feminism in the '80s may seem like a very messy affair compared with what it was. It is, I suppose, messy as well as being unresolved and, at times, painful. But if it is harder to find answers now, maybe it is because we are asking better questions.[24]

History and nostalgia are not the only issues. As Ruth McManus writes, the problem is also in part about the manner of feminism's entry into the academy, where it loses its capacity to bridge practice and theory, or to relate the romance of the historical movement to life in Wishaw.

> I immersed myself in academic feminism, looking for its secret. I learned that academic feminism, like everything else, is bound by the contexts of its practitioners. This is not a 'bad' thing in itself, it just means that it is very difficult to communicate across differences, even within the relative openness of an academic feminist discussion group ... I was seen as a 'white, Northern [do you mean Britain or England?] working-class girl' – a label I accepted. The working-class voice was accepted under false pretences. To do this course at all meant having a degree and finding money privately to pay my fees. Both these things distanced me from what I saw as a working-class identity.[25]

The optimism of *Surviving the Blues* resides in the notion of better questions, that the existence and acknowledgment of differences between women might be seen, not in terms of the fragmentation and weakness of feminism in the 1980s, as compared with the past, but as part of a great strength. If 'universal sisterhood' has been exclusive in its drive for uniformity, if feminism has become associated in some contexts with privilege through its failure to recognize and value differences, then out of a recognition and understanding of those differences must come a strategy for political change which embraces 'Blackwomen, working-class women, lesbians, women with disabilities', and others, 'conscious of the differences in their oppression as women'.[26] *Surviving the Blues* commits itself to this project, with autobiographical contributors speaking for themselves, resisting misleading stereotypes of collective experience, whilst maintaining the struggle against the oppression of women.

> The women writing here do not falsely presume that their personal histories might be representative of 'young women's experience today', but show instead an acute awareness of both what is specific to their individual circumstances and what is specific to them as members of a larger group, including their gender group – women.[27]

These arguments within feminism have been instrumental in informing and continuing to energize the project of using autobiography politically, in relation to which the women's movement has retained the momentum, despite the many difficulties. Two basic premises have also been retained. One is that to articulate the experience of oppression first-hand is a precondition for social and political change. The other is that collective testimony is one of the best means of achieving this, so that neither author nor reader sees the autobiographical project as a matter of individualism. It is when 'the personal' is sunk in individualism, or loses its relationship to the condition of oppression, that the project fails to have a political edge, whether the emphasis is on history, nostalgia, fame or feminist identity itself. (It would be a painful irony if it were feminism itself, rather than patriarchy, which had begun to render some women's perceptions of their own experiences and personal histories as, again, 'uninteresting, meaningless or trivial' – in comparison with those of the supposedly fully-fledged, adult feminist, legitimated by the historical accident of being alive in 'the second wave'). But, if feminist politics retains its commitment to 'younger and different women's perspectives', in 'actively making room' for all those who want to be there, via whatever means, including the uses of autobiography, then feminism can continue to shape a politics of women's liberation for this and the next century.[28] That way, 'the personal is political' will have lost none of its original force.

Notes

1   William Blake and William Wordsworth are obvious examples of radical individuals often cited as in the mainstream of the Western European literary tradition, as in James Olney (1972) *Metaphors of Self; The Meaning of Autobiography*, Princeton University Press.

2   Raphael Samuel (Ed.) (1981) *People's History and Socialist Theory*, London: Routledge, airs a number of these debates, making reference to Ken Worpole, Centerprise publications of the people's autobiography of Hackney, and others, including those in Jerry White's list of further reading on page 42.

3   John Burnett (Ed.) (1982) *Destiny Obscure: Autobiographies of Childhood, Education and Family from the 1820s to the 1920s*, 1984 edition, Harmondsworth: Penguin; and David Vincent (1982) *Bread, Knowledge and Freedom: A Study of Nineteenth-Century Working Class Autobiography*, London: Methuen.

4   Merylyn Cherry's paper (1994) 'Towards Recognition of Working Class Women Writers', published as a Working Press Research Pamphlet, rehearses important arguments about working-class women's fiction and autobiography; my own (1985) *Victorian Writing and Working Women: The Other Side of Silence*, Cambridge: Polity, draws attention to some arguments about definitions of class, as well as to the existence of working-class women's autobiographies in the Victorian period.

5   Simone de Beauvoir (1958) *Memoirs of a Dutiful Daughter*, 1963 edition, Harmondsworth: Penguin. See Kate and Edward Fullbrook (1993) *Simone de Beauvoir and Jean-Paul Sartre: The Remaking of a Twentieth Century Legend*,

Hemel Hempstead: Harvester Wheatsheaf, for a striking reappraisal of de Beauvoir's autobiographical writings.

6   Co-operative Working Women (1931) *Life as We Have Known It*, 1977 edition, London: Virago.

7   Jean McCrindle and Sheila Rowbotham, (Eds) (1977) *Dutiful Daughters: Women Talk About Their Lives*, 1979 edition, Harmondsworth: Penguin.

8   McCrindle and Rowbotham 1977, Introduction, p. 9.

9   Linda Peffer in McCrindle and Rowbotham 1977, pp. 359–96.

10 McCrindle and Rowbotham 1977, Introduction, p. 9.

11 See Angie Sandhu 'Texts and Contexts: Contemporary Feminist Negotiations of Class, Race and Gender', unpublished PhD thesis, Loughborough University of Technology, for an excellent account of the politics of 'difference'.

12 Liz Heron (Ed.) (1985) *Truth, Dare or Promise: Girls Growing Up in the Fifties*, London: Virago.

13 Heron 1985, Introduction.

14 Heron 1985.

15 Heron 1985.

16 Sara Maitland (Ed.) (1988) *Very Heaven: Looking Back at the 1960s*, London: Virago.

17 Maitland 1988, Introduction.

18 Maitland 1988.

19 Maitland 1988.

20 Joan Scanlon (Ed.) (1990) *Surviving the Blues: Growing Up in the Thatcher Decade*, London: Virago.

21 Scanlon 1990, Introduction.

22 Norah Al-Ani, 'Don't Ask Her, She's Just the Cleaner', in Scanlon 1990, pp. 11–15.

23 Louise Donald, 'A Deafening Silence', in Scanlon 1990, pp. 91–104.

24 Mary Smeeth, 'Can You Hear Me at the Front?', in Scanlon 1990, pp. 24–33.

25 Ruth McManus, 'Getting Here', in Scanlon 1990, pp. 134–47.

26 Scanlon 1990, Introduction.

27 Scanlon 1990.

28 Scanlon 1990.

Contributors

Clare Blake wrote her contribution when she was an undergraduate at Homerton College, Cambridge, where she specialised in English and in 'early years' education. It came out of work she did for a dissertation on the autobiographies of Brian Keenan and John McCarthy.

Gillie Bolton is a poet, freelance writer, and tutor of writing. She directs the Stories at Work project for the professional development of doctors, teachers, etc.; and runs Creative Writing, Writing as Therapy training, and Spiritual Writing workshops. Her own autobiography is partly published in poetry of course; the unwritten bit includes Derbyshire gritstone, mudpies in Essex, and bicycling in Cambridge.

Janet Bottoms is a Senior Lecturer in English at Homerton College, Cambridge, where she specialises in Shakespeare and Renaissance studies, with a particular interest in issues related to the use of Shakespeare in schools. She has also taught courses on English and American literature to adult classes through the Continuing Education departments of Sheffield and Cambridge Universities. It was one such course, on diaries and diarists, that originally introduced her to Alice James.

Peter Cunningham (see Bobbie Wells).

Pam Hirsch is centrally interested in women who have taken risks, in their lives and in their work. She is addicted to the company of women, both in their books and in their living presence. Including a PhD thesis, she has written on Mary Wollstonecraft, George Eliot, Barbara Bodichon and Charlotte and Emily Bronte. She is currently researching and writing a new biography of Barbara Bodichon to be published in Spring, 1997 (Chatto & Windus).

Maroula Joannou is Senior Lecturer in English Studies at Anglia Polytechnic University and author of *'Ladies, Please Don't Smash These Windows': Women's Writing, Feminist Consciousness and Social Change 1918–1938* and co-editor with David Margolies of *Heart of the Heartless World: Essays in Cultural Resistance in Memory of Margot Heinemann.* She is currently co-editing *New Feminist Essays on the Women's Suffrage Movement* with June Purvis.

Margaretta Jolly is researching on women's letters and letter-writing during the Second World War for a PhD at the University of Sussex. She has enjoyed working with older women in reminiscence projects and is an enthusiastic member of Brighton Women's Workers' Educational Association.

Mary Lea holds degrees in Sociology and Applied Linguistics, and has in the past held posts in social work, social research and teaching. In common with many other women, she has juggled the development of her career with bringing up a family of four children. At present, she is based at the University of Kent, where she works as a researcher and advisor in learning in higher education, with a specific interest in the relationship between learners, identities and institutions, and the implications that this relationship has for curriculum development.

Claire MacDonald is a theatre writer and critic currently writing a book on feminism and performance art for Routledge. She is co-editor of the forthcoming journal *Performance Research* and is a Senior Lecturer and Research Fellow in Performing Arts at De Montfort University, Leicester.

Laura Marcus is Lecturer in English and Humanities at Birkbeck College, University of London. She has published widely on autobiography, literary and feminist theory, and women's writing and is author of *Auto/biographical Discourses: Theory, Criticism, Practice* (Manchester University Press, 1994).

Sarah Meer is a research student at Cambridge University. She is finishing a thesis about the debate on American slavery in the 1850s and hopes to soon begin work on a project on African American writing from later in the nineteenth century.

Cheryl-Ann Michael is a South African graduate student at Jesus College, Cambridge, and is currently working on a PhD thesis on South African women's autobiographical narratives.

Ato Quayson did his PhD for the Faculty of English, University of Cambridge, on the conceptual and other links between the work of Rev Samuel Johnson, Amos Tutuola, Wole Soyinka and Ben Okri and is now Lecturer in International and Commonwealth literature at Cambridge. His current interests are African theatre and film with particular reference to South Africa, Zimbabwe, Ghana and Nigeria.

Brian Ridgers is currently completing his PhD thesis at Queen Mary and Westfield College, University of London. It is entitled, *Gendered Interventions: The Construction of Women's Writing in the Nineteenth-Century.*

Morag Styles is Language Co-ordinator at Homerton College, Cambridge, where she teaches courses on Language in the Primary School and Children's literature, to undergraduates, postgraduates and teachers. She also runs occasional writing workshops for adults. She is passionate about poetry, and is currently writing *From the Garden to the Street; Three Hundred Years of Poetry for Children* on the history of children's verse. With co-editors Eve Bearne and Victor Watson, she has helped to write and produce two volumes on children's literature, *After Alice* and *The Prose and the Passion. Voices Off* is forthcoming in 1996.

Julia Swindells works for the English Department of Homerton College, Cambridge. Her publications include *Victorian Writing and Working Women, The Other Side of Silence*, and with Lisa Jardine, *What's Left? Women in Culture and the Labour Movement.* She also writes with Joan Scanlon for the radical feminist magazine, *Trouble and Strife*, and is an active member of Cambridge Labour Party.

Ruth Symes studied English at Queens' College, Cambridge, and has worked as a teacher in London, Warrington, Brighton and York. She has recently completed a PhD thesis entitled, *Educating Women: The Preceptress and her Pen*, 1780–1820, at York University.

Alistair Thomson works at the Centre for Continuing Education in the University of Sussex, where he is responsible for a Certificate in Life History Work and an MA in Life Histories and Learning; in 1996 he plans to bring these courses and research degrees together in A Centre for Life History Work. He is a co-editor of the journal *Oral History*, and author of *Anzac Memories: Living with the Legend* (Oxford, 1994).

Jane Unsworth describes herself as a 26-year-old undergraduate, who is an evangelical convert to the pursuit of learning.

Nadia Valman is researching her doctoral thesis on gender and Jewishness in nineteenth-century British literature at Queen Mary and Westfield College, University of London.

Bobbie Wells and **Peter Cunningham** are social historians and former schoolteachers engaged in the professional education and training of teachers at Homerton College, Cambridge. They share a profound interest in the educational process and a commitment to exploring this through recapturing past experiences of teaching and learning.

Linden West is Lecturer in the Theory and Practice of Continuing Education at the University of Kent and Director of Studies of a Diploma, MA and research degree programme in Continuing Education. He also runs a Unit for the Study of Continuing Education. He has written extensively in the field of adult and continuing education over many years and is presently writing a book, *Beyond Fragments, adults, motivation and higher education*. He is married with five children.

David Whitley is a Senior Lecturer in English at Homerton College, Cambridge. His research interests include Medieval and Renaissance literature, the Aesopic fable, and Media Education. Within his chequered past he has travelled quite widely, failed to complete a degree in Biochemistry and worked for a number of years with emotionally disturbed adolescents. If these parts of his life do not seem to have any obvious relation to each other, it may at least account for an interest in autobiography!

Index

Note: 'n.' after a page reference indicates the number of a note on that page.